LEGAL AID FOR THE POOR AND THE LEGAL SERVICES CORPORATION

GRANTS AND FUNDING

Additional books in this series can be found on Nova's website
under the Series tab.

Additional E-books in this series can be found on Nova's website
under the E-books tab.

GRANTS AND FUNDING

LEGAL AID FOR THE POOR AND THE LEGAL SERVICES CORPORATION

CARL T. DONOVAN
EDITOR

Nova Science Publishers, Inc.
New York

For permission to use material from this book please contact us:
Telephone 631-231-7269; Fax 631-231-8175
Web Site: http://www.novapublishers.com

Additional color graphics may be available in the e-book version of this book.

LIBRARY OF CONGRESS CATALOGING-IN-PUBLICATION DATA

Legal aid for the poor and the Legal Services Corporation / editors, Carl T. Donovan.
p. cm.
Includes index.
ISBN 978-1-61668-939-1 (hardcover)
1. Legal Services Corporation. 2. Legal assistance to the poor--United States. I. Donovan, Carl T.
KF336.L433 2010
344.7303'258--dc22

2010027152

Published by Nova Science Publishers, Inc. ✝ New York

CONTENTS

PREFACE

At a time when poor Americans are struggling to keep their jobs, homes and basic necessities for their families, it is crucial for the federal government to address the civil legal needs of these vulnerable people as a national priority. The Legal Services Corporation (LSC) is a private, nonprofit, federally funded corporation that helps provide legal assistance to low-income people in non-criminal (i.e., civil) matters. The primary responsibility of the LSC is to manage and oversee the congressionally appropriated federal funds that it distributes in the form of grants to local legal service providers, which in turn give legal assistance to low-income clients in all 50 states. This book explores the Legal Services Corporation, its background and funding, and addresses government accountability and weaknesses in the program.

Chapter 1 – In August 2007, GAO reported (GAO-07-993) that Legal Services Corporation (LSC) had not kept up with evolving reforms aimed at strengthening governance, accountability and internal controls. In December 2007, GAO reported (GAO-08-37) weaknesses in LSC's internal controls over grants management and oversight of grantees. GAO was asked to testify on the status of accountability practices of the LSC. GAO's testimony is primarily a summary of our prior reporting, but includes follow up work conducted between May and October 2009 to obtain information on the status of our prior recommendations.

Chapter 2 - The Legal Services Corporation (LSC) is a private, nonprofit, federally funded corporation that helps provide legal assistance to low-income people in civil (i.e., non-criminal) matters. The primary responsibility of the LSC is to manage and oversee the congressionally appropriated federal funds that it distributes in the form of grants to local legal services providers, which in turn give legal assistance to low-income clients. The LSC appropriation for FY2009 is $390 million.

Since its inception, the legal services program has been controversial. Congress, through the LSC Act and various annual appropriation laws, has imposed many restrictions on activities of LSCfunded legal services programs. The Obama Administration and certain Congressional proposals would eliminate some of these restrictions.

Under current law, LSC-funded legal services programs may not: (1) engage in partisan litigation related to redistricting; (2) attempt to influence regulatory, legislative, or adjudicative action at the federal, state, or local level; (3) attempt to influence oversight proceedings of the LSC; (4) engage in litigation related to abortion; (5) engage in litigation related to school desegregation; (6) engage in litigation related to draft registration or desertion from the military; (7) initiate or participate in any class action suit; (8) represent certain categories of aliens, except that both LSC and non-LSC funds may be used to represent aliens who have been victims of domestic violence or child abuse; (9) conduct advocacy training on a public policy issue or encourage political activities, strikes, or demonstrations; (10) claim or collect attorneys' fees; (11) represent clients in eviction proceedings if the eviction was based on drug-related activities; (12) represent federal, state, or local prisoners; (13) participate in efforts to reform a federal or state welfare system; (14) solicit clients; or (15) engage in activities related to assisted suicide, euthanasia, or mercy killing.

The Obama Administration's FY2010 budget proposed that funding for the LSC be increased to $435 million for FY2010 (which would exceed the previous all-time high level of $400 million), and that LSC restrictions on class action suits and attorneys' fees be eliminated. H.R. 2847, the FY2010 appropriations bill from the House Appropriations Subcommittee on Commerce, Justice, Science and Related Agencies (CJS), as passed by the House (on June 18, 2009) would increase funding for the LSC to $440 million for FY20 10 and would keep the current restrictions on LSC activities, except for the one relating to attorneys' fees. H.R. 2847, as passed by the Senate (on November 5, 2009), would increase funding for the LSC to $400 million for FY2010 and would, in effect, allow non-federal funds that are received by LSC-funded legal services programs to be used to pay for activities that are prohibited by the LSC, except for litigation involving abortion or prisoners. By contrast, the proposed Civil Access to Justice Act of 2009, S. 718, introduced by Senator Harkin (et al.) on March 26, 2009 (and the House companion bill H.R. 3764, introduced by Representative Robert "Bobby" Scott (et al.) on October 8, 2009), would increase LSC funding to $750 million per year and remove most of the restrictions on activities performed by legal services programs that receive LSC funds.

This report provides background information on the LSC, presents some of the arguments for and against the imposition of the current restrictions on LSC funds, and provides information on when the restrictions were enacted. This report will be updated as warranted.

Chapter 3 - The Legal Services Corporation (LSC) is a private, nonprofit, federally funded corporation that helps provide legal assistance to low-income people in civil (i.e., non-criminal) matters. The primary responsibility of the LSC is to manage and oversee the congressionally appropriated federal funds that it distributes in the form of grants to local legal services providers, which in turn give legal assistance to *low-income* clients in all 50 states, the District of Columbia, the U.S. territories of American Samoa, Guam, and the Virgin Islands, the Commonwealth of Puerto Rico, and Micronesia (including the Commonwealth of the Northern Mariana Islands, the Republic of the Marshall Islands, and Palau).

Although the authorization of appropriations for the LSC expired at the end of FY1980, the LSC has operated for the past 29 years under annual appropriations laws. The LSC is currently funded at $390 million for FY2009 (P.L. 111-8). Current LSC funding remains below the LSC's highest funding level of $400 million in FY1994 and FY1995. The Obama Administration's FY2010 budget request included $435 million for the LSC. On June 18, 2009, the House passed legislation (H.R. 2847) that would appropriate $440 million for the LSC for FY2010. On November 5, 2009, the Senate passed legislation (H.R. 2847, amended) that would appropriate $400 million for the LSC for FY2010.

Under the LSC's competitive process, legal services providers in every jurisdiction bid to become the LSC grantee for a designated service area in a state. During 2008, the LSC funded 137 local programs/grantees in 918 offices employing about 4,100 attorneys. Local programs establish their own eligibility criteria, in which clients served may not have income that exceeds 125% of the federal poverty guidelines. In 2008, 73% of LSC clients were females and 27% were males. The majority of LSC clients (85%) were between the ages of 18 and 59, 13% were age 60 or older, and 2% were under the age of 18. Almost 47% of LSC clients were non-Hispanic white, 25% were non-Hispanic black, 8% were of other races, and 20% were Hispanic. In 2008, LSC grantees closed 889,155 cases involving issues primarily related to families (divorce, child support, etc.), housing, income maintenance, consumer finance, and individual rights.

Although the LSC is the largest single source of funding for the civil legal services system in the United States, it is not the only source of funding. Local legal services programs supplement their LSC grants with funds from a variety of governmental and private sources. LSC funding accounts for 40% of all funding for civil legal services for the poor in the United States. This report will be regularly updated.

Chapter 4 - As the institution charged by Congress with the administration of the federally-funded civil legal assistance program for those who would otherwise be unable to afford adequate legal counsel, the Legal Services Corporation (LSC) has a responsibility to communicate to Congress what is required to secure *necessary access to civil legal assistance*—that is, the level of assistance that would be required across the nation to respond appropriately to the civil legal needs of low-income individuals and families.

The civil legal problems of low-income people involve essential human needs,. such as protection from abusive relationships, safe and habitable housing, access to necessary health care, disability payments to help lead independent lives, family law issues including child support and custody actions, and relief from financial exploitation.

The difference between the level of legal assistance available and the level that is necessary to meet the needs of low-income Americans is the "justice gap."

In September 2005, LSC issued a comprehensive report, *Documenting the Justice Gap in America: The Current Unmet Civil Legal Needs of Low-Income Americans*, which used a variety of methodologies to document the justice gap and to quantify necessary access to civil legal assistance.

This report updates the 2005 Justice Gap Report, using new data. Analysis of this data confirms that the conclusion of the 2005 Justice Gap Report remains valid: there continues to be a major gap between the civil legal needs of low-income people and the legal help that they receive.

Chapter 5 - This is an edited, excerpted and augmented version of a Legal Services Corporation Fact Book, dated August 2009.

Chapter 6 - LSC is the single largest provider of civil legal aid for the poor in the nation. Established by Congress in 1974, LSC operates as an independent 501(c)(3) nonprofit corporation that promotes equal access to justice and provides grants for high-quality civil legal assistance to low-income Americans. LSC distributes more than 95 percent of its total funding to 137 independent nonprofit legal aid programs with 918 offices that provide legal assistance to low-income individuals and families throughout the nation.

LSC promotes equal access to justice by awarding grants to legal services providers through a competitive grants process; conducting compliance reviews and program visits to oversee program quality and compliance with statutory and regulatory requirements as well as restrictions that accompany LSC funding; and by providing training and technical assistance to programs. LSC encourages programs to leverage limited resources by partnering and collaborating with other funders of civil legal aid, including state and local governments, IOLTA, access to justice commissions, the private bar, philanthropic foundations, and the business community.

The Corporation is headed by a bipartisan board of directors whose 11 members are appointed by the President and confirmed by the Senate. The board is chaired by Frank B. Strickland. Helaine M. Barnett, a career legal aid lawyer, has served as president of LSC since January 2004.

Chapter 7 – This is a testimony of Helaine M. Barnett before the Subcommittee on Commercial and Administrative Law, Committee on the Judiciary on October 27, 2009.

Chapter 8 - This is a testimony of Harrison D. Mciver, III before the Subcommittee on Commercial and Administrative Law, Committee on the Judiciary on October 27, 2009.

Chapter 9 - This is a testimony of Michael D. McKay before the Subcommittee on Commercial and Administrative Law, Committee on the Judiciary on October 27, 2009.

Chapter 10 - This is a testimony of Donald Saunders before the Subcommittee on Commercial and Administrative Law, Committee on the Judiciary on October 27, 2009.

Chapter 11 - This is a testimony of H. Thomas Wells, Jr. before the Subcommittee on Commercial and Administrative Law, Committee on the Judiciary on October 27, 2009.

In: Legal Aid for the Poor and the Legal Services Corporation ISBN: 978-1-61668-939-1
Editor: Carl T. Donovan

Chapter 1

LEGAL SERVICES CORPORATION: SOME PROGRESS MADE IN ADDRESSING GOVERNANCE AND ACCOUNTABILITY WEAKNESSES, BUT CHALLENGES REMAIN

Susan Ragland

WHY GAO DID THIS STUDY

In August 2007, GAO reported (GAO-07-993) that Legal Services Corporation (LSC) had not kept up with evolving reforms aimed at strengthening governance, accountability and internal controls. In December 2007, GAO reported (GAO-08-37) weaknesses in LSC's internal controls over grants management and oversight of grantees. GAO was asked to testify on the status of accountability practices of the LSC. GAO's testimony is primarily a summary of our prior reporting, but includes follow up work conducted between May and October 2009 to obtain information on the status of our prior recommendations.

WHAT GAO RECOMMENDS

In its August 2007 report, GAO made 8 recommendations to LSC's Board of Directors to improve LSC's governance and accountability practices and four recommendations to management to improve key management processes. GAO also provided a matter for congressional consideration on whether LSC could benefit from additional mandated governance and accountability requirements. In its December 2007 report, GAO made 1 recommendation to LSC's Board and 4 recommendations to management to improve LSC's internal control and oversight of grantees. LSC agreed with our recommendations and has addressed 9 of GAO's 17 recommendations as of October 20, 2009. GAO will continue to monitor LSC's corrective actions.

WHAT GAO FOUND

In August 2007, GAO reported that the governance practices of LSC's board fell short of the modern practices employed by other nonprofit corporations and public companies. Although the board members had demonstrated active involvement in LSC through regular board meeting attendance and participation, we pointed out several areas where LSC's governance practices could be strengthened. LSC's management practices had also not kept up with the current practices for key processes in risk assessment, internal control, and financial reporting. We pointed out certain areas where management's practices could be strengthened. GAO concluded that a properly implemented governance and accountability structure might have prevented incidents, such as compensation rates in excess of statutory caps, questionable expenditures, and potential conflicts of interest. GAO made 12 recommendations – 8 to the board and 4 to management. LSC's management has implemented all 4 recommendations to improve its management practices. The board has fully implemented 3 recommendations, but it needs to take additional actions to fully implement the other 5 recommendations. For example, LSC's board has fully implemented the key recommendation to establish an audit committee. However, another key recommendation for the board to implement procedures to periodically evaluate key management processes has not yet been fully implemented. LSC told GAO that it plans to take additional actions to more fully address the five recommendations.

In December 2007, GAO reported weaknesses in LSC's internal controls over grants management and oversight of grantees that negatively affected LSC's ability to provide assurance that grant funds were being used for their intended purposes in compliance with applicable laws and regulations. Effective internal controls over grants and grantee oversight are critical to accomplishing LSC's mission because it relies extensively on grantees to provide legal services to individuals who otherwise could not afford to pay for legal counsel. GAO made 5 recommendations to address these issues. LSC management fully implemented two of our report recommendations, including following up on identified improper or potentially improper uses of grants funds. However, LSC has only partially implemented three key recommendations, including only limited action to implement an approach for selecting grantees for review using consistently applied, risk-based criteria.

In order to improve LSC's board and management's ability to maintain accountability over LSC's mission, it will be critical for LSC's board and management to maintain priority focus on fully implementing all remaining GAO recommendations.

Mr. Chairman and Members of the Subcommittee:

I am pleased to be here today to discuss our prior work on the Legal Services Corporation's (LSC) governance, accountability, and grants management practices and the status of LSC's efforts to address the seventeen recommendations we made as a result of that work.[1]

Today I will highlight our key findings and conclusions from our prior reports on LSC's governance and accountability practices, as well as the internal control improvements needed in LSC grants management and oversight. Our August and December 2007 reports[2] contain a detailed description of our findings, conclusions, and recommendations. In addition, I will also provide the current status of LSC's action to implement the recommendations contained within those reports directed at improving governance and management and grants management internal controls.

LSC's mission is to make federal funding available for legal assistance in civil matters to low-income individuals throughout the United States on everyday legal problems. LSC pursues this mission by making grants[3] to legal service providers (grant recipients) who serve low-income members of the community who would otherwise not be able to afford legal assistance (clients). Established by a federal charter[4] in 1974[5] as a federally funded, private nonprofit corporation, LSC is highly dependent on federal appropriations for its operations. LSC received $390 million in appropriations for fiscal year 2009.[6] For fiscal year 2010 and 2011, LSC has requested $485.8 million and $516.5 million, respectively.

LSC distributes funding to local legal-service providers based on the number of low-income individuals living within a service area.[7] LSC management is responsible for ensuring that grant funds are used for their intended purposes and in accordance with laws and regulations. Thus, LSC is accountable for the effectiveness of its own internal controls and for providing oversight and monitoring of grantees' internal controls, use of grant funds, and compliance with laws and regulations. LSC's Board of Directors is responsible for carrying out fiduciary duties in overseeing LSC management's operations and use of appropriated funds.

Effective governance and accountability, including internal control are key to maintaining trust and credibility. Governance can be described as the process of providing leadership, direction, and accountability in fulfilling the organization's mission, meeting objectives, and providing stewardship of public resources, while establishing clear lines of responsibility for results. Accountability represents the processes, mechanisms, and other means—including financial reporting and internal controls—by which an entity's management carries out its stewardship and responsibility for resources and performance. Internal control is an integral component of an organization's management that provides reasonable assurance that the objectives of effectiveness and efficiency of operations, reliability of financial reporting, and compliance with applicable laws and regulations are being achieved.[8]

We conducted the work for the August 2007 and December 2007 reports on which this testimony was based from November 2006 through June 2007, and September 2006 through September 2007, respectively, in accordance with generally accepted government auditing standards. Those standards require that we plan and perform the audit to obtain sufficient, appropriate evidence to provide a reasonable basis for our findings and conclusions based on our audit objectives. We believe the evidence obtained provided a reasonable basis for our audit findings and conclusions based on our audit objectives. In addition, between May 2009 and October 2009 we obtained and reviewed available documentation and discussed with LSC officials the status of actions to implement our August and December 2007 recommendations.

LSC Has Made Improvements in its Governance and Management Practices But Key Actions Still Need to Be Completed

While LSC's board and management have taken actions to improve its governance and accountability practices towards fully implementing the recommendations from our August 2007 report additional actions to fully implement the other key recommendations are needed. In August 2007 we reported, that since its inception over 30 years ago, LSC's governance and accountability practices, including its financial reporting and internal control, had not kept pace with evolving governance and accountability practices and as a result, its practices had fallen behind those of federal agencies, U.S. government corporations, [9] and other nonprofit corporations.

LSC's board and management agreed with all twelve of our recommendations in this area, the board has implemented corrective actions for three of the eight recommendations made to the board and management has implemented all four recommendations made to management. For instance, in response to one of our eight recommendations to the board, in March 2008 the board established an audit committee, which filled an oversight gap of LSC's internal control, financial reporting and audit processes. However, another key recommendation directed at the board developing and implementing procedures to periodically evaluate key management processes, has yet to be developed and fully implemented. This recommendation is key in that it contributes to establishing an effective, supporting internal control environment at LSC as well as assists the board in fulfilling its oversight duties. As the board transitions to new board members,[10] it will be important for the new board to provide priority focused attention on fully implementing the other five of our recommendations.

Governance Practices

In August 2007 we reported that the governance practices of LSC's board fell short of the modern practices employed by boards of nonprofit corporations and public companies. Although the board members had demonstrated active involvement in LSC through their regular board meeting attendance and participation, we pointed out several areas where LSC's governance practices could be strengthened. Those areas included a more comprehensive orientation program for new board members and an ongoing training program that enables board members to stay current on governance practices, the regulatory environment, and key management practices. Although the LSC board had four committees, including finance and operations and regulations, it did not have audit, ethics, or compensation committees' functions, important governance mechanisms commonly used in corporate governance structures. The board had also not assessed the performance, collectively or individually, of its board members. Finally, the board had not implemented certain procedures that are key to helping it carry out its fiduciary duties for overseeing LSC, including evaluating key management processes, such as risk assessment, risk mitigation, internal controls and financial reporting.

Our August 2007 report recommendations to improve and modernize the governance processes and structure of LSC along with our views on the status of LSC's efforts to implement these recommendations (as of October 20, 2009) are summarized in table 1.

LSC data we obtained and analyzed as part of our follow up work conducted between May 2009 and October 2009, showed that the board had fully implemented three of the eight recommendations, and had taken some action on the remaining five recommendations. But full implementation will be needed in order for the board's actions to be fully effective. The following summary highlights LSC actions and work that remains to be done on the five recommendations that our analysis showed were partially implemented.

- In response to our recommendation that the board establish and implement a comprehensive orientation program, LSC created a "wiki,"[11] which contains relevant information for LSC board members. However, LSC management informed us that they are waiting for the pending board member nominations to be confirmed by the U.S. Senate prior to holding a formal orientation program.
- In response to our recommendation that the board develop a plan for providing regular training. LSC's management informed us there have been discussions about a training program and that the organizational updates for training the board occurs during the quarterly board meetings and that additional training needs of the board are determined by the self- assessments that the board members complete. LSC officials also stated that since this is an overall experienced board, the recent self-assessments did not indicate a need for training outside the organizational update. Officials told us that LSC management is currently documenting a training program, which we will evaluate when completed and implemented.
- We recommended that the board establish a compensation committee function to oversee compensation matters including LSC officers and LSC's overall compensation structure. Currently, the board's Governance and Performance Review Committee's charter requires the committee to annually review and report on LSC's president and inspector general performance and compensation. An LSC official told us that during the October board meeting the board will be discussing and voting on a new charter for the Governance and Performance Review Committee.
- In response to our recommendation that the board conduct a periodic self- assessment of the board's, the committees' and each member's individual performance, the board has conducted and documented assessments for the board and individuals. According to an LSC official, the committee self-assessment process is still under discussion.
- We recommended that the board develop and implement procedures to periodically evaluate key management processes including at a minimum, processes for risk assessment and mitigation, internal control and financial reporting. The recently established audit committee's charter provides the audit committee with responsibility over internal controls and therefore the evaluation of management's processes. Although the audit committee was established in March 2008, it has not yet completed this key action.

Table 1. Status of August 2007 GAO Report Recommendations on Governance Practices to LSC Board of Directors

Recommendation	Status
Establish an audit committee function to provide oversight to LSC's financial reporting and audit processes either through creating separate audit committee or by rewriting the charter of the board's finance committee.	Implemented
Establish charters for the Board of Directors and all existing committees and any newly developed committees to clearly establish committees' purposes, duties, and responsibilities.	Implemented
Establish a shorter time frame (e.g., 60 days) for issuing LSC's audited financial statements	Implemented
Establish and implement a comprehensive orientation program for new board members to include key topics such as fiduciary duties, IRS requirements, and interpretation of the financial statements.	Partially implemented
Develop a plan for providing a regular training program for board members that includes providing updates or changes in LSC's operating environment and relevant governance and accountability practices.	Partially implemented
Establish a compensation committee function to oversee compensation matters involving LSC officers and overall compensation structure either through creating a separate compensations committee or by rewriting the charter of the board's annual performance review committee.	Partially implemented
Implement a periodic self-assessment of the board's, the committees', and each individual member's performance for purposes of evaluating whether improvements can be made to the board's structure and processes.	Partially implemented
Develop and implement procedures to periodically evaluate key management processes, including, at a minimum, processes for risk assessment and mitigation, internal control and financial reporting.	Partially implemented

Source: GAO analysis of LSC data.

Management Practices

In August 2007, we reported that LSC's management practices did not reflect current practices in the areas of risk assessment, internal control, and financial reporting. We pointed out areas where management's practices could be strengthened. We found that management had not implemented a systematic or formal risk assessment that evaluated the risks the corporation faces from both external and internal sources. Such an assessment provides a structure for implementing internal control and other risk mitigation policies. In addition, senior management had not established comprehensive policies or procedures regarding conflicts of interest or other issues of ethical conduct. Without such policies and procedures, LSC was at risk of not identifying potential conflicts of interest and not taking appropriate actions to avoid potentially improper transactions or actions on the part of LSC personnel. Also, management had not conducted analysis of accounting standards to determine the most appropriate standards for LSC to follow.

Our August 2007 report recommendations to improve and modernize key management processes at LSC, along with our views on the status of LSC's efforts to implement those recommendations (as of October 20, 2009) are summarized in Table 2.

Table 2. Status of August 2007 GAO Report Recommendations on Management Practices to LSC Management

Recommendation	Status
Conduct and document a risk assessment and implement a corresponding risk management program that is part of a comprehensive evaluation of internal control.	Implemented
With the board's oversight evaluate and document relevant requirements of the Sarbanes-Oxley Act of 2002 and practices of New York Stock Exchange and American Bar Association that are used to establish a comprehensive code of conduct, including ethics and conflict-of-interest policies and procedures for employees and officers of the corporation.	Implemented
Establish a comprehensive and effective continuity of operations plan (COOP) program, including conducting a simulation to test the established program.	Implemented
Conduct an evaluation to determine whether Government Accounting Standards Board (GASB) should be adopted as a financial reporting standard for LSC's annual financial statements.	Implemented

Source: GAO analysis of LSC data.

IMPROVED INTERNAL CONTROLS NEEDED OVER GRANTS MANAGEMENT AND OVERSIGHT

While LSC has taken some actions with respect to our prior report's grants management-related recommendations, LSC has only partially implemented some key recommendations in this area. LSC management fully implemented two of our December 2007 report recommendations, including following up on identified improper or potentially improper uses of grants funds. However, LSC has only partially implemented three key recommendations, including limited action on implementing an approach for selecting grantees for review using consistently applied, risk-based criteria. Full implementation of all of the remaining recommendations is needed in order to ensure that LSC management has effective control over its mission-critical grantees.

Our December 2007 review of grants management and oversight at LSC identified weaknesses in LSC's internal controls over grants management and oversight that negatively affected LSC's ability to monitor and oversee grants and left grant funds vulnerable to misuse.[12] At grantees we visited, we also found poor fiscal practices and improper or potentially improper expenditures that LSC could have identified with more effective oversight. Although LSC has taken action to address two of the four recommendations we made to management in our December 2007 report, it has not yet implemented the two recommendations focused on oversight of grantees use of funds. In order to strengthen the organizational structure and governance of grantee oversight and monitoring, we made a recommendation to the board to develop and implement policies that clearly delineate organizational roles and responsibilities.

In December 2007 we reported on weakness in LSC's control environment regarding the lack of a clear definition of the authority and responsibilities between two of the three organizational units that oversee the work of grantees. At the time of our review, LSC management shared fiscal oversight and monitoring of grantees with the OIG. Management's oversight role was conducted through two offices—the Office of Program Performance (OPP) and the Office of Compliance and Enforcement (OCE). We found that the roles and the division of responsibilities were not clearly communicated between the OIG and OCE. The result was staff confusion about the types and scope of grantee fiscal reviews that LSC management could undertake on its initiative and strained relations between management and the OIG. In addition, communication and coordination between OCE and OPP was not sufficient to prevent gaps and unnecessary duplication between the offices' respective oversight activities.

Regarding its oversight of grantees, the scope of LSC's control activities for monitoring grantee fiscal compliance was limited and feedback to grantees not timely. In determining the timing and scope of grantee oversight visits, LSC did not employ a structured or systematic approach for assessing the risk of noncompliance or financial control weaknesses across its 137 grantees. Without an analytically sound basis for assessing risk and distributing its oversight resources, LSC did not have a basis for knowing whether its oversight resources were being used effectively to mitigate and reduce risk among its grantees.

LSC's monitoring of grantee internal control systems needed to be strengthened, because the scope of work in OCE's fiscal reviews was not sufficient in assessing grantee internal control and compliance for purposes of achieving effective oversight. In the OCE site visits we observed, staff did not follow up on questionable transactions and relied heavily on information obtained through interviews. LSC also was not timely in follow-up on an investigation into an alleged instance of noncompliance referred to it by the OIG. Feedback to grantees was often slow. As of September 2007, LSC had not yet issued reports to grantee management for almost 19 percent (10 out of 53) of the 2006 site visits. Without timely communications about the results of site visits, grantee management does not have information about deficiencies and the related corrective actions needed. In a grantee exit conference we observed, the LSC review team did not communicate a number of findings they had concluded were significant and in need of immediate attention. Effective grantee monitoring is especially important for LSC because LSC has limited options for sanctioning poorly performing grantees due to the recurring nature of many of its grants.

In the limited reviews we performed at 14 grantees, we identified internal control weaknesses at 9 grantees that LSC could have identified with more effective oversight reviews. While control deficiencies at the grantees were the immediate cause of the improper expenditures we found, weaknesses in LSC's controls over its oversight of grantees did not assure effective monitoring of grantee controls and compliance or prevent the improper expenditures. We also identified various weaknesses and improper expenditures at grantees we visited. These weaknesses and improper expenditures can result in a loss of credibility to the grantee and grantor and also allow instances of fraud to take place if not addressed.

Our December 2007 report recommendations to improve its internal control and oversight of grantees, along with our views on the status of LSC's efforts to implement those recommendations (as of October 20, 2009) are summarized in Table 3.

Table 3. Status of December 2007 GAO Report Recommendations on Grants Management to LSC Management and Board

Recommendation	To	Status
Develop and implement policies and procedures for information sharing among the OIG, OCE and OPP and coordination of OCE and OPP site visits.	Management	Implemented
Perform follow-up on each of the improper or potentially improper uses of grant funds that GAO identified in the *LSC Improved Internal Controls Needed in Grants Management and Oversight*report (GAO-08-37).	Management	Implemented
Implement an approach for selecting grantees for internal control and compliance reviews that is founded on risk-based criteria, uses information and results from oversight and audit activities and is consistently applied.	Management	Partially implemented
Implement procedures to improve the effectiveness of the current LSC fiscal compliance reviews by revising LSC current guidelines to provide • a direct link to the results of OPP reviews and OIG and IPA audit findings, • guidance for performing follow-up on responses from grantee interviews, and • examples of fiscal and internal control review procedures that may be appropriate based on individual risk factors and circumstances at grantees.	Management	Partially implemented
Develop and implement policies that clearly delineate organizational roles and responsibilities for grantee oversight and monitoring including grantee internal controls and compliance.	Board	Partially implemented

Source: GAO analysis based on LSC data.

As a result of our follow-up work conducted between May 2009 and October 2009, we determined that LSC management had fully implemented two of the four recommendations we made to management. The remaining two, as well as the recommendation to the board were partially implemented. Based on our evaluation, the following summary highlights LSC actions and work that remains to be done on the three recommendations that remain partially implemented.

- In response to our recommendation that LSC management use an approach for selecting grantees for internal control and compliance reviews that is founded on risk-based criteria and consistently applied, LSC revised its OPP and OCE manuals to include criteria for use in selecting grantees for reviews. Although LSC officials told us that the risk- based criteria was issued, they have not provided us with sufficient evidence to demonstrate that the criteria is consistently applied. We will evaluate LSC's implementation as part of our current ongoing work.
- We recommended that LSC address three factors—revise current guidelines of fiscal compliance reviews to provide (1) a direct link of results of OPP reviews and other audit findings, (2) guidance for performing follow up responses during interviews,

and (3) examples of fiscal and internal control review procedures relative to individual risk factors. LSC has updated its written guidelines for the fiscal component of OCE's regulatory and compliance reviews; however, the updates do not include the three factors. LSC officials told us they will analyze their current manuals and incorporate interview guidelines and other information as needed. We will reevaluate this recommendation after LSC management completes its analysis.

- In response to our recommendation that the board develop and implement policies and procedures that clearly delineate organizational roles and responsibilities for grantee oversight and monitoring, the board-approved updated descriptions of organizational roles and responsibilities. However, internal controls discussed in the board approved descriptions are limited to fiscal internal controls and do not include operational or other internal controls that OPP and OCE are responsible for monitoring. According to LSC's management, the board's description combined with OPP and OCE manuals and documents address more than fiscal internal controls. We will reevaluate this recommendation after LSC management analyzes and gathers additional documentation to determine whether further actions are needed to ensure clear organizational roles and responsibilities.

CONCLUSION

LSC's Board of Directors and management have made progress on implementing our prior recommendations including fully implementing nine recommendations. The improvements that LSC has made in its governance and accountability provide a good foundation for completing implementation of the elements needed for a strong program of governance and internal controls. Although management has implemented the key recommendation of conducting and documenting a risk assessment, ongoing risk assessment and a robust risk management program is important to LSC's overall internal control structure.

Further, although the board has implemented the key recommendation of establishing an audit committee, the board must continue its efforts to implement another key recommendation of developing and implementing procedures to periodically evaluate management processes, including risk assessment, mitigation, internal control and financial reporting. It will also be important for the board to provide ongoing oversight of management's risk assessment and risk management program. Periodically evaluating management will assist the board in fulfilling its oversight duty. Fully implementing the remaining recommendations, will enable the board and management to achieve the level of governance and internal control needed to provide adequate assurance that LSC's governance and internal control structures are effective, and that grant funds are being used as intended and in accordance with laws and regulations.

A strong governance structure and well established management practices and internal controls will be crucial for LSC to maintain stable operations during the upcoming board transition. Strong internal controls, with ongoing risk assessment, monitoring, and oversight will also be key to providing both the board and management with assurance that LSC funds are being used for their intended purposes, in accordance with laws and regulations and enable LSC to effectively adjust to evolving practices and risks.

This concludes my prepared statement.

End Notes

[1] GAO, *Legal Services Corporation: Governance and Accountability Practices Need to Be Modernized and Strengthened*, GAO-07-993 (Washington, D.C.: Aug. 15, 2007) and GAO, *Legal Services Corporation: Improved Internal Controls Needed in Grants Management and Oversight*, GAO-08-37 (Washington, D.C.: Dec. 28, 2007).

[2] GAO-07-993 and GAO-08-37.

[3] As used in this testimony, the term grant encompasses all of the agreements LSC uses to distribute federal funding to providers of civil legal assistance to low-income persons, and the term grant recipient refers to those who enter into such agreements. Although LSC distributes most financial assistance through grants, it sometimes uses contracts.

[4] As used in this tstimony, the term federal charter refers to a congressional act, or the written instrument documenting this act as in a statute, that establishes or authorizes the establishment of a corporation and includes requirements governing the corporation's operations.

[5] Legal Services Corporation Act of 1974, Pub. L. No. 93-355, 88 Stat. 378 (July 25, 1974), codified, as amended, at 42 U.S.C. §§ 2996 – 2996l (LSC Act).

[6] Omnibus Appropriations Act, 2009, Pub. L. No. 111-8, div. B, title IV, 123 Stat. 524, 593 (Mar. 11, 2009); Consolidated Security, Disaster Assistance, and Continuing Appropriations Act, 2009, Pub. L. No. 110-329, div. A, § 101, 122 Stat. 3574 (Sep. 30, 2008), as amended by Joint Resolution, Pub. L. No. 111-6, 123 Stat. 522 (Mar. 6, 2009).

[7] Under 45 C.F.R. § 1634.2(c), the service area is the geographic area defined by LSC to be served by grants or contracts to be awarded on the basis of a competitive bidding process.

[8] GAO, *Standards for Internal Control in the Federal Government*, GAO/AIMD-00-21.3. 1 (November 1999).

[9] In general, our review of government corporations was limited to those corporations subject to chapter 91 of title 31of the U.S. Code (commonly known as the Government Corporation Control Act).

[10] As of October 2009, all but one of the Board members term has expired. As new Board members are confirmed by the Senate, the Board members with expired terms will leave LSC's Board.

[11] A wiki is a Web site that uses wiki software, allowing the easy creation and editing of interlinked web pages.

[12] GAO-08-37.

In: Legal Aid for the Poor and the Legal Services Corporation ISBN: 978-1-61668-939-1
Editor: Carl T. Donovan

Chapter 2

LEGAL SERVICES CORPORATION: RESTRICTIONS ON ACTIVITIES

Carmen Solomon-Fears

SUMMARY

The Legal Services Corporation (LSC) is a private, nonprofit, federally funded corporation that helps provide legal assistance to low-income people in civil (i.e., non-criminal) matters. The primary responsibility of the LSC is to manage and oversee the congressionally appropriated federal funds that it distributes in the form of grants to local legal services providers, which in turn give legal assistance to low-income clients. The LSC appropriation for FY2009 is $390 million.

Since its inception, the legal services program has been controversial. Congress, through the LSC Act and various annual appropriation laws, has imposed many restrictions on activities of LSCfunded legal services programs. The Obama Administration and certain Congressional proposals would eliminate some of these restrictions.

Under current law, LSC-funded legal services programs may not: (1) engage in partisan litigation related to redistricting; (2) attempt to influence regulatory, legislative, or adjudicative action at the federal, state, or local level; (3) attempt to influence oversight proceedings of the LSC; (4) engage in litigation related to abortion; (5) engage in litigation related to school desegregation; (6) engage in litigation related to draft registration or desertion from the military; (7) initiate or participate in any class action suit; (8) represent certain categories of aliens, except that both LSC and non-LSC funds may be used to represent aliens who have been victims of domestic violence or child abuse; (9) conduct advocacy training on a public policy issue or encourage political activities, strikes, or demonstrations; (10) claim or collect attorneys' fees; (11) represent clients in eviction proceedings if the eviction was based on drug-related activities; (12) represent federal, state, or local prisoners; (13) participate in efforts to reform a federal or state welfare system; (14) solicit clients; or (15) engage in activities related to assisted suicide, euthanasia, or mercy killing.

The Obama Administration's FY2010 budget proposed that funding for the LSC be increased to $435 million for FY2010 (which would exceed the previous all-time high level of $400 million), and that LSC restrictions on class action suits and attorneys' fees be eliminated. H.R. 2847, the FY2010 appropriations bill from the House Appropriations Subcommittee on Commerce, Justice, Science and Related Agencies (CJS), as passed by the House (on June 18, 2009) would increase funding for the LSC to $440 million for FY20 10 and would keep the current restrictions on LSC activities, except for the one relating to attorneys' fees. H.R. 2847, as passed by the Senate (on November 5, 2009), would increase funding for the LSC to $400 million for FY2010 and would, in effect, allow non-federal funds that are received by LSC-funded legal services programs to be used to pay for activities that are prohibited by the LSC, except for litigation involving abortion or prisoners. By contrast, the proposed Civil Access to Justice Act of 2009, S. 718, introduced by Senator Harkin (et al.) on March 26, 2009 (and the House companion bill H.R. 3764, introduced by Representative Robert "Bobby" Scott (et al.) on October 8, 2009), would increase LSC funding to $750 million per year and remove most of the restrictions on activities performed by legal services programs that receive LSC funds.

This report provides background information on the LSC, presents some of the arguments for and against the imposition of the current restrictions on LSC funds, and provides information on when the restrictions were enacted. This report will be updated as warranted.

INTRODUCTION

The Legal Services Corporation (LSC) is a private, nonprofit, federally funded corporation that helps provide legal assistance to low-income people in civil (i.e., non-criminal) matters. The primary responsibility of the LSC is to manage and oversee the congressionally appropriated federal funds that it distributes in the form of grants to local legal services providers, which in turn give legal assistance to low-income clients in all 50 states, the District of Columbia, the U.S. territories of American Samoa, Guam, and the Virgin Islands, the Commonwealth of Puerto Rico, and Micronesia (including the Commonwealth of the Northern Mariana Islands, the Republic of the Marshall Islands, and Palau).[1]

The LSC does not provide legal services directly. Rather, it funds local legal services providers/programs. Legal services providers/programs may include nonprofit organizations that have as a purpose the provision of legal assistance to eligible clients, private attorneys, groups of private attorneys or law firms, state or local governments, and certain sub-state regional planning and coordination agencies. During 2008, the LSC funded 137 legal services programs in 918 offices.

Although the authorization of appropriations for the LSC expired at the end of FY1980, the LSC has operated for the past 29 years by virtue of annual appropriations laws. The LSC is currently funded at $390 million for FY2009 (P.L. 111-8).

Since its inception, the legal services program has been controversial, and Congress has imposed restrictions on activities of LSC-funded legal services programs. Debate existed from the start among policymakers as to whether the LSC's role should be similar to that of its predecessor,[2] namely, using lawsuits and other means to resolve broad underlying difficulties of the poor, or whether the focus should be more narrowly defined to addressing small, specific situations. Although there is widespread agreement that individuals who cannot afford an attorney should have their "day in court,"[3] many observers contend that federal dollars should not be used to promote broad social causes.

LSC ATTORNEYS MAY NOT

- engage in partisan litigation related to redistricting;
- attempt to influence regulatory, legislative, or adjudicative action at the federal, state, or local level;
- attempt to influence oversight proceedings of the LSC;
- engage in litigation related to abortion;
- engage in litigation related to school desegregation;
- engage in litigation related to draft registration or desertion from the military;
- initiate or participate in any class action suit;
- represent certain categories of aliens, except that both LSC and non-LSC funds may be used to represent aliens who have been victims of domestic violence or child abuse;
- conduct advocacy training on a public policy issue or encourage political activities, strikes, or demonstrations;
- claim or collect attorneys' fees;
- represent clients in eviction proceedings if the eviction was based on drug-related activities;
- represent federal, state, or local prisoners;
- participate in efforts to reform a federal or state welfare system;
- solicit clients; or
- engage in activities related to assisted suicide, euthanasia, or mercy killing.

DEBATE OVER RESTRICTIONS

Proponents of reducing the number of restrictions on the LSC argue that the restrictions deny those represented by LSC-funded attorneys access to basic legal tools, such as claiming court- ordered attorneys' fee awards[4] and participating in class actions that are available to all other litigants.[5] They contend that their adversaries grossly exaggerate their activist activities, they claim that they spend the vast majority of their time providing assistance to poor individuals who are trying to resolve family issues such as divorce and separation, custody and visitation, and domestic abuse, or housing issues such as eviction.[6] Some LSC advocates also counter that class action suits are an efficient and effective way to represent clients who face a common problem and to resolve the legal problems of large numbers of persons in similar situations.[7]

Opponents of reducing the number of restrictions on the LSC argue that without the restrictions LSC attorneys in far too many instances would seek the flamboyant social cause-oriented class action cases, rather than cases that address the urgent, routine, day-to-day legal needs of low- income individuals. They maintain that LSC attorneys, prior to the restrictions, were abusing their statutory directive by pursuing a liberal agenda.[8] Some fear that hundreds of legal services attorneys would unleash a barrage of lawsuits in the nation's federal and state courts to advance a liberal political agenda if the restrictions were not in place.[9]

The authorizing statute (P.L. 93-355) of the LSC contains restrictions against lobbying, political activities, class actions except under certain conditions, and cases involving abortion, school desegregation, and draft registration or desertion from the military. Additional restrictions have been included in annual appropriations laws over the years. However, it was the 1996 appropriations law that stipulated that the restrictions were to apply to all LSC activities, not just those funded by LSC appropriations.[10] This meant that all of the resources of a LSC-funded legal services programs, whether they came from the LSC appropriation, other federal funds, state or local appropriations, state Interest on Lawyers' Trust Account (IOLTA) programs, contracts, private donations, foundation grants or other funding sources, were subject to the same restrictions as LSC funds.[11] Some attorneys claimed that this provision in effect enabled Congress to restrict the work of attorneys working for the poor far beyond the scope of the federal appropriation.[12] Others referred to the restriction as the "program integrity" restriction, and claimed that the limit on the use of non-LSC funds is crucial. They asserted that because most, if not all, LSC grantees (i.e., legal services programs) receive money from private or other government sources, without the "program integrity" rule, the other restrictions would be rendered virtually meaningless because grantees could simply claim that they are using non-LSC money. [13] Although more theoretical than practical, it is important to mention the proviso that LSC-funded legal services programs can provide some of the restricted activities if they do so through a legally and physically separate entity. Such an undertaking is viewed by most legal services programs as too expensive to contemplate.

Some commentators contend that the restrictions prevent LSC attorneys from helping many low- income persons in urgent need of assistance. The current recession, along with a variety of problems such as consumer fraud, domestic violence, and flawed housing practices,[14] have resulted in some policymakers supporting increased funding and fewer restrictions on the LSC.[15]

During a recent hearing on the LSC, Representative Alan Mollohan, chairman of the House Appropriations Subcommittee on Commerce, Justice, Science, and Related Agencies (CJS), made the following statement:

> The ongoing recession is driving more and more Americans below the poverty thresholds that establish eligibility for legal aid services. This growing population of eligible clients is confronted with legal needs that are increasing in both number and complexity. Many clients face the prospect of foreclosure or foreclosure-related eviction. With job losses increasing, there are more clients needing assistance gaining access to food stamp benefits, unemployment compensation or Medicaid services. There is also substantial evidence that economic distress increases family distress, including divorce and domestic violence. All of these factors are driving up demand for legal aid services at precisely the same time that the supply of those services is dwindling. Legal aid providers across the country have been forced to make significant budget cuts due to state government deficits and diminishing charitable and private support.[16]

The House-passed CJS Appropriations bill (H.R. 2847) would increase funding for the LSC to $440 million in FY20 10 (an increase of $50 million over current year funding) and would keep the current restrictions on LSC activities, except for the one relating to attorneys' fees. According to the House report on H.R. 2847:

> A general provision in Title V of the bill revises the administrative provision in order to permit grantees to pursue the recovery of attorneys' fees when recovery is permitted or required under Federal or State law. The Committee believes that this action will level the playing field between legal aid attorneys and their counterparts in the private sector and provide a potentially crucial source of additional revenue to legal aid providers in a year in which state and private funding sources are decreasing.[17]

The Senate-passed CJS Appropriations bill (H.R. 2847) would increase funding for the LSC to $400 million in FY2010 (an increase of $10 million over current year funding). The Senate- passed version of the bill would also continue existing limitations on the use of federal funds, except that it would eliminate the restrictions on the use of non-federal funds except in litigation involving abortion and cases involving prisoners.[18] The bill will go to conference to resolve the differences between the House and Senate versions of the bill.

By contrast, the proposed Civil Access to Justice Act of 2009, S. 718, introduced by Senator Harkin (et al.) on March 26, 2009 (and the House companion bill H.R. 3764, introduced by Representative Robert "Bobby" Scott (et al.) on October 8, 2009), would reauthorize the LSC for six years, increase funding to $750 million per year (for each of the fiscal years FY2010 through FY2015), remove most of the restrictions on activities performed by legal services programs that receive LSC funds,[19] and revise the governance of the LSC. In his introduction of the bill, Senator Harkin said:

> Unfortunately, as the economy continues to wane, those needing legal assistance increase. Yet, the Federal commitment to legal services and LSC is not as effective as it needs to be. LSC has not been authorized since 1981, and since 1995 Congress has slashed funding for legal services for the poor, from $415 million to $350 million in fiscal year 2008, with only a recent increase to $390 million for fiscal year 2009. Further, severe restrictions on LSC funded attorneys impede the ability of legal aid attorneys to provide the most meaningful legal representation to low-income Americans. The result is that access to justice and quality representation has become far from a reality for too many of our citizens.[20]

On June 17, 2009, speaking in opposition of funding the LSC, Representative Hensarling stated: " ... it's a program that's been unauthorized since 1980, reported instances of waste, fraud and abuse. And should we actually be taxing taxpayers to force them to subsidize their neighbors to turn around and sue them? I don't think so." He asserted that there are other options for providing legal services to the poor, such as pro bono law firms and lawyers that work on contingent fees.[21]

The following section provides information on when the current restrictions were first enacted. (See box on page 1 for a list of the current restrictions.)

LEGISLATIVE HISTORY OF RESTRICTIONS ON LSC ACTIVITIES

Generally speaking, Democrats and other advocates of the LSC have consistently argued that the poor should receive the same range of legal assistance through the LSC that is available to those who could afford to hire private attorneys. By contrast, Republicans generally have asserted that LSC attorneys should deal with the day-to-day needs of the poor and should be barred from dealing with controversial political issues.

The legislation authorizing the LSC was signed by President Nixon in 1974. During the Ford Administration, the LSC was reauthorized through FY1980. During the 1980s there were several attempts by the Reagan Administration to abolish the LSC. Although the George H.W. Bush Administration did not try to eliminate the LSC or drastically cut its funding, it supported more restrictions on the LSC. During the early years of the Clinton Administration the LSC reached its highest funding level of $400 million; however, funding was reduced significantly in 1996 due to pressure from a majority Republican Congress to reduce LSC funding and impose more restrictions on the types of permissible LSC activities. According to many sources, imposing restrictions on LSC activities was the compromise that enabled the LSC to continue to exist.[22] During the George W. Bush Administration funding for the LSC gradually increased and several more restrictions on LSC activities were imposed. The Obama Administration has proposed that funding for the LSC be increased to $435 million for FY2010 (which would exceed the previous all-time high level of $400 million), and that LSC restrictions on class action suits and attorneys' fees be eliminated.

The LSC Act and various annual appropriation laws contain restrictions on activities in which recipients of LSC funds may engage, and on types of cases in which LSC-funded legal services providers/programs may provide legal representation.[23]

LSC Authorizing Legislation (P.L. 93-355; Enacted July 25, 1974)[24]

The LSC was the result of a bipartisan agreement between members of Congress who supported the predecessor OEO legal services program and those who opposed the OEO program. Supporters of the predecessor OEO program maintained that law reform through the use of litigation, lobbying, and community organization was the most effective approach to obtain social justice for poor people. However, opponents maintained that OEO legal services program efforts in cases pertaining to integration, abortion, and union organizing had generated significant controversy. P.L. 93-355 authorized an independent, national nonprofit organization to oversee provision of legal services to the nation's poor (i.e., the LSC), while simultaneously refocusing legal services advocacy toward basic representation of individual clients and away from law reform by prohibiting LSC funds to be used for lobbying, and policy advocacy.[25]

Since its inception, Congress has imposed restrictions on the activities of LSC attorneys. The authorizing statute (P.L. 93-355) contains restrictions against lobbying, political activities, class actions (except under certain conditions), and cases involving abortion, school desegregation, and draft registration or desertion from the military.

P.L. 96-68 (Appropriations Bill)—September 24, 1979

A provision that prohibited LSC funds from being used to assist any alien in the United States with regard to immigration, exclusion, deportation, or expulsion matters was first included in P.L. 96-68.

P.L. 97-377 (Appropriations Bill)—December 21, 1982

The prohibition against using LSC funds to assist aliens was modified so that LSC funds could be used to help certain categories of resident aliens (i.e., immigrants) who were lawfully present in the United States. This modified provision was first included in P.L. 97-377.

P.L. 104-134 (Appropriations Bill)—April 26, 1996

P.L. 104-134 made numerous changes to the LSC. In 1996, the LSC was still a very contentious topic of debate. The LSC had been unauthorized for many years; which resulted in controversial issues surrounding the LSC being addressed through the inclusion of a number of administrative provisions in annual appropriations acts. In 1995, the House had adopted a budget resolution that assumed that the funding for the LSC would be cut by one-third for FY1996, two-thirds for FY1997, and eliminated thereafter. Many members of Congress concluded that to prevent the elimination of the LSC they would have to accept significant budget cuts to the LSC and more restrictions on LSC activities.[26] The political compromise that was reached preserved the LSC, but reduced its funding, changed the way in which LSC funds were distributed, imposed additional restrictions on the use of LSC funds,[27] and also stipulated that non-LSC funds received by individual legal services programs were subject to the same restrictions as LSC funds. The compromise did not include the reauthorization of the LSC.

P.L. 104-134 included provisions that prohibited *any* funds received by LSC legal services providers/programs to be used for (1) efforts related to redistricting; (2) attempts to influence regulatory, legislative or adjudicative action at the federal, state, or local level; (3) grassroots lobbying; (4) attempts to influence oversight proceedings of the LSC; (5) class action suits; (5) representation of certain categories of aliens; (6) conducting advocacy training on a public policy issue or encouraging political activities, strikes, boycotts or demonstrations; (7) claiming or collecting attorneys' fees; (8) litigation related to abortion; (9) representation of federal, state, or local prisoners; (10) efforts to reform a federal or state welfare system; (11) representation of clients in eviction proceedings brought by a public housing agency if the eviction was based on drug-related activities;[28] and (12) solicitation[29] of clients.

P.L. 104-134 also mandated that LSC-funded providers/programs must establish priorities, and staff must agree in writing not to engage in activities outside these priorities. Moreover, P.L. 104- 134 prohibited the LSC from receiving nonfederal funds, and legal services providers/programs are prohibited from receiving non-LSC funds, unless the source of funds is told in writing that these funds may not be used for any activities prohibited by the LSC Act or the appropriations law pertaining to the LSC.

P.L. 104-208 (Appropriations Bill)—September 30, 1996

The prohibition against using LSC funds to assist certain categories of aliens was modified to allow both LSC and non-LSC funds to be used to represent aliens who have been victims of domestic violence or child abuse. This modification was first added by P.L. 104-208.

P.L. 105-12 (Assisted Suicide Funding Restriction Act of 1997)— April 30, 1997

A provision that prohibited LSC funds from being used for activities related to assisted suicide, euthanasia, or mercy killing was first added by P.L. 105-12.

P.L. 105-119 (Appropriations Bill)—November 26, 1997

Among other things, this law incorporated previous restrictions on LSC activities by reference to P.L. 104-134 and also made some modifications to some of the 1996 restrictions. All subsequent annual appropriations bills that include LSC-related provisions incorporate the restrictions on LSC-funded activities by reference to this law (P.L. 105-119) and/or P.L. 104-134.

CONCLUSION

Although polls indicate majority support for the existence of, and federal funding for, the nonprofit provision of legal assistance to the poor,[30] determining the appropriate funding level of the LSC and agency/program parameters remains an issue.

According to 21 state justice commissions,[31] restrictions placed on programs receiving LSC funds adversely affected many low-income persons. The justice commission in New Jersey asserted that the restrictions have a "negative impact," "in actual practice (causing great inefficiencies in the way applicants for service must be processed and referred) and principle (denial of essential and fundamental legal assistance to some who need it)." The Texas commission maintained that the restrictions are "major obstacles ... for achieving 'equal access' for disfavored clients and politically unpopular cases."[32]

Some commentators contend that "access to justice" for poor people is inherently unequal when it is subject to restrictions that are not imposed on clients who can afford to pay for their attorneys.[33] Others assert that "access to justice" for the poor is a fallacy because LSC is unable to meet the demands of the current eligible low-income population.[34] They assert that eliminating the restrictions on LSC activities would only widen the gap of unmet need. Many in the legal services community are supporting proposals that would both increase LSC funding and eliminate some of the restrictions on LSC activities. Others opposed to providing any funding for the LSC contend that the LSC has been unauthorized since 1980 for legitimate reasons. They maintain that instead of increasing the national debt by spending $440 million on the LSC, other non-federal resources are more appropriate sources of funding for legal services programs for the poor.[35]

End Notes

1 For basic information on the LSC, see CRS Report RL34016, *Legal Services Corporation: Background and Funding*, by Carmen Solomon-Fears.

2 The federal government has administered a program of legal services for the poor since 1966. Originally, the program was administered through the Office of Economic Opportunity (OEO), a now-defunct agency that had led the War on Poverty in the mid-1960s. In 1971, President Nixon proposed establishment of a separate corporation to deliver legal services to insulate the program from political pressure. In his special message to the Congress on May 5, 1971, proposing the establishment of a Legal Services Corporation, President Nixon stated that the legal services program "*has not been without travail. Much of the litigation initiated by legal services has placed it in direct conflict with local and State governments. The program is concerned with social issues and is thus subject to unusually strong political pressures. Even though surrounded by controversy, this program can provide a most effective mechanism for settling differences and securing justice within the system and not on the streets.*"

3 Most of the cases handled by LSC are resolved through advice and referral. In 2007, only about 13% of cases were resolved in court, primarily because they involved family law issues (e.g., protective orders, child support, etc.) in which court action was required by state law.

4 A general practice of law is for the winning parties to ask the court to require the other side to pay court costs and attorneys' fees. Many commentators maintain that countering trial delays by opposing counsel with a reminder that if they lose they will not only have to change the rule or policy but that they will also have to pay attorneys' fees is a legal strategy (i.e., leverage) that is not available to LSC-funded attorneys (pursuant to annual appropriation laws, starting with P.L. 104-134). Some observers also point out that the prohibition against accepting attorneys' fees also reduces the resources that potentially could have been available to LSC-funded legal services programs to provide more aid to low- income persons. In other words, they contend that during these times of tight budgets, attorneys' fees could be a significant source of funding for many LSC-funded programs.

5 Brennan Center for Justice (New York University School of Law), "Restricting Legal Services: How Congress Left the Poor With Only Half a Lawyer," 2000. Also see Statement of Rebekah Diller (deputy director) before the U.S. Senate Committee on the Judiciary, May 22, 2008.

6 *The Congressional Digest*, vol. 60, no. 5, "Controversy Over the Federal Legal Aid Program," May 1981. See also Brennan Center for Justice (New York University School of Law), "Restricting Legal Services: How Congress Left the Poor With Only Half a Lawyer," 2000.

7 American Civil Liberties Union (ACLU), "Upsetting Checks and Balances: Congressional Hostility Toward the Courts in Times of Crisis," November 1, 2001, p. 46-47.

8 *The Congressional Digest*, vol. 60, no. 5, "Controversy Over the Federal Legal Aid Program," May 1981. See also John Carlisle, "Legal Services Unleashed," The American Spectator, special report, April 3, 2009.

9 John Carlisle, "Legal Services Unleashed," The American Spectator, special report, April 3, 2009. See also Rael Jean Isaac, "Illegal Services—When Congress passed restrictions on the Legal Services Corporation, the LSC call in its lawyers," *National Review*, vol. 49, March 24, 1997, p. 42-45, and p. 60.

10 Although the LSC is the largest single source of funding for the civil legal services system in the United States, it is not the only source of funding. Local legal services programs supplement their LSC grants with funds from a variety of governmental and private sources. Non-LSC funding sources include state and local grants; state Interest on Lawyers' Trust Accounts (IOLTAs) programs; federal programs such as the Title XX Social Services Block Grant, the Older Americans Act, the Violence Against Women Act, and Community Development Block Grants; and private grants from entities such as the United Way, foundations, and national, state, and local bar associations. In addition, private attorneys accept referrals to provide legal services to the poor, primarily through LSC-funded pro bono programs. In 2007, LSC funding accounted for about 42% of the $844.4 million spent in the U.S. for civil legal services for the poor.

11 Alan Houseman and Linda Perle, "Restrictions on Providing a Full Range of Services," Memorandum to Peter Edelman, February 6, 2009. http://www.law.stanford.edu/display/images Houseman_Perle_LSC_Restrictions_Memo.pdf

12 American Civil Liberties Union (ACLU), "Upsetting Checks and Balances: Congressional Hostility Toward the Courts in Times of Crisis," November 1, 2001, p. 47.

13 John Carlisle, "Legal Services Unleashed," The American Spectator, special report, April 3, 2009.

14 P.L. 106-185 (Civil Asset Forfeiture Reform Act of 2000; enacted April 25, 2000) included a provision whose purpose is to ensure that an indigent individual whose primary residence is subject to civil forfeiture is represented by an LSC attorney in such civil action.

15 Some advocates of eliminating the restrictions on LSC activities contend that the opportunity to stop the fraudulent practices of some lenders in the mortgage market was missed because legal services programs were prohibited from lobbying and filing class action suits. They assert that civil legal aid attorneys serve as a detection and warning system for problems plaguing low-income communities. They note that as the people most familiar with the legal problems of the communities in which they work, often they are the first to learn of new legal abuses occurring in those communities. They point out that historically, civil legal aid lawyers were the ones who spoke out and prompted change when the police refused to respond to domestic violence calls, when foster care agencies placed children in unsafe foster homes, and when local employers repeatedly failed to pay the minimum wage. Source: Laura K. Abel (Brennan Center for Justice—New York University), "Lawyers for the Poor Muzzled in Subprime Mess," The Nation, January 16, 2008.

16 U.S. Congress, Hearing on the Legal Services Corporation, statement of Chairman Alan Mollohan, House Appropriations Subcommittee on Commerce, Justice, Science, and Related Agencies, April 1, 2009.

17 U.S. Congress. House. Commerce, Justice, Science, and Related Agencies Appropriations Bill, 2010, to accompany H.R. 2847 (111th Congress, 1st Session), H.Rept. 111-149, June 12, 2009, p. 163.

18 The Senate report (S.Rept. 111-34, June 25, 2009, p. 143) deletes section 504(d) of P.L. 104-134. This section prohibits legal services programs that are funded partly by LSC funds from using non-federal (e.g., state, local, or private) funds to pay for activities that are prohibited by the LSC. However, S.Rept. 111-34 also stipulates that no funds (federal or non-federal) can be used for activities specified in section 504(a)(14) or section 504(a)(15) of P.L. 104-134 (respectively, these two sections pertain to abortion litigation and litigation involving persons incarcerated in a federal, state, or local prison).

19 S. 718 would eliminate LSC restrictions related to attorneys' fees, lobbying with non-federal funds, and class action suits (if the class action is based on established law). It would modify the restriction pertaining to public housing evictions so that LSC-funded legal services programs could serve persons who have been acquitted of drug-related charges or against whom such charges were dropped. It would modify the restriction related to inmates of federal, state, and local prisons so that services could be provided to prisoners trying to successfully re-enter society. In addition, the bill would eliminate all restrictions on the use of non-LSC funds with the exception of cases related to abortion.

20 *Congressional Record*, Senate, Remarks of Senator Harkin on S. 718, March 26, 2009, p. S3916.

21 *Congressional Record*. House. Amendment No. 6 to H.R. 4287 offered by Representative Hensarling, p. H6936-H 6937.

22 Alan W. Houseman, "Civil Legal Assistance for the 21st Century: Achieving Equal Justice for All," Center for Law and Social Policy, May 1998, pp. 10-11, https://www.policyarchive.org/bitstream/handle/10207/13767/civil_legal_assistance_for_the_21st_century.pdf?sequence=1.

23 The LSC Act can be found at 42 U.S.C. §2996 et seq.; the restrictions can be found at 42 U.S.C. §2996e and §2996f. The LSC regulations can be found at 45 C.F.R. Part 1600 et seq.

24 The public laws listed below indicate the first time the restriction was included in law. Subsequent legislation also included the previously mentioned restrictions. LSC restrictions have been renewed every year since 1996. However, many of the appropriation bills that included provisions related to the LSC are not mentioned in this report because they did not include new restrictions.

25 Alan W. Houseman and Linda E. Perle, "Securing Equal Justice For All: A Brief History of Civil Legal Assistance in the United States," Center for Law and Social Policy, revised January 2007, pp. 19-22, http://www.clasp.org/admin/ site/publications/files/0158.pdf. Also see Michael B. Wallace, "Out of Control: Congress and the Legal Services Corporation," American Enterprise Institute for Public Policy Research (AEI studies 485), 1989, pp. 169-173.

26 Mauricio Vivero, "From "Renegade" Agency to Institution of Justice: The Transformation of Legal Services Corporation," *Fordham Urban Law Journal*, vol. XXIX, no. 3, February 2002, p. 1325-1333.

27 P.L. 104-134 recodified some of the previous restrictions and added some new restrictions.

28 Section 504(a)(17) of P.L. 104-134 stipulates that LSC-funded legal services programs may not defend a person in a proceeding to evict the person from a public housing project if (1) the person has been charged with the illegal sale or distribution of a controlled substance, and (2) the eviction proceeding is brought by a public housing agency because the illegal drug activity of the person threatens the health or safety of another tenant residing in the public housing project or employee of the public housing agency.

29 Federal regulations (Title 45 U.S. Code, part 1638) state that the purpose of the restriction is to ensure that LSC-funded legal services programs do not solicit clients. The regulations clarify that providing information regarding legal rights and responsibilities and advertising the program's services are not considered solicitation.

30 In a 2009 Harris poll commissioned by the American Bar Association, 83% of the survey respondents agreed that it is essential that a non-profit provider of legal services is available to assist those who could not otherwise afford legal help. Also, 68% of respondents said they support federal funding to help Americans who need legal resources and advice when they are in crisis.

31 Access to Justice Commissions have been created by many states as a strategy for developing and implementing initiatives designed to expand access to and enhance the quality of justice in civil legal matters for low-income people.

32 Brennan Center for Justice (New York University School of Law), "Reports from 21 States Identify Federal Legal Services Corporation Restrictions as a Barrier to Justice," May 8, 2009.

33 Brennan Center for Justice (New York University School of Law), "Letter to OMB Asks President Obama to Change Administration's Stance on Legal Services Restrictions," January 30, 2009.

34 A 2005 report indicated that only about 20% of persons eligible for LSC-funded services actually had access to those services when they needed them. (Source: Legal Services Corporation, "Documenting the Justice Gap in America: The Current Unmet Civil Legal Needs of Low-Income Americans," September 2005, p. 18.) Note: LSC-funded legal services programs may not provide services to persons who have income above 125% of the federal poverty guidelines. According to the Census Bureau, in 2007, approximately 50 million persons had income below 125% of the poverty level.

35 *Congressional Record*. House. Amendment No. 6 to H.R. 4287 offered by Representative Hensarling, p. H6936-H 6937.

In: Legal Aid for the Poor and the Legal Services Corporation ISBN: 978-1-61668-939-1
Editor: Carl T. Donovan

Chapter 3

LEGAL SERVICES CORPORATION: BACKGROUND AND FUNDING

Carmen Solomon-Fears

SUMMARY

The Legal Services Corporation (LSC) is a private, nonprofit, federally funded corporation that helps provide legal assistance to low-income people in civil (i.e., non-criminal) matters. The primary responsibility of the LSC is to manage and oversee the congressionally appropriated federal funds that it distributes in the form of grants to local legal services providers, which in turn give legal assistance to *low-income* clients in all 50 states, the District of Columbia, the U.S. territories of American Samoa, Guam, and the Virgin Islands, the Commonwealth of Puerto Rico, and Micronesia (including the Commonwealth of the Northern Mariana Islands, the Republic of the Marshall Islands, and Palau).

Although the authorization of appropriations for the LSC expired at the end of FY1980, the LSC has operated for the past 29 years under annual appropriations laws. The LSC is currently funded at $390 million for FY2009 (P.L. 111-8). Current LSC funding remains below the LSC's highest funding level of $400 million in FY1994 and FY1995. The Obama Administration's FY2010 budget request included $435 million for the LSC. On June 18, 2009, the House passed legislation (H.R. 2847) that would appropriate $440 million for the LSC for FY2010. On November 5, 2009, the Senate passed legislation (H.R. 2847, amended) that would appropriate $400 million for the LSC for FY2010.

Under the LSC's competitive process, legal services providers in every jurisdiction bid to become the LSC grantee for a designated service area in a state. During 2008, the LSC funded 137 local programs/grantees in 918 offices employing about 4,100 attorneys. Local programs establish their own eligibility criteria, in which clients served may not have income that exceeds 125% of the federal poverty guidelines. In 2008, 73% of LSC clients were females and 27% were males. The majority of LSC clients (85%) were between the ages of 18 and 59, 13% were age 60 or older, and 2% were under the age of 18. Almost 47% of LSC clients were non-Hispanic white, 25% were non-Hispanic black, 8% were of other races, and 20% were Hispanic. In 2008, LSC grantees closed 889,155 cases involving issues primarily related to families (divorce, child support, etc.), housing, income maintenance, consumer finance, and individual rights.

Although the LSC is the largest single source of funding for the civil legal services system in the United States, it is not the only source of funding. Local legal services programs supplement their LSC grants with funds from a variety of governmental and private sources. LSC funding accounts for 40% of all funding for civil legal services for the poor in the United States. This report will be regularly updated.

INTRODUCTION

The Legal Services Corporation (LSC) is a private, nonprofit, federally funded corporation that helps provide legal assistance to low-income people in non-criminal (i.e., civil) matters. The LSC is governed by an 11-member board appointed by the President and confirmed by the Senate, of whom no more than six members may be of the same political party. The primary responsibility of the LSC is to manage and oversee the congressionally appropriated federal funds that it distributes in the form of grants to local legal services providers, which in turn give legal assistance to *low-income* clients in all 50 states, the District of Columbia, the U.S. territories of American Samoa, Guam, and the Virgin Islands, the Commonwealth of Puerto Rico, and Micronesia (including the Commonwealth of the Northern Mariana Islands, the Republic of the Marshall Islands, and Palau).

The federal government has administered a program of legal services for the poor since 1966. Originally, the program was administered through the Office of Economic Opportunity, a now-defunct agency that had led the War on Poverty in the mid-1960s. In 1971, President Nixon proposed establishment of a separate corporation to deliver legal services to insulate the program from political pressure.[1] Authorizing legislation was enacted in 1974 (P.L. 93-355), and the LSC came into existence the following year. In 1977, the LSC was extended through FY1980 (P.L. 95-222). Although Congress has not reauthorized the LSC statute since FY1980, it has continued to fund LSC every year, and has included legislative language affecting LSC activities in the annual appropriations laws.

PROGRAM MECHANICS

The LSC does not provide legal services directly. Rather, it funds local legal services providers, referred to by the LSC as "grantees." Grantees may include nonprofit organizations that have as a purpose the provision of legal assistance to eligible clients, private attorneys, groups of private attorneys or law firms, state or local governments, and certain sub-state regional planning and coordination agencies.

During 2008, the LSC funded 137 local programs in 918 offices employing about 4,100 attorneys. These numbers are reduced from 1994, when 320 local programs employed about 4,500 attorneys. Each local program is governed by its own board of directors, of which a majority are attorneys and one-third are eligible clients. Local programs establish their own eligibility criteria, under which a client's household income may not exceed 125% of the federal poverty guidelines.[2] Each local program must spend an amount equal to at least 12.5% of its basic grant to encourage private attorneys to provide pro bono legal aid to the poor.

LSC LAWS AND APPROPRIATIO

P.L. 93-355 (July 25, 1974)
P.L. 95-222 (Dec. 28, 1977)
P.L. 105-12 (Apr. 30, 1997)
P.L. 106-185 (Apr. 25, 2000)
P.L. 104-134 (Apr. 26, 1996)
P.L. 104-208 (Sept. 30, 1996)
P.L. 105-119 (Nov. 26, 1997)
P.L. 105-277 (Oct. 21, 1998)
P.L. 106-113 (Nov. 29, 1999)
P.L. 106-553 (Dec. 21, 2000)
P.L. 107-77 (Nov. 28, 2001)
P.L. 108-7 (Feb. 20, 2003)
P.L. 108-199 (Jan. 23, 2004)
P.L. 108-447 (Dec. 8, 2004)
P.L. 109-108 (Nov. 22, 2005)
P.L. 110-5 (Feb. 15, 2007)
P.L. 110-161 (Dec. 26, 2007)
P.L. 110-329 (Sept. 30, 2008)

Since April 1996 (P.L. 104-134), LSC grantees (i.e., legal services agencies/providers/ programs) have been selected on a competitive basis.[3] Under the LSC's competitive process, legal services providers in every jurisdiction bid to become the LSC grantee for a designated service area in a state. Pursuant to its 1998 State Planning Initiative, the LSC has sought to streamline its delivery system. During the competition process, the LSC evaluates applications according to established quality standards and awards grants to those providers judged best qualified to provide high- quality legal services in accordance with applicable legal requirements. Federal regulations (Title 45 C.F.R. Part 1634) stipulate the procedures to be followed in awarding LSC grants. Grants are made for one to three years. Multi-year awardees must submit reports and grant renewal forms as part of the annual grant renewal process.

Before the implementation of the 1998 State Planning Initiative, LSC grantees often were unaware of other LSC grantees in the state. Work and training collaborations and other cooperative endeavors were rare among LSC grantees in the same state, and practically nonexistent among LSC grantees in other states. Further, most legal services programs only had superficial relationships and minimal contact with law firms and local judges. In anticipation of reduced federal funding, the LSC first encouraged and later directed grantees to form partnerships with the judiciary, private bar associations, and with each other. The 1998 State Planning Initiative was the means by which the LSC sought to ensure that LSC funds were efficiently and effectively used to provide legal services to poor persons in all areas of the states and jurisdictions. Pursuant to the 1998 Initiative, the LSC made participation in statewide civil legal services delivery systems a condition of receipt of LSC funding.[4]

It is generally agreed that poor persons in need of legal assistance have benefitted from the LSC's statewide delivery system approach. The LSC has done this by requiring federally funded legal services providers to coordinate their work with other persons and organizations within a state, including groups historically considered funding "competitors" (other nonprofit organizations and non-LSC legal services programs) or "unlikely partners" (judges, legislators, bar leaders).[5]

Restrictions on Activities

Since its inception, the legal services program has been controversial, and Congress has imposed restrictions on activities of local attorneys. The authorizing statute contains restrictions against lobbying, political activities, class actions except under certain conditions, and cases involving abortion, school desegregation, and draft registration or desertion from the military. Additional restrictions have been included in appropriations laws each year. Under the current appropriations law, LSC grantees may not:

- engage in partisan litigation related to redistricting;
- attempt to influence regulatory, legislative, or adjudicative action at the federal, state, or local level;
- attempt to influence oversight proceedings of the LSC;
- initiate or participate in any class action suit;
- represent certain categories of aliens, except that both LSC and non-LSC funds may be used to represent aliens who have been victims of domestic violence or child abuse;
- conduct advocacy training on a public policy issue or encourage political activities, strikes, or demonstrations;
- claim or collect attorneys' fees;
- engage in litigation related to abortion;
- represent clients in eviction proceedings if the eviction was based on drug-related activities;
- represent federal, state, or local prisoners;
- participate in efforts to reform a federal or state welfare system;
- engage in activities related to assisted suicide, euthanasia, or mercy killing; or
- solicit clients.

LSC grantees must establish priorities, and staff must agree in writing not to engage in activities outside these priorities. Moreover, federal law prohibits the LSC from receiving nonfederal funds, and grantees are prohibited from receiving non-LSC funds, unless the source of funds is told in writing that these funds may not be used for any activities prohibited by the LSC Act or the appropriations law.[6]

CLIENTS AND CASES

Legal services provided through LSC funds are available only in civil matters to individuals with household incomes of less than 125% of the federal poverty guidelines. The LSC places primary emphasis on the provision of routine legal services. Legal services cases deal with a variety of issues, including family-related issues (divorce, separation, child custody, support, adoption, spousal abuse, child abuse or neglect); housing issues (evictions, foreclosures); welfare or other income maintenance program issues (access to health care, unemployment compensation benefit claims); consumer and finance issues (consumer fraud, debt collection); and individual rights (employment, health, juvenile, and education).

LSC CASES CLOSED

FY2002: 978,834
FY2003: 935,793
FY2004: 901,067
FY2005: 906,338
FY2006: 895,488
FY2007: 906,507
FY2008: 889,155

During 2008, legal services attorneys closed 889,155 cases. Family issues such as divorce and separation, custody and visitation, domestic abuse, and child support were the substance of about 35% of cases handled by field offices; housing issues, including eviction cases, comprised about 26% of cases; income maintenance issues represented another 11% of cases; and consumer finance (12.2%), health (3.5%), employment (3%), education (0.8%), and individual rights (1.5%) issues comprised 21% of cases. Most of the cases handled by LSC are resolved through advice and referral. In 2008, only about 13% of cases were resolved in court, primarily because they involved family law issues (e.g., protective orders, child support, etc.) in which court action was required by state law.[7]

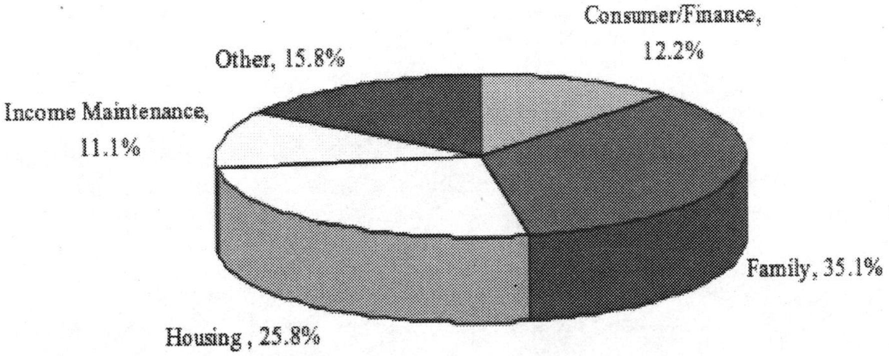

Source: Figure prepared by the Congressional Research Service.

Figure 1. LSC Cases Closed in 2008, by Legal Problem.

LSC grantees have closed about 1 million cases annually for the last several years. In addition, they have handled another 4 million legal service "matters" such as helping self-represented (i.e., pro se) litigants obtain the information they need to pursue their lawsuits, disseminating legal services materials in communities, referring clients to appropriate services, and providing mediation assistance.[8]

According to the LSC Fact Book for 2008, LSC clients were of all races and ethnic groups. LSC clients include the working poor, veterans, family farmers, people with disabilities, battered women, women seeking divorces or child support, and victims of natural disasters. In 2008, 73% of LSC clients were females and 27% were males. Approximately 85% of LSC clients were between the ages of 18 and 59, 13% were age 60 or older, and about 2% were under age 18.

RACE AND ETHNICITY OF LSC CLIENTS, 2008

White, not Hispanic	46.5%
Black, not Hispanic	24.9%
Hispanic	20.4%
Native American	2.3%
Asian or Pacific Islander	1.6%
Other	4.3%

In 2005, LSC staff were directed by the LSC to document the extent to which the civil legal needs of low-income persons were not being met. In September 2009, the report was updated. The new report confirms the findings of the earlier report. The LSC found that (1) 50% of potential clients requesting legal assistance were denied assistance because the LSC did not have the resources to help them; (2) at least 80% of persons who were eligible for LSC services do not get access to either a legal services attorney or a private attorney (pro bono or paid) when they need such assistance; and (3) there is one legal services attorney for every 6,415 low-income persons—the comparable number for the general population is one attorney for every 429 persons, a difference of 15 to 1.[9]

FUNDING HISTORY

When the LSC was first established, its initial goal was to provide all low-income people with at least "minimum access" to legal services, defined as the equivalent of one legal services attorney for every 5,000 poor persons. This goal was briefly achieved in FY1980, but not maintained due to inflation and subsequent budget cuts. For example, in FY2004, the LSC estimated an appropriation of $683 million would have been needed for minimum access; however, the LSC received $335 million in appropriations that year. According to a 2009 LSC study (cited above), there is one legal services attorney for every 6,415 poor persons.

Table 1. LSC Appropriations History ($ in millions)

FY	$	FY	$	FY	$	FY	$	FY	$
1976	92	1990	317	1995	400	2000	304	2005	331
1980	300	1991	328	1996	278	2001	329	2006	327
1984	275	1992	350	1997	283	2002	329	2007	349
1988	306	1993	357	1998	283	2003	337	2008	351
1989	309	1994	400	1999	300	2004	335	2009	390

Source: Table prepared by the Congressional Research Service.

Funds for the LSC are included in the annual appropriation for Science, the Departments of State, Justice, and Commerce, and Related Agencies (House) and Commerce, Justice, Science, and Related Agencies (Senate). **Table 1** shows LSC appropriations for selected years from FY1976 (the first full year of LSC operations) to FY2009. Current funding remains below the LSC's highest funding level of $400 million in FY1994 and FY1995. LSC funding accounts for less than half (40%) of all funding for civil legal services for the poor in the United States (discussed in more detail later in this report).

FY1996

From its inception through FY1995, LSC appropriations gradually increased. However, for FY1996, Congress funded the LSC at $278 million, for a reduction of almost 31% from the previous year. In its FY1996 budget resolution, the House assumed a three-year phase-out of the LSC, recommending appropriations of $278 million in FY1996, $141 million in FY1997, and elimination by FY1998. The House Budget Committee stated in its report (H.Rept. 104-120):

> Too often, ... lawyers funded through federal LSC grants have focused on political causes and class action lawsuits rather than helping poor Americans solve their legal problems.... A phase out of federal funding for the LSC will not eliminate free legal aid to the poor. State and local governments, bar associations, and other organizations already provide substantial legal aid to the poor.

The FY1996 appropriation for the LSC entirely eliminated funding for supplemental legal assistance programs, including Native American and migrant farm worker support, national and state support centers, regional training centers, and other national activities.

FY1997-FY2001

The phase-out of the LSC envisioned by the House budget resolution did not occur. Instead, between FY1996 and FY2001, LSC funding was gradually increased. For FY1997, Congress funded the LSC at $283 million (P.L. 104-208). For FY1998, Congress again funded the LSC at $283 million (P.L. 105-119). For FY1999, Congress funded the LSC at $300 million (P.L. 105- 277). For FY2000, Congress funded the LSC at $305 million, but also included a provision in the legislation that mandated a 0.3 8% government-wide rescission of discretionary budget authority for FY2000. The funding for the LSC for FY2000 was thereby decreased to $304 million (P.L. 106-113).

For FY2001, the Clinton Administration requested $340 million for the LSC. The Clinton Administration had requested $340 million every year since FY1997, in an effort to partially restore the 1996 cutback in funding. P.L. 106-553 included $330 million for LSC for FY2001, and was signed by President Clinton on December 21, 2000. P.L. 106-554 mandated a 0.22% government-wide rescission of discretionary budget authority for FY200 1 for almost all government agencies. Thus, the $330 million appropriation for LSC for FY2001 was reduced to $329.3 million.

FY2002-FY2005

For FY2002 through FY2005, the Bush Administration requested $329.3 million in annual appropriations for the LSC. In carrying out the LSC's vision of an effective and efficient statewide system of delivering legal services to the poor, grantees had been merging and reconfiguring their legal services programs to better use every federal dollar allocated to them.[10] The House report (H.Rept. 107-139) indicated concern about the LSC overruling, without appeal, certain configurations implemented by grantees via the state planning process. The House report directed the LSC to review the state planning process and report back to the committee with a proposal that outlined the reconfiguration standards and the process for states to appeal LSC's decisions. P.L. 107-77 included $329.3 million for LSC for FY2002.

For FY2003, Congress funded the LSC at $336.6 million (P.L. 108-7); this funding level included a $9.5 million allotment to offset decennial Census funding reallocations (i.e., to partially compensate some service areas for smaller LSC funding levels for FY2003 than the area received for FY2002 as a result of the change in state poverty populations based on census data for 2000), and a mandated 0.65% government-wide rescission.

For FY2004, Congress funded the LSC at $335.3 million (P.L. 108-199); this funding level included a 0.59% across-the-board government-wide rescission and an additional 0.465% uniform rescission applicable only to funding for the Commerce, Justice, State, and Related Agencies appropriation (which included the LSC).

For FY2005, Congress funded the LSC at $330.8 million (P.L. 108-447); this funding level included a provision that allowed the LSC to spend up to $1 million of prior-year funding balances for a school student loan repayment pilot program, a 0.8% across-the-board government- wide rescission, and an additional 0.54% uniform rescission applicable only to funding for the Commerce, Justice, State, and Related Agencies appropriation (which included the LSC).

FY2006-FY2008

For FY2006, the Bush Administration requested $318.3 million for the LSC. P.L. 109-108 included $330.8 million for the LSC for FY2006—the same amount originally passed by the House, instead of $358.5 million, as passed by the Senate. P.L. 109-108 also included a general rescission equal to 0.28% of funding for the Science, State, Justice, Commerce, and Related Agencies appropriation (which includes the LSC). P.L. 109-148 included a 1% government-wide rescission on discretionary programs. Thus, the LSC appropriation for FY2006 was lowered to $326.6 million.

For FY2007, the Bush Administration requested $310.9 million for the LSC. P.L. 110-5 included language that specified that the LSC would be funded at $348.6 million for FY2007. P.L. 110-5 incorporated the fourth continuing resolution for FY2007 (H.J.Res. 20), which included provisions to fund most of the government agencies, including the LSC, through FY2007.

For FY2008, the Bush Administration requested $311 million for the LSC. The Administration's budget request included $289 million for basic field programs and requires independent audits; almost $13 million for management and administration; $5 million for client self-help and information technology; and $3 million of the Office of the Inspector General.

For FY2008, the Senate Appropriations Committee recommended $390 million for the LSC (S. 1745), a $41.4 million increase above the FY2007 LSC appropriation, and $79.1 million above the Administration's FY2008 budget request for the LSC. During the Senate debate on the bill (H.R. 3093), an amendment by Senator Bingaman was passed to permit LSC-funded legal services programs to provide legal assistance to "H2B" workers—temporary foreign workers employed in the forestry industry—in matters directly related to their employment. LSC-funded programs are currently prohibited from serving H2B workers. The Senate-passed bill provided $390 million for the LSC for FY2008.

For FY2008, the House Appropriations Committee recommended $377 million for the LSC, a $28.4 million increase above the FY2007 LSC appropriation, $66.1 million above the Administration's FY2008 budget request for the LSC, and $13 million below the Senate-passed bill. The House-passed bill (H.R. 3093) included $377 million for the LSC for FY2008.

Pursuant to a continuing appropriations resolution (H.J.Res. 52), enacted September 29, 2007, the LSC operated at FY2007 funding levels through November 16, 2007 (P.L. 110-92). Pursuant to a second continuing appropriations resolution in the FY2008 Department of Defense appropriation (H.R. 3222), enacted November 13, 2007, the LSC operated at FY2007 funding levels through December 14, 2007 (P.L. 110-116). Pursuant to a third continuing appropriations resolution (H.J.Res. 69), enacted December 14, 2007, the LSC operated at FY2007 funding levels through December 21, 2007 (P.L. 110-137). Pursuant to a fourth continuing appropriations resolution (H.J.Res. 72), the LSC operated at FY2007 funding levels through December 31, 2007 (P.L. 110- 137).

P.L. 110-161, the Consolidated Appropriations Act, 2008 (H.R. 2764—enacted December 26, 2007), included $350.5 million for the LSC for FY2008. This amount is $1.9 million above the FY2007 appropriation for the LSC and $39.6 million above the Administration's FY2008 budget request for the LSC. However, it is below the amounts that were passed by the House and the Senate. The FY2008 appropriation for the LSC includes $332.4 million for basic field programs and required independent audits, $12.5 million for management and administration, $2.1 million for client self-help and information technology, $3.0 million for the Office of the Inspector General, and $0.5 million for loan repayment assistance. According to the LSC, pursuant to P.L. 110-161, LSC-funded legal services programs can now provide limited representation to temporary forestry workers.

FY2009

For FY2009, the Bush Administration requested $311.0 million for the LSC.[11] The Administration's budget request included $290.1 million for basic field programs and required independent audits; $12.8 million for management and administration; $5.0 million for client self- help and information technology; and $3.0 million for the Office of the Inspector General.

For FY2009, the House Appropriations Committee approved $390 million for the LSC. The House committee-approved draft bill provided 11% more than the FY2008 LSC appropriation and 25% more than the FY2009 request for the LSC. It included $367 million for basic field programs and required independent audits, $16 million for management and administration, $3 million for client self-help and information technology, $3 million for the Office of the Inspector General, and $1 million for loan repayment assistance.

For FY2009, the Senate Appropriations Committee, like the House committee, also approved $390 million for the LSC. However, the Senate committee bill (S. 3182) included $369 million for basic field programs and required independent audits, $13 million for management and administration, $3.8 million for client self-help and information technology, $3.2 million for the Office of the Inspector General, and $1 million for loan repayment assistance.

P.L. 110-289, the Housing and Economic Recovery Act of 2008 (enacted July 30, 2008), included a provision that provides $30 million for pre-foreclosure and legal counseling through a new grant program. Under the new program, the Neighborhood Reinvestment Corporation, a congressional chartered nonprofit organization, is required to make grants to housing counselors to hire LSC attorneys to assist homeowners who have legal issues directly related to the homeowner's foreclosure, delinquency, or short sale. [12]

P.L. 110-315, the College Opportunity and Affordability Act of 2008 (enacted August 14, 2008), included a provision that authorizes $10 million for the U.S. Department of Education to distribute as loan repayment assistance grants (up to $6,000 per year, $40,000 for a lifetime) to full-time civil legal aid lawyers who agree to remain employed as such for at least three years.[13] Although the loan repayment program was authorized, funding for the program has not yet been appropriated.

P.L. 110-329, the Consolidated Security, Disaster Assistance, and Continuing Appropriations Act, 2009 (enacted September 30, 2008), among other things, required that the LSC continue to operate at FY2008 funding levels (i.e., $350.5 million) until March 6, 2009, or until LSC's regular FY2009 appropriation is enacted.

P.L. 111-8, the Omnibus Appropriations Act, 2009 (enacted March 11, 2009), includes $390.0 million for the LSC for FY2009. This amount is $39.5 million above the FY2008 appropriation for the LSC and $79.0 million above the Bush Administration's FY2009 budget request for the LSC. The FY2009 appropriation for the LSC includes $365.8 million for basic field programs and required independent audits, $16.0 million for management and administration, $3.0 million for client self-help and information technology, $4.2 million for the Office of the Inspector General, and $1.0 million for loan repayment assistance.

It is important to note that since FY1996, all of the LSC appropriations laws have included language stipulating the provisions restricting the activities of LSC grantees enacted in previous LSC appropriations laws.[14] (See the earlier section titled "Restrictions on Activities.") **Table 2** shows LSC appropriations for FY2001-FY2009, by component of funding.

FY2010

For FY2010, the Obama Administration requested $435 million for the LSC.[15] This amount is $45 million (11.5%) above the FY2009 appropriation of $390 million for the LSC. The Administration's budget request included $410.4 million for basic field programs and required independent audits; $17 million for management and grants oversight; $3.4 million for client self- help and information technology; $3.2 million for the Office of the Inspector General; and $1 million for loan repayment assistance. The Obama Administration also proposed that LSC restrictions on class action suits and attorneys' fees be eliminated.

For FY2010, the House Appropriations Committee approved $440 million for the LSC (H.Rept. 111-149). The House bill (H.R. 2847) provides almost 13% more than the FY2009 LSC appropriation and 1% more than the Administration's FY20 10 budget request for the LSC. The House approved $440 million for the LSC on June 18, 2009. The House voted to continue existing limitations on the use of LSC funds (and non-LSC funds) except for the restriction on the ability of LSC-funded programs to collect attorneys' fees. The House bill also included funds for a loan repayment assistance program to help legal services programs recruit and retain talented attorneys.

For FY20 10, the Senate Appropriations Committee approved $400 million for the LSC (S.Rept. 111-34). The Senate version of the bill (H.R. 2847) provides about 3% more than the FY2009 LCS appropriation and 8% less than the Administration's FY20 10 request for the LSC. The Senate passed H.R. 2847 on November 5, 2009. The Senate-passed version of the bill included $400 million in funding for the LSC and would continue existing limitations on the use of federal funds but would eliminate the restrictions on the use of non-federal funds except in litigation involving abortion and cases involving prisoners.[16]

DISTRIBUTION OF LSC FUNDS AND NON-LSC RESOURCES

LSC funds appropriated for basic field programs are distributed to the states and jurisdictions on a per capita basis, according to U.S. Bureau of the Census data[17] on the number of "poor" persons in each service area.[18] Grantees within each state or jurisdiction then compete among themselves for funding.

Table 2. LSC: Funding for Program Components, FY2001 -FY2009 ($ in millions)

LSC Program Components	FY2001	FY2002	FY2003	FY2004	FY2005	FY2006	FY2007	FY2008	FY2009
Basic field programs	309.3	310.0	308.0	316.4	312.4	308.4	330.8	332.5	365.8
Management and administration	10.8	12.4	13.2	13.0	12.8	12.7	12.7	12.5	16.0
Client self-help and information technology	6.9	4.4	3.4	1.3	1.3	1.2	2.1	2.1	3.0
Office of the Inspector General	2.2	2.5	2.6	2.6	2.5	2.5	3.0	3.0	4.2
Offset for census-based reallocations	0.0	0.0	9.4	1.8	1.8	1.8	0.0	0.0	0.0
Student loan repayment program	0.0	0.0	0.0	0.0	0.0	0.0	0.0	0.5	1.0
Total	329.3	329.3	336.6	335.3	330.8	326.6	348.6	350.5	390.0

Source: Table prepared by the Congressional Research Service.

Note: These data reflect appropriations after all rescissions; numbers may not add to total due to rounding.

Although the LSC is the largest single source of funding for the civil legal services system in the United States, it is not the only source of funding. Local legal services programs supplement their LSC grants with funds from a variety of governmental and private sources. Non-LSC funding sources include state and local grants; state Interest on Lawyers' Trust Accounts (IOLTAs) programs;[19] federal programs such as the Title XX Social Services Block Grant, the Older Americans Act, the Violence Against Women Act, and Community Development Block Grants; and private grants from entities such as the United Way, foundations, and national, state, and local bar associations. In addition, private attorneys accept referrals to provide legal services to the poor, primarily through LSC-funded pro bono programs.[20]

As shown in Table 3, in 2008, LSC funding accounted for about 40% of the $881.0 million spent in the United States for civil legal services for the poor.[21]

Table 3. Funding for LSC and Non-LSC Programs, by Jurisdiction, FY2008

State	LSC Funding	Number of LSC Programs	Non-LSC Funding	Total Funding	LSC Funding as % of Total
Alabama	6,391,069	1	1,004,547	7,395,616	86.4
Alaska	1,309,799	1	1,562,390	2,872,189	45.6
Arizona	10,002,746	3	5,046,865	15,049,611	66.5
Arkansas	3,965,429	2	1,957,345	5,922,774	67.0
California	45,972,139	11	44,104,270	90,076,409	51.0
Colorado	3,652,360	1	9,612,933	13,265,293	27.5
Connecticut	2,510,388	1	738,948	3,249,336	77.3
Delaware	645,563	1	582,564	1,228,127	52.6

State	LSC Funding	Number of LSC Programs	Non-LSC Funding	Total Funding	LSC Funding as % of Total
District of Columbia	999,250	1	1,450,252	2,449,502	40.8
Florida	19,138,324	7	19,644,504	38,782,828	49.3
Georgia	9,346,744	2	14,162,194	23,508,938	39.8
Hawaii	1,615,005	2	5,517,378	7,132,383	22.6
Idaho	1,406,165	1	954,685	2,360,850	59.6
Illinois	12,194,108	3	19,029,266	31,223,374	39.1
Indiana	5,468,579	1	3,093,466	8,562,045	63.9
Iowa	2,390,194	1	5,822,688	8,212,882	29.1
Kansas	2,319,730	1	6,027,645	8,347,375	27.8
Kentucky	6,267,511	4	11,600,142	17,867,653	35.1
Louisiana	8,174,746	4	5,506,883	13,681,629	59.7
Maine	1,375,222	1	4,831,543	6,206,765	22.2
Maryland	3,973,707	1	18,442,066	22,415,773	17.7
Massachusetts	5,466,702	4	1,766,614	7,233,316	75.6
Michigan	9,771,150	6	13,936,372	23,707,522	41.2
Minnesota	3,705,231	5	14,364,126	18,069,357	20.5
Mississippi	5,326,377	2	3,059,155	8,385,532	63.5
Missouri	5,793,058	4	12,182,075	17,975,133	32.2
Montana	1,404,379	1	1,962,672	3,367,051	41.7
Nebraska	1,477,438	1	806,918	2,284,356	64.7
Nevada	2,054,121	1	692,426	2,746,547	74.8
New Hampshire	706,841	1	172,530	879,371	80.4
New Jersey	7,005,564	6	42,010,077	49,015,641	14.3
New Mexico	4,142,386	1	2,381,466	6,523,852	63.5
New York	25,828,654	7	64,991,724	90,820,378	28.4
North Carolina	9,956,235	1	12,536,437	22,492,672	44.3
North Dakota	1,010,696	1	978,085	1,988,781	50.8
Ohio	10,770,476	6	47,784,601	58,555,077	18.4
Oklahoma	5,670,197	2	5,858,296	11,528,493	49.2
Oregon	3,685,556	1	4,764,828	8,450,384	43.6
Pennsylvania	12,712,462	8	26,258,559	38,971,021	32.6
Rhode Island	1,078,675	1	2,770,103	3,848,778	28.0
South Carolina	5,659,072	1	4,956,674	10,615,746	53.3
South Dakota	1,900,907	2	813,738	2,714,645	70.0
Tennessee	7,350,782	4	12,343,509	19,694,291	37.3
Texas	30,161,864	3	22,362,294	52,524,158	57.4
Utah	1,995,174	1	1,937,900	3,933,074	50.7
Vermont	607,175	1	64,567	671,742	90.4
Virginia	6,093,972	6	11,008,894	17,102,866	35.6
Washington	6,648,388	1	15,433,796	22,082,184	30.1
West Virginia	2,890,210	1	4,659,954	7,550,164	38.3
Wisconsin	4,991,219	2	6,021,488	11,012,707	45.3
Wyoming	658,722	1	0	658,722	100.0
Guam	312,133	1	614,178	926,311	33.7

Table 3. (Continued)

State	LSC Funding	Number of LSC Programs	Non-LSC Funding	Total Funding	LSC Funding as % of Total
Micronesia	1,624,748	1	695,250	2,319,998	70.0
Puerto Rico	16,754,963	2	4,093,509	20,848,472	80.4
Virgin Islands	313,062	1	1,347,133	1,660,195	18.9
Total (States and DC)	335,642,461	132	519,572,452	855,214,913	39.2
Total (States, DC, and Territories)	354,647,367	137	526,322,522	880,969,889	40.3

Source: Table prepared by the Congressional Research Service, using data from the Legal Services Corporation, *Legal Services Corporation Fact Book 2008*, August 2009, This report can be found at https://grants.lsc.gov/ Easygrants_Web_LSC/Implementation/Modules/ Login/Controls/PDFs/ factbook2008forRIN.pdf. Compilation of state and territory program data is based on information from the LSC website, http://www.lsc.gov/map/ index.php.

End Notes

[1] Center for Law and Social Policy. *Securing Equal Justice for All: A Brief History of Civil Legal Assistance in the United States*, by Alan W. Houseman and Linda E. Perle, Revised January 2007, p. 19, http://www.clasp.org/ admin/ site/publications/files/0158.pdf. See also President Nixon, *Special Message to the Congress Proposing Establishment of a Legal Services Corporation*, May 5, 1971, http://www.presidency

[2] In 2007, 125% of the federal poverty guidelines was $25,813 for a household of four (higher in Alaska and Hawaii).

[3] This system supplanted the previous system of presumptive refunding for LSC grantees. The LSC is prohibited from granting any preference to current or previous grantees of LSC funds (Section 503(e) of P.L. 104-134, enacted April 26, 1996).

[4] Legal Services Corporation. *State Planning—A Five Year Overview*, 2005, pp. 1-7, http://www.lsc.gov/pdfs/ 030194_sp5yrrprt.pdf.

[5] Ibid., p. 8.

[6] For additional information, see CRS Report R40679, *Legal Services Corporation: Restrictions on Activities.*

[7] Legal Services Corporation, *Legal Services Corporation Fact Book 2008*, August 2009, https://grants.lsc.gov/ Easygrants_Web_LSC/Implementation/Modules/Login/Controls/PDFs/factbook2008forRIN.pdf.

[8] Testimony before the House Judiciary Committee Subcommittee on Commercial and Administrative Law Submitted by LSC President Helaine M. Barnett, March 31, 2004, http://www.lsc.gov/government testimony_detail_T1 16_R2.php.

[9] Legal Services Corporation, "Documenting the Justice Gap in America—The Current Unmet Civil Legal Needs of Low-Income Americans," September 2005, available at http://www.lsc.gov/press/documents/ LSCJusticeGap_FINAL_1001.pdf. See also Legal Services Corporation, "Documenting the Justice Gap in America— The Current Unmet Civil Legal Needs of Low-Income Americans," September 2009, available at http://www.lsc.gov/ pdfs/documenting_thejustice_gap_in_america_2009.pdf.

[10] Legal Services Corporation, A Special Report to Congress, *State Planning & Reconfiguration*, September 2001, pp. 2-3, 10.

[11] Each year the LSC submits its own budget request to Congress. In most years, the LSC budget request is significantly higher than the amount that appears in the President's annual budget. For FY2009, the LSC requested an appropriation of $471.4 million, a 52% increase over the President's budget request of $311 million for the LSC. The reasons cited for the significant increase included legal problems of existing and new clients stemming from the recent crises in the mortgage and housing industries, the ongoing impact of natural disasters, and widespread domestic violence, along with recent LSC findings that there is significant unmet need among America's poorest populations with regard to civil legal assistance.

[12] See sections 2305 and 2401 of P.L. 110-289.

[13] See section 431 of P.L. 110-315.

[14] Although the authorizing statute contains some restrictions on LSC activities, many more restrictions were added by P.L. 104-134 in 1996. Other restrictions and modifications or clarifications were added in 1997 (P.L. 105-

119) and 1998 (P.L. 105-277). All LSC appropriation laws enacted after 1996 have included language referencing the restrictions in prior appropriation laws.

[15] Each year the LSC submits its own budget request to Congress. In most years, the LSC budget request is significantly higher than the amount that appears in the President's annual budget. For FY20 10, the LSC requested an appropriation of $485.1 million, an 11.5% increase over the President's budget request of $435 million for the LSC. The reasons cited for the significant increase included legal problems of existing and new clients stemming from the recent crises in the mortgage and housing industries, the ongoing impact of natural disasters, and widespread domestic violence, along with recent LSC findings that there is significant unmet need among America's poorest populations with regard to civil legal assistance.

[16] S.Rept. 111-34 (page 143) deletes section 504(d) of P.L. 104-134 (pertaining to the use of non-federal funds for activities prohibited by the LSC), but also stipulates that no funds (federal or non-federal) can be used for activities specified in section 504(a)(14) or section 504(a)(15) of P.L. 104-134 (respectively, these two sections pertain to abortion litigation and litigation involving persons incarcerated in a federal, state, or local prison).

[17] The census data is based on the most recent decennial census—currently, the year 2000.

[18] In other words, if a specific state has 12% of the U.S. poverty population, that state generally would receive about 12% of the LSC funding amount allocated for local legal services programs.

[19] These funds represent interest earned on sums deposited by clients with attorneys for short periods of time.

[20] In 2008, approximately 36,000 private attorneys accepted referrals to help LSC clients.

[21] Legal Services Corporation, *Legal Services Corporation Fact Book 2008*, August 2009, https://grants.lsc.gov/Easygrants _Web _LSC/Implementation/Modules/Login/Controls/PDFs/factbook2008forRIN.pdf.

In: Legal Aid for the Poor and the Legal Services Corporation ISBN: 978-1-61668-939-1
Editor: Carl T. Donovan

Chapter 4

DOCUMENTING THE JUSTICE GAP IN AMERICA: THE CURRENT UNMET CIVIL LEGAL NEEDS OF LOW-INCOME AMERICANS

Legal Services Corporation

"Equal justice under law is not merely a caption on the facade of the Supreme Court building. It is perhaps the most inspiring ideal of our society...it is fundamental that justice should be the same, in substance and availability, without regard to economic status."
—U.S. Supreme Court Justice Lewis Powell, Jr.

EXECUTIVE SUMMARY

As the institution charged by Congress with the administration of the federally-funded civil legal assistance program for those who would otherwise be unable to afford adequate legal counsel, the Legal Services Corporation (LSC) has a responsibility to communicate to Congress what is required to secure *necessary access to civil legal assistance*—that is, the level of assistance that would be required across the nation to respond appropriately to the civil legal needs of low-income individuals and families.

The civil legal problems of low-income people involve essential human needs, such as protection from abusive relationships, safe and habitable housing, access to necessary health care, disability payments to help lead independent lives, family law issues including child support and custody actions, and relief from financial exploitation.

The difference between the level of legal assistance available and the level that is necessary to meet the needs of low-income Americans is the "justice gap."

In September 2005, LSC issued a comprehensive report, *Documenting the Justice Gap in America: The Current Unmet Civil Legal Needs of Low-Income Americans*, which used a variety of methodologies to document the justice gap and to quantify necessary access to civil legal assistance.

This report updates the 2005 Justice Gap Report, using new data. Analysis of this data confirms that the conclusion of the 2005 Justice Gap Report remains valid: there continues to be a major gap between the civil legal needs of low-income people and the legal help that they receive.

- Data collected in the spring of 2009 show that for every client served by an LSC-funded program, one person who seeks help is turned down because of insufficient resources.
- New state legal needs studies have added depth to a body of social science knowledge that has produced consistent findings for a decade and a half, documenting that only a small fraction of the legal problems experienced by low-income people (less than one in five) are addressed with the assistance of either a private attorney (pro bono or paid) or a legal aid lawyer.
- Analysis of the most recent available figures on attorney employment shows that nationally, on the average, only one legal aid attorney is available for every 6,415 low-income people. By comparison, there is one private attorney providing personal legal services (those meeting the legal needs of private individuals and families) for every 429 people in the general population who are above the LSC poverty threshold.
- New data indicate that state courts, especially those courts that deal with issues affecting low- income people, in particular lower state courts and such specialized courts as housing and family courts, are facing significantly increased numbers of unrepresented litigants. Studies show that the vast majority of people who appear without representation are unable to afford an attorney, and a large percentage of them are low-income people who qualify for legal aid. A growing body of research indicates that outcomes for unrepresented litigants are often less favorable than those for represented litigants.

The first three findings are derived from three different methodologies, which were also employed in the 2005 report. The fourth finding is derived from a review and analysis of data on litigants appearing in court without representation, which was recommended in the 2005 report for which LSC did not have sufficient data at that time.

- **Methodology #1:** ***Unable to Serve:*** *National count of people seeking legal help from LSCfunded providers who are denied services because programs lack sufficient resources.* LSC asked its 137 grantee programs, with 918 offices, to document the number of people seeking assistance from the program who could not be served due to insufficient program resources. LSCfunded programs collected this data over a two-month period in March-May 2009, the same time period during which this data was collected for the 2005 Justice Gap Report.
- **Methodology #2:** ***Continuing Documentation of Unmet Legal Needs:*** *Analysis and comparison of recent state legal needs studies.* Since 2005, seven states have conducted legal needs studies using similar methodologies. For this report, the methodologies and findings of the seven recent state studies were compared to one another to draw currently valid, nationally applicable conclusions from them. The findings of these studies were also compared to the nine state studies conducted

during 2000-200 5 that were discussed in the 2005 report and the Comprehensive Legal Needs Study funded by the American Bar Association and released in 1994.

- **Methodology #3: *Attorneys Per Capita:*** *Attorneys Per Capita: National count of legal aid attorneys; comparison of ratio of legal aid attorneys to low-income population and ratio of private attorneys providing personal legal services to general population.* The count of legal aid attorneys included attorneys in all programs providing civil legal help to low-income people, not just those in LSC programs. The count of private attorneys providing personal legal services to the general population was based on estimates obtained from the American Bar Association. This report used U.S. Census population figures and estimates for the number of attorneys from the year 2007, the most recent year for which all figures were available.
- ***New Data on Unrepresented Litigants:*** Although there are no national statistics on unrepresented litigants, data was obtained from a compilation prepared by the National Center for State Courts of reports from state and federal courts, as well as individual reports from several states. The impact of the current economic crisis on caseloads and unrepresented litigants was documented by a survey of judges conducted by the Self-Represented Litigation Network in the spring of 2009. The available social science research on this topic also was reviewed.

Closing the justice gap and securing *necessary access to civil legal assistance* will require a multifaceted approach which will include a partnership of individual lawyers, the organized bar, federal and state governments, private funders and concerned private parties. In addition to increased funding for staffed legal aid programs, closing the justice gap will require increased pro bono efforts by the nation's lawyers. As the primary conduit for the federal government's share, the Legal Services Corporation bears responsibility for leading the way.

The findings reported here suggest a phased approach to addressing the unmet need. First, LSC's 2005 and 2009 "Unable to Serve" data show that only half of those seeking legal help from LSC grantees are able to be served. As an initial critical goal, there must be enough funding to serve all of those *currently* seeking help from LSC grantees. This requires a doubling of LSC funds and a doubling of the state, local, and private funds that also support LSC grantees.

Second, state legal needs studies conducted from 2000 to 2009 generally indicate that less than one in five low-income persons get the legal assistance they need. To fund this need, the federal share must grow to be five times greater than it is now, or $1.6 billion. IOLTA and other state, local and private funding sources, which are being hard hit by the economic downturn at present, will also have to grow in the future to contribute their proportionate share of the increase necessary to fund civil legal services.

In order to keep faith with our national commitment to equal access to justice, it is essential that the nation move toward the necessary funding levels in firm, measured strides that are designed to close the justice gap as quickly as possible.

Introduction

The 2005 Justice Gap Report

In September 2005, the Legal Services Corporation (LSC) issued a comprehensive report, *Documenting the Justice Gap in America: The Current Unmet Civil Legal Needs of Low-Income Americans*, which used a variety of methodologies to document the civil legal needs of low-income individuals and families and to quantify *necessary access to civil legal assistance*—that is, the level of assistance that would be required across the nation to respond appropriately to those needs.

The civil legal problems of low-income people involve essential human needs, such as protection from abusive relationships, safe and habitable housing, access to necessary health care, disability payments to help lead independent lives, family law issues including child support and custody actions, and relief from financial exploitation.

The difference between the level of legal assistance available and the level that is necessary to meet the needs of low-income Americans is the "justice gap."

The 2005 Justice Gap Report was the first nationwide report on the civil legal needs of low-income people since the Comprehensive Legal Needs Study funded by the American Bar Association and released in 1994.[1] The Justice Gap Report was based on data collected from LSC-funded programs in 2004 and 2005, as well as data from other state legal needs studies, the U.S. Census Bureau, and other sources covering the period 2000-200 5. The report synthesized and compared the findings of the existing studies from this period, as well as those from the 1994 ABA study.

LSC's Responsibility to Assess Legal Needs

Congress, in creating the Legal Services Corporation in 1974, determined that there is "need to provide equal access to the system of justice in our nation for those who would be otherwise unable to afford adequate legal counsel." Congress explicitly recognized in the LSC Act that, "providing legal assistance to those who face an economic barrier to adequate legal counsel will serve best the ends of justice, assist in improving opportunities for low-income persons," and "has reaffirmed faith in our government of laws."

The goal of providing equal access to justice for those who cannot afford to pay an attorney remains the reason for LSC's existence and the benchmark for its efforts. In developing the budget mark it submits to Congress, therefore, LSC has a duty to assess what has been accomplished in meeting the need, what still needs to be achieved, and the role that federal funding should play in doing so. This was the basis for the determination by the LSC Board of Directors that LSC should undertake the 2005 Justice Gap Report.

The 2009 Justice Gap Report

Since the first Justice Gap Report was issued in 2005, major developments have occurred that potentially affect levels of need for civil legal assistance and the ability of legal aid providers to meet it.

- The current economic crisis, with its attendant problems of high unemployment, home foreclosures and family stress, has resulted in legal problems relating to consumer credit, housing, employment, bankruptcies, domestic violence and child support, and has pushed many families into poverty for the first time.
- Just before the 2005 report was issued, Hurricane Katrina struck the Gulf Coast, resulting in legal needs that are still being experienced by low-income residents of Louisiana, Mississippi, and Texas, where many victims of the disaster have relocated. Hurricanes Ike and Gustav hit this region in 2008, a year that also saw widespread, record floods in the Midwest.
- While a long-term trend of increased state funding for civil legal aid has continued, budget crises have put this funding at risk in some states. Revenues from state Interest on Lawyers' Trust Accounts (IOLTA) programs rose in some states with new revenue enhancement techniques, but have recently fallen precipitously in many states as a result of low interest rates and the declining economy, reducing trust account deposits.
- According to the U.S. Census Bureau, the number of individuals living below 125 percent of the federal poverty level in the United States increased from 49.6 million in 2005 to 53.8 million in 2008.[2]
- At the federal level, an increase of $40 million in LSC funding for FY 2009 was signed into law in March 2009. (The increase was reflected in LSC grants beginning in April 2009, and its impact is not reflected in any of the data in this report.)

This report updates the findings and analysis of the 2005 report. As in 2005, LSC President Helaine M. Barnett convened a Justice Gap Advisory Committee to assist in the preparation of the report. In addition to LSC staff, the committee included representatives of the ABA Standing Committee on Legal Aid and Indigent Defendants (SCLAID) and the National Legal Aid and Defender Association (NLADA), both of which have traditionally provided their own recommendations on LSC funding and have independently undertaken efforts to develop new data on the unmet legal needs of low-income people, in addition to representatives of LSC-funded field programs and other members of the legal services community with expertise in documenting legal needs.[3]

The 2009 Justice Gap Advisory Committee concurred with the judgment of the 2005 group that the likely cost of more than $1 million to conduct a new national legal needs survey would not be justified, and that the justice gap could best be illuminated by using the same three methodologies employed in the 2005 report, each of which has particular strengths and provides a different perspective. In addition, as recommended in the 2005 Justice Gap Report, the committee also reviewed and analyzed available data and research on litigants appearing in court without representation. Together, these different sources offer a broad picture of the justice gap.

The information in this updated report confirms the findings of the 2005 Justice Gap Report and is consistent with a body of social scientific literature that has been growing for two decades. Of those people who seek assistance from LSC-funded legal aid programs, one is turned away because of limited resources for every one helped. Only a small fraction of the legal needs of low-income people are addressed with the assistance of an attorney. There are more than ten times as many private lawyers providing personal legal services to persons in the general population above the LSC poverty threshold as there are legal aid attorneys in relation to the low-income population they serve.[4] State courts are being overwhelmed by a rising tide of unrepresented litigants, many of them low-income people eligible for LSC-funded assistance who have been unable to obtain an attorney.

All of these findings support the conclusion that there remains a significant justice gap in the United States: the difference between the level of legal assistance available and the level that is necessary to meet the civil legal needs of low-income Americans.

METHODOLOGY #1: UNABLE TO SERVE

Count of People Seeking Assistance from LSC-Funded Programs Who Cannot be Served Due to Lack of Resources

To document the justice gap at the legal aid program level, LSC collected data on the number of people currently seeking help from LSC-funded legal aid programs who cannot be served due to insufficient program resources. Data was obtained from every state in the country.[5]

This count indicates that almost one million cases (944,376) per year are currently being rejected because programs lack sufficient resources to handle them. This figure does not include the many people who do not reach an LSC-funded program to ask for help, for whatever reason. Other studies indicate that those who seek help from legal aid programs represent only a fraction of the low- income people with legal needs.

Comparison of this data to statistics on cases handled in 2008 indicates that *for every client served by an LSC-funded program, at least one person seeking help will be turned down* due to limited resources. This conclusion is almost identical to the "Unable to Serve" finding of the 2005 study.

Methodology

LSC asked its grantee programs to collect data on numbers of people who could not be served during a two-month period, from Monday, March 16, through Friday, May 15, 2009. This period replicates that of the 2005 survey, which was taken March 14 through May 13, 2005.

Programs were asked to count the number of people who sought legal help from the program (in person, by phone, or online) for problems within LSC's statutory mandate and were denied services because the program lacked sufficient resources.[6]

It is important to keep in mind that the data yielded by this methodology is *under-inclusive* as a representation of the justice gap in several ways:

- Data was collected only from LSC-funded programs. The count does not include people who may have sought help unsuccessfully from other programs. This limitation is particularly significant in a few states and grantee service areas where intake is not primarily performed by the LSC grantees, which could consequently count only a small percentage of the total number of persons who were turned down for service.[7]
- The count of people who could not be served does not include clients who received some service, but not the level of service that they actually needed. LSC programs frequently provide advice and counsel to people when they cannot provide full representation. These cases do not appear as denials of service because the client has actually received a service (Advice and Counsel or Limited Action).[8]
- Many people who were counted as turned away for a single legal problem are likely to have had more than one legal problem. Legal aid programs regularly find that people who have contacted them for assistance with one problem have other legal problems as well.[9] State legal needs studies confirm that a large percentage of people with at least one legal problem have more than one problem (see Methodology #2).[10]
- The count does not include people who sought unsuccessfully to reach LSC-funded programs. Legal aid programs have a finite capacity to provide legal assistance to eligible clients and, because of limited resources, often must limit intake to certain hours and a limited number of phone lines and intake advocates.[11]
- More broadly, the methodology does not capture people with serious legal needs who did not contact any legal aid provider. Many factors may keep people from seeking help:
  - People with legal problems frequently do not understand that they need legal help (see Appendix C).
  - People with legal problems frequently do not know where to turn to obtain that help, or may not know that they are eligible for legal aid (see Appendix D).
  - People who meet the eligibility requirements for free legal services may not seek help from the program because they believe that the program will not be able to assist them. Legal aid providers observe that calls for assistance involving particular problem types tend to rise when the program is providing services in this area and to fall when intake is limited or closed in this area. A number of factors are typically involved in this phenomenon: for example, social services agencies and community workers are not making referrals; people are being told by others in the community that the program will not be able to help; and conversely, people are not hearing from others that they have obtained help from the program for a similar problem. Thus the number of calls tends to drop during periods when it is unlikely that clients will be able to obtain help, reflecting the understanding of the community about whether services are likely to be available.

- Other barriers, such as geographical distance and isolation, low literacy, physical or mental disability, limited English proficiency, culture and ethnic background, and apprehension about the courts and the legal system, also pose impediments.

This data provides *specific* documentation of the magnitude of unmet need. It is unique in that, through an extensive, nationwide sample, it documents legal problems for which people have *actually* sought, and been denied, help. It is also understated because it does not include many other people with pressing legal problems who also need assistance, but did not contact an LSC-funded program. [12]

Findings

The annualized figures for different case types are reported in Table 1.

To obtain an annualized figure, the data from the two-month survey was multiplied times six as a projection for an entire year.[13] For comparison, the number of cases in which service was *provided* by LSC-funded programs in 2008 is also set out in Table 1.[14]

The table shows that there will be roughly 944,000 people seeking legal help in 2009 that LSC programs will be unable to serve at all. In comparison, approximately 889,000 people were served by LSC-funded programs in 2008.[15] This means that *for every client served by an LSC-funded program, at least one eligible person seeking help will be turned down.*

This methodology yielded a similar ratio in the 2005 study, which estimated that 1,086,000 people would be turned away over the course of the year, while in the previous year, LSC programs had served 900,000 clients (see Appendix E, Table 2005-1).

Table 1. Unable to Serve

Type of Legal Problem Categories	Unable to Serve Twelve Month Projections	Calendar Year 2008 Cases Closed
Consumer	98,214	108,404
Education	8,874	6,839
Employment	42,264	26,896
Family	391,038	312,046
Juvenile	18,780	15,143
Health	22,230	30,802
Housing (Other than Foreclosure)	113,706	219,592
Foreclosure	21,756	9,920
Income	49,236	98,257
Individual	39,216	13,250
Miscellaneous*	139,062	48,006
Total	**944,376**	**889,155**

*Includes such services as wills and estates, advance directives and powers of attorney.

The fact that the 2009 "Unable to Serve" survey did not show a national increased demand for service during a period when such an increase would have been expected, due to the economic crisis, may be attributable in part to several of the limitations of the survey identified above. In particular, the limited intake capacity of many programs means that an increased number of callers would not necessarily result in an increased number of callers who actually reach the program. Another factor that may prevent increased demand from resulting in increased requests for assistance is that many potential clients and sources of referrals learn when legal aid programs are unable to accept new cases and stop calling or making referrals.

Conclusion to Methodology #1

This methodology indicates that, as in 2005, *roughly one-half of the people who seek help from LSCfunded legal aid providers are being denied service because of insufficient program resources*. Almost one million cases will be rejected this year for this reason.

Because this figure does not include people seeking help from non-LS C-funded programs, people who cannot be served fully, and people who for whatever reason are not seeking help from any legal aid program, it represents only a fraction of the level of unmet need. The methodology reported in the next section provides information about the size of this larger group of low-income people with civil legal needs.

Methodology #2: Continuing Documentation of Legal Needs

Analysis and Comparison of State Legal Needs Studies 2006-2009

Over the past four years, seven states have conducted large-scale, survey-based studies to determine the kinds of legal problems experienced by low-income residents and the extent to which these needs are being met. These seven studies were conducted by independent research entities, according to rigorous social science survey standards. The states that produced these studies are Virginia (2007), Utah (2007), Wisconsin (2007), Nevada (2008), Alabama (2009), Georgia (2009) and New Jersey (2009).

These seven studies add to a body of knowledge that has been building since the ABA study in 1994. For this report, the methodologies and findings of these seven studies were compared to one another to determine the extent to which it is possible to draw nationally applicable conclusions from them.[16] The findings and methodologies were also compared to those in the nine state studies considered in the 2005 Justice Gap Report, as well as those in the 1994 ABA study, to assess the continuing validity of the earlier findings.

In the six recent studies based on random telephone surveys, the sample size met the statistical threshold necessary to be able to generalize findings to the state low-income population (and in most instances was well above it). These findings can thus be considered very reliable.[17] Analysis of the seven recent state studies shows that their findings are broadly consistent with one another. This consistency of findings from state to state (and researcher to researcher) reinforces their validity and indicates that they are likely to be predictive of needs at the national level.

Key points of comparison are as follows. (Each is described in more detail in a subsequent section.)

- The seven recent state studies found that low-income households experience a per-household average of legal needs ranging up to three legal needs per year.
- All seven state studies found that only a small fraction of the legal problems experienced by low-income people (less than one in five) is addressed with the assistance of a private or legal aid lawyer.
- Those studies that ask respondents to rank the importance of the problems they experienced show that even if the legal problems included are limited to those considered to be "very important" or "most serious" or that "caused trouble" by the household experiencing it, a large majority of the problems are not addressed with the help of a lawyer.

These key findings of the seven recent state study findings are consistent with the analogous findings in the nine studies reported in the 2005 Justice Gap Report and the 1994 ABA study.

Methodology

Table 2. shows the studies considered in this report.

Table 2. State Legal Needs Surveys of Low-Income People 2006-2009

State	Released	Sponsor/Funder	Survey/Analysis By
Virginia	2007	Legal Services Corporation of Virginia	Schulman, Ronca, & Bucuvalas, Inc.
Utah	2007	Utah Legal Serices/ "And Justice for All"	Sociology Department, Portland State University/D. Michael Dale
Wisconsin	2007	State Bar of Wisconsin	Gene Kroupa & Associates
Nevada	2008	Supreme Court of Nevada Access to Justice Commission	Gene Kroupa & Associates; Social Entrepreneurs, Inc.
Alabama	2009	Alabama Access to Justice Commission/Alabama Bar Foundation	Southeast Research, Inc.
Georgia	2009	Georgia Supreme Court Equal Justice Commission, Committee on Civil Justice	A.L. Burruss Institute of Public Service and Research, Kennesaw State University/D. Michael Dale
New Jersey	2009	Legal Services of New Jersey	Schulman, Ronca, & Bucuvalas, Inc./Poverty Research Institute, Legal Services of New Jersey, in consultation with Institute for Survey Research, Temple University

All seven of these state studies used a fundamentally similar methodology, based on the well-established social science survey methodology used in the 1994 ABA study. This is the same methodology used in the nine studies reported in the 2005 Justice Gap Report:

- A statistically valid sample of low-income households was identified either through a random telephone survey or, in Utah, according to an alternative "cluster sampling" methodology (for a description of this methodology, see Appendix B).
- In an interview (by telephone, in the states using a random telephone survey; in person, in Utah, according to the "cluster sampling" methodology), respondents were presented with descriptions of various circumstances constituting potential legal problems and asked whether anyone in their household had experienced these circumstances during the preceding year. The survey questionnaire was reviewed by attorneys to ensure that the situations described to the respondents contained a legal issue and met a threshold of seriousness.
- When respondents reported having experienced such circumstances, follow-up questions were asked about what the household did (or did not do) about the situation and what contacts, if any, they had with the civil justice system.

As shown above in Table 2, the sponsors and funders of the studies were different in each state, and the surveys on which they were based were conducted or overseen by a variety of different independent academic or private research entities. The survey questionnaires varied somewhat to reflect local circumstances and concerns. Other details of the methodology also varied somewhat. (See Appendix B for variations). However, in all seven states, the survey samples were broadly representative of low-income people in the state and the survey questions about legal needs were sufficiently similar to allow the resulting findings to be compared meaningfully to one another.

Findings: Legal Needs

The studies found that on the average low-income households experienced from 1.3 to 3.0 legal needs per year, as shown in Table 3.[18]

Table 3. Legal Needs

State	Average number of legal needs in preceding year per low-income household
Virginia	2.4
Utah	1.3[19]
Alabama	1.7
Georgia	3.0
State	Average number of *categories* of legal needs in which low-income houselholds experiencing at least one problem experienceda problem in the preceding year
Wisconsin	2.1[20]
Nevada	2.4[21]
State	Average number of *new* legal needs in preceding year per low-income individual experiencing at least one problem
New Jersey	2.3[22]

Findings. Legal Help Sought/Received – Unmet Legal Needs

All seven state studies found a similarly large gap between the level of legal needs reported by low- income households and the percentage of those needs for which legal help was received.

The various studies report their findings on this fundamental issue in somewhat different ways, as shown in Table 4. Some studies report a figure for legal help *received*, either by a percentage of overall problems or by a percentage of respondents who obtained help (either *individuals* or *households*, depending on the study). Others report legal help received as a subset of legal help *sought*.[23]

Consequently, not all of the percentages shown are able to be compared directly to one another. However, the gap between the overall level of needs identified and the percentage of those for which legal help was received or sought is similarly large in each instance.

Overall, what these studies demonstrate is that only a small fraction of the legal problems experienced by low-income people (less than one in five) are addressed with the assistance of a private attorney or legal aid lawyer.

Table 4. Legal Help Received/Sought

State	***Received* legal help (by percentage of problems)**
Alabama	15.9 percent of problems, legal assistance received
Georgia	9.1 percent of problems, legal assistance received
	***Received* legal help (by percentage of households with problems)**
Utah	13.0 percent of households with problems received help from an attorney
Nevada	9 percent of households with problems received help from a lawyer for all the problems they identified; 20 percent received help for at least one, but not all of the legal problems they identified.
Virginia	17 percent of households with a legal need used a private lawyer or legal aid to assist them with that problem
	***Received* legal help (by percentage of households with problems *that sought help*)**
Wisconsin	37 percent of households with legal problems sought help from a lawyer for at least one problem; 27 percent of this group received help from a lawyer for at least one problem; 12 percent of this group received help for all the problems they identified
	Received legal help (by percentage of individuals who sought help or believed they needed help from a lawyer); soughtlegal help (by percentage of problems)
New Jersey	30.6 percent of respondents who tried to get the help of a lawyer of believed they needed the help of a lawyer were able to get assistance; 19.4 percent of problems, help sought from a lawyer.

Findings. Importance of Problems

Several of the state studies also collected data about the respondent's assessment of the seriousness of the problem involved and/or the respondent's understanding of whether a lawyer was necessary to resolve it, yielding data about percentages of the most immediate, serious problems.

- **Utah:** Respondents characterized 55.1 percent of the problems identified as "extremely important" and an additional 27.3 percent as "very important."
- **Georgia:** 40.4 percent of respondents reported that the problem had caused "significant trouble" and almost 66 percent replied that their problem had caused some level of trouble.
- **New Jersey:** Respondents with lower incomes rated 58.2 percent of their legal problems as "most serious."

Comparison of State Findings on Unmet Need 2006-2009 to State Findings on Unmet Need 2000-2005 and 1994 ABA Study

The 2005 Justice Gap Report considered nine state legal needs studies issued from 2000-200 5: Oregon (2000), Vermont (2001), New Jersey (2002), Connecticut (2003), Massachusetts (2003), Washington (2003), Tennessee (2004), Illinois (2005) and Montana (2005). These were the only survey-based legal needs studies of low-income people released during this period.

Like those considered in this update, these nine studies were sponsored and funded by a variety of different bar, court and funding entities, and the surveys on which they were based were conducted or overseen by different independent academic or private research entities. Like the 20 06- 2009 group of state studies, the sample size in all of the studies based on random surveys met the statistical threshold necessary to be able to generalize findings to the state low-income population (and in most instances was well above it). Again, especially given the consistency of findings from study to study, these findings can thus be considered very reliable. See Appendix E, Tables 2005-2 and 2005-5.

The findings of the seven studies considered here are wholly consistent with those of the nine studies reported in the 2005 Justice Gap Report. They are also consistent with those of the 1994 ABA study, which remains the only *national* study ever undertaken of this subject.

- The findings on the average number of legal needs per low-income household per year are within the same range: in the 2006-2009 group, from 1.3 to 3.0; in the earlier group, from 1.1 to 3.5 (See Appendix E, Table 2005-3). The ABA study found an annual average of 1.1 needs per low-income household. Only one state study, Vermont (2001), found a level of need as low as that in the ABA study. The ABA study thus represents the *lowest* figure available for estimating the number of legal needs experienced by low-income Americans.
- The findings on the level of *unmet* legal needs are within the same range: in all seven states, only a small fraction of the legal needs experienced by the household were

addressed with the assistance of an attorney—less than one in five. In the 2000-200 5 state studies that reported the percentage of total problems identified for which legal help was obtained (the most consistent way of measuring unmet legal need among the studies), the range was from 9 to 18.1 percent. (See Appendix E, Table 2005-4). The ABA study, at the low end of the range of study findings on *unmet* legal needs (i.e., showing a high percentage of *met* legal needs), concluded that roughly one out of every five of the legal needs of low-income people was addressed with the assistance of a private attorney or legal aid lawyer.

- As in the studies considered in 2005, those studies that asked respondents to rank the seriousness of their legal problems found that most people considered a majority of the problems identified to be serious (see Appendix E, Table 2005-6).

Conclusion to Methodology #2

Each of the seven state legal needs studies considered in this section—as well as the nine state studies considered in the 2005 Justice Gap Report—provides a full picture of the legal needs of low- income people in a particular state and the extent to which they are being met or not met. These studies look at the full range of legal needs, including those that never reach an attorney's office or a courthouse, and they consider legal services provided to low-income people from *all* sources, including pro bono attorneys and private attorneys charging full or reduced fees.

The seven new studies add to a body of knowledge that has been building since the ABA's 1994 national study. They confirm the findings of these earlier studies, all of which are consistent with one another, and support the conclusion that the findings of these state studies are generally applicable at the national level.

These studies confirm that *only a small fraction of the legal problems experienced by low-income people (less than one in five) are addressed with the assistance of either a private attorney (pro bono or paid) or a legal aid lawyer.*

METHODOLOGY #3: ATTORNEYS PER CAPITA

Legal Aid Lawyers Compared to Private Lawyers

Another perspective on the justice gap is provided by data on the numbers of legal aid attorneys serving the nation's low-income people. For this report, ABA and LSC staff collected data on the number of legal aid attorneys in the country in 2007, the most recent year for which data is available in most categories. A count was sought of *all* legal aid attorneys, not just those in LSC programs.

The count shows that despite the expansion of non-LSC funded programs since the mid-1990s, a majority of attorneys serving the poor still work in LSC-funded programs: there were 4,231 lawyers in LSC-funded programs (this figure includes all lawyers in the program, including those funded with state, private and other funds) and an estimated 3,700 in programs that do not receive LSC funding. The LSC-funded network thus remains the major source—and in many areas, the only source—of civil legal aid for low-income Americans.

The number of legal aid attorneys available to serve the poor provides a simple demonstration of the justice gap when compared to the number of attorneys serving the general public. The number of attorneys in private practice can be presumed to reflect a market response to the legal needs of the U.S. population. Nationally, there are *well over ten times more* private attorneys providing personal legal services to people in the general population[24] than there are legal aid attorneys serving the poor. While there is only one legal aid lawyer (including all sources of funding) per 6,415 low- income people in the country, this report estimates that there is one lawyer providing personal legal services (that is, services aimed at meeting the legal needs of private individuals and families) for every 429 people in the general population.

Methodology

ABA and LSC staff collected data on the number of legal aid attorneys in the country in 2007. "Legal aid attorneys" were not limited to those in LSC-funded programs; rather, the number of full-time-equivalent attorneys working in all programs providing free civil legal services to low-income people was sought. Reports from LSC-funded programs (not limited to federally-funded attorneys) were used as a starting point. Additional information was sought from state IOLTA programs or other contacts in each state, with special priority given to states with substantial non-LSC funding. For states where it was not possible to obtain actual attorney counts, ABA staff made projections based on resource data from the ABA Project to Expand Funding for Legal Services (PERLS), an initiative of the ABA Standing Committee on Legal Aid and Indigent Defendants. The ratio of legal aid attorneys to low-income people was calculated from the U.S. Census Bureau's Current Population Survey estimate of the low-income population for 2007, using 125 percent of the federal poverty guidelines as a definition of low-income.

For comparison, ABA estimates for the number of attorneys in private practice in the United States were obtained for the year 2007.[25] This yielded a count of 849,862 attorneys in private practice.

A rough estimate of the number of attorneys providing personal legal services to the general population was made based on information from the American Bar Foundation, which has found that 68 percent of attorneys in private practice are solo practitioners or in firms of ten attorneys or fewer.[26] These attorneys are those most likely to specialize in meeting the personal legal needs of private individuals and families. While some of these solo practitioners and small firm attorneys provide criminal defense or services falling outside the area of personal legal services, this is offset by the many attorneys in larger firms who do provide personal legal services in addition to corporate services. This analysis indicates that there are roughly 577,906 attorneys in the U.S. providing personal legal services to the general population.

The attorney figures were compared to the population of the United States from the 2007 Current Population Survey to obtain the ratio of private attorneys per capita in the general population.

Findings

As shown in Table 5, roughly 53 percent of all legal aid attorneys work in LSC-funded programs. The LSC network thus remains the major source of civil legal aid for low-income Americans. In many areas, the LSC-funded program is the only provider of civil legal aid.

Comparing the estimated number of legal aid attorneys in the nation in 2007 (7,931) to the number of people estimated to be living at 125 percent of poverty or lower by the Current Population Survey for 2007 (50,876,000) yields a ratio of one attorney per 6,415 low-income people.

In contrast, nationally, as calculated above, there were roughly 577,906 attorneys providing personal legal services to the general population numbering 247,826,000 in 2007. This yields a ratio of one attorney per 429 people in the general population—well over ten times the ratio of legal aid attorneys to the population they serve.[27] The difference between the level of resources available to the general population and those available to the low-income population is enormous.

Changes from 2005 Justice Gap Report

The 2005 Justice Gap Report considered the number of legal aid attorneys in 2002, compared to the number of attorneys serving the general population in 2000, the most recent year for which figures were available.

Between 2002 and 2007, the number of attorneys working in LSC-funded programs increased by 10 percent, from an estimated 3,845 to an estimated 4,231. The number of attorneys working in non-LS C-funded programs increased from an estimated 2,736 to an estimated 3,700. The overall estimated increase was 1,350, from 6,581 to 7,931, roughly 20 percent.

Table 5. Total Number of Legal Aid Attorneys—7,931 (*Calendar Year 2007*)

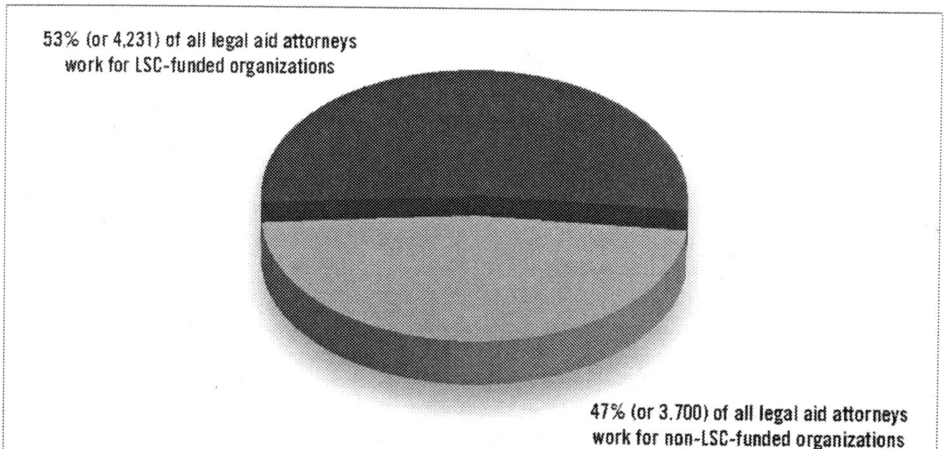

Table 6. Comparison of Private Lawyers to General Population and Legal Aid Lawyers to Low-Income Population

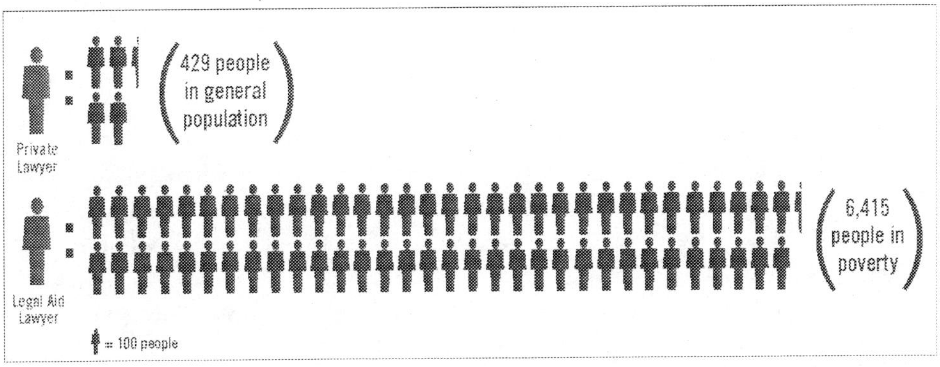

However, due to the growth of the U.S. poverty population, there was little change in the ratio of legal aid lawyers to the low-income population: the 2002 ratio was 1:6586; the 2007 ratio was 1:6415. The percentage of lawyers working in LSC-funded programs has fallen slightly, from 58 percent to 53 percent.

Conversely, lawyers have grown in relation to the general population: the ratio of lawyers providing legal services to the general population in 2007 was 1:429, compared to 1:525 in 2000. The gap between the services available to the general public and the services available to low-income people has increased.

Pro Bono Efforts

Although this methodology does not include a count of the private attorneys who provided pro bono services to low-income individuals and families, pro bono assistance is essential to helping close the justice gap.[28] Since the 2005 report, LSC has undertaken a major initiative to increase the involvement of private attorneys in LSC-funded programs. The LSC Board of Directors adopted a private attorney action plan, "Help Close the Justice Gap, Unleash the Power of Pro Bono," which included a call to grantees to adopt resolutions that recognize and celebrate the involvement of private attorneys in the delivery of civil legal services. LSC provided guidance in 2007 to grantees on resources and innovative approaches available to more effectively integrate private attorneys into the delivery of civil legal assistance.[29] LSC recommended that grantees develop long-term relationships with large law firms, corporate and government attorneys and offer support to small firms, solo practitioners and judicare attorneys so that they may more effectively provide services. In addition, the guidance encourages grantees to engage law schools and law students in pro bono services. Just as importantly, the American Bar Association has for many years sought to stimulate and support pro bono contributions by private lawyers. Pro bono has always been and will continue to be an important resource in closing the justice gap.[30] But pro bono efforts by private attorneys alone will not be enough to meet the legal needs of low-income individuals and families across the nation. Legal aid programs will need to have both the additional resources necessary to employ more staff and to enhance their efforts to engage the private bar in providing pro bono services.

Conclusion to Methodology #3

Nationally, on the average, there is one legal aid attorney (including those funded by *all* sources) available to serve 6,415 poor people. This ratio has not changed significantly since the 2002 figure reported in the last report. In comparison, there is one private attorney providing personal legal services for every 429 people in the general population.

Despite the expansion of non-LSC-funded programs in the past decade, a majority of attorneys serving the poor still work in LSC-funded programs. The LSC network thus remains the primary source of civil legal aid for low-income Americans.

NEW DATA ON UNREPRESENTED LITIGANTS

In the 2005 study, the Justice Gap Committee explored the possibility of obtaining data from courts and administrative agencies about the percentage of litigants who appear without representation in particular categories of cases typically involving low-income people. LSC conducted a pilot project involving four states to test the feasibility of collecting such data. However, the pilot states were able to provide only isolated bits of data, and the 2005 Justice Gap Report identified analysis of court data as a methodology that should be considered in future efforts.

Since the 2005 Justice Gap Report, more data has become available on this subject. In 2006, the National Center for State Courts issued a compilation of reports on "self-represented"—or more accurately, unrepresented—litigants in lower state courts (the category of courts in which low- income people appear most frequently), as well as appellate state courts, and federal courts.[31] In addition, reports from several states provide information about the income levels of unrepresented litigants.

In the spring of 2009, the Self-Represented Litigation Network, a coalition of major national organizations including the Conference of Chief Justices, Conference of State Court Administrators, National Association for Court Management, and LSC, hosted by the National Center for State Courts, conducted a survey of judges and self-help programs to determine the impact of the current economic downturn on the number of unrepresented litigants.[32]

Based on their own observations and currently available data, many judges, court administrators, members of the legal aid community, and commentators have raised concerns about unrepresented litigants, arguing that most people who appear in court without an attorney do so because they cannot afford one, and that the outcome for the litigant (as well as the impact on the courts) can be negative. A number of reports from state Supreme Court task forces and similar entities have called for increased funding for civil legal assistance as one response to the crisis in the courts caused by unrepresented litigants.

The following excerpts from reports by state blue-ribbon commissions in Iowa, New Hampshire, and Massachusetts all address the link between overburdened legal aid programs and the rise in unrepresented litigants, as well as the potentially overwhelming challenges that unrepresented litigants face in presenting their cases and the resulting impact on the court system.

- "Because of their unfamiliarity with the law and court procedures, pro se litigants have trouble negotiating the court system and require judicial staff to spend additional time explaining and assisting litigants through the process.... Legal services programs serving low-income Iowans are forced to routinely turn away large numbers of applicants for services due to limited staff or are only able to provide clients with advice over the telephone or through a pamphlet.

Although the increase in pro se litigants may be attributable to many factors, the limited and decreasing availability of legal services to low-income Iowans is clearly a significant factor.... While there are measures that can be taken and have been recommended to permit better access to the courts for pro se litigants, representation by a competent attorney is still the best alternative. However, decreased access to an attorney forces many desperate litigants to approach the legal system pro se. Consequently, additional funding must be obtained to improve the likelihood that those who are not financially able to hire a private attorney can access an attorney either through a legal services program or through a pro bono project."

Report of the Joint Iowa Judges Association and Iowa State Bar Association Task Force on Pro Se Litigation, May 2005

- "Recommendation #7: The State of New Hampshire should fully fund legal services staffing for traditional civil legal services.

The Commission recognizes that the current network of civil legal assistance is excellent, and in many ways a model in terms of the quality of representation and level of cooperation among providers. That being said, the system is woefully overburdened.... The Commission urges that this system be fully funded.... The rise in the number of pro se litigants presents many challenges: pro se parties are not trained in the law and hence often do an inadequate job of representing themselves. Justice is therefore compromised, resulting in pro se litigants being deprived of their full rights. The increase in the number of untrained litigants also undermines the smooth functioning of the courts by introducing delays and inefficiencies, adding further to legal costs for all."

New Hampshire Citizens Commission on the State Courts, Report and Recommendations, June 2006

- "Studies have shown that, even though there may be other contributing factors, the primary reason for the growth in self-representation is lack of financial resources. Because of budget constraints, legal services programs are forced to turn away many of those eligible for free legal assistance.... Given the current economic downturn, there is every reason to expect that still more individuals will find it necessary to bring or defend civil cases of great personal importance—involving family, housing, employment, and financial issues—without the benefit of counsel."

Assessing the Needs of Self-Represented Litigants in Our Courts, Final Report and Recommendations Massachusetts Supreme Judicial Court Steering Committee on Self-Represented Litigants, November 2008

Unrepresented by Necessity

Currently available data bears out these concerns, indicating that the vast majority of people who appear without representation do so because they are unable to afford an attorney, and that a large percentage of these are low-income people who qualify for legal aid.[33] For example:

- A 2005 study of unrepresented litigants in New York City Family and Housing Courts found that 57 percent had incomes under $20,000 per year and 83 percent had incomes of under $30,000 per year.[34]
- A 2003 California Report to the Legislature found that more than 90 percent of the 450,000 people who use court self-help programs in the state each year earn less than $2,000 per month.[35]

Growing Number of Unrepresented Litigants

Although there is no national compilation of statistics on unrepresented litigants in court, data from some court systems shows extremely high numbers, often clustered in those courts in which low-income people are particularly likely to appear, such as family and housing courts:

- The state lower court data collected in the 2006 compilation from the National Center for State Courts demonstrates high numbers of people proceeding without representation in a number of states.[36] For example:
    - A New Hampshire report found that one party was pro se in 85 percent of all civil cases in the district court and 48 percent of all civil cases in the superior court. In superior court domestic relations cases, almost 70 percent of cases had one pro se party, while in district court domestic violence cases, 97 percent of the cases have one pro se party.
    - A Utah study found that 49 percent of petitioners and 81 percent of respondents in family law cases were unrepresented.
    - A California study found that 67 percent of petitioners and 80 percent of respondents in family law cases were unrepresented; in unlawful detainer (eviction) cases, over 90 percent of defendants and 34 percent of petitioners at filing were unrepresented. In domestic violence restraining order cases, litigants are reported to be pro se over 90 percent of the time.
    - A Wisconsin study reported that 70 percent of litigants in family cases were unrepresented.

Table 7. Percentage of Judges Reporting an Impact of the Economic Crisis on Unrepresented Litigation (*Survey by Self-Represented Litigation Network, Spring 2009*)

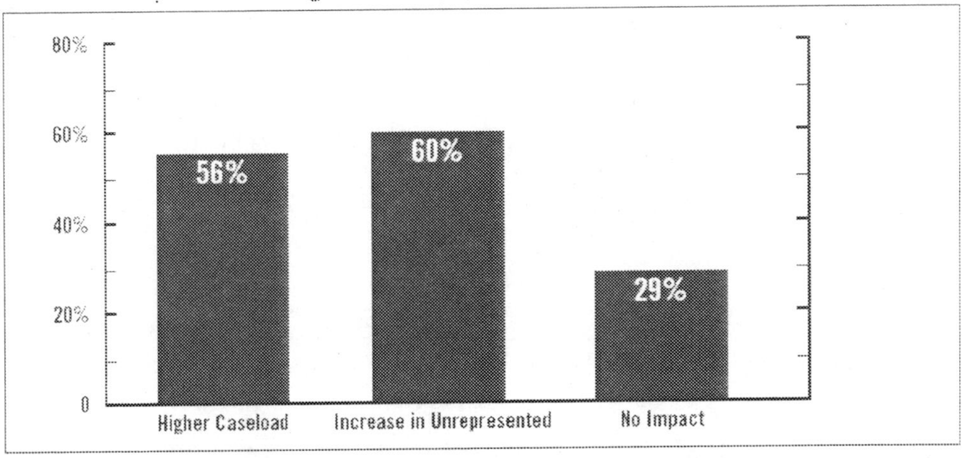

- More recently, the 2008 Massachusetts Supreme Judicial Court Steering Committee on Self- Represented Litigants Report estimated that at least 100,000 litigants were currently representing themselves in civil matters. In the Probate and Family Court, as many as 80 percent of family law cases involved at least one unrepresented party. In the housing court, self-representation is the general rule among tenants and is increasing among landlords. Based on past experience and nationwide trends, the report predicts that these numbers will only increase in the future.[37]
- The 2008 District of Columbia legal needs study reported that 98 percent of both petitioners and respondents in the Domestic Violence Unit of the DC Superior Court were unrepresented; approximately 77 percent of plaintiffs in divorce/ custody/ miscellaneous cases in Family Court were unrepresented; more than 98 percent of respondents in paternity and child support cases were unrepresented; 97 percent of respondents in housing court cases were unrepresented.[38]

Recent Increases as a Result of the Economic Crisis

While recent national court data on unrepresented litigants is not available, in a survey conducted in the spring of 2009 by the Self-Represented Litigation Network, 60 percent of the judges responding reported more unrepresented litigants in their courtrooms in that quarter than in the corresponding quarter of the previous year.

Unrepresented Litigants and the Justice Gap

The rising level of unrepresented litigants in state courts raises critically important questions relating to LSC's mandate of providing equal access to justice for those who cannot afford to pay an attorney. There is a growing body of research indicating that outcomes for unrepresented litigants are often less favorable than those for represented litigants.[39] Coordinated collection and analysis of data as well as additional research would be helpful to provide national information on how many people are appearing in court without representation, how many of them are doing so because they cannot afford or otherwise obtain counsel, the types of cases involved, and the impact of lack of representation on case outcomes.[40] To the extent that litigants are proceeding without counsel because they cannot afford an attorney, and the outcome of their case is being compromised by lack of representation, equal justice is at risk.

CONCLUSION

Providing Necessary Access to Civil Legal Assistance

The challenge confronting the nation in providing equal access to justice is large, urgent and complex, as the research and analysis in this report shows. The serious shortage of civil legal assistance identified in the 2005 Justice Gap Report still exists. The progress that has been made in providing civil legal assistance to the nation's poor remains at risk because of a depressed economy and the competition for scarce government funds.

Legal aid clients are the most vulnerable among us and are as diverse as our nation, encompassing all races, ethnic groups and ages, including the working poor, homeowners and renters facing foreclosure or eviction, families with children, veterans, farmers, people with disabilities, victims of domestic violence and victims of natural disasters. Three out of four clients are women—many of whom are struggling to keep their children safe and their families together. According to the U.S. Census Bureau, nearly 54 million Americans are eligible for LSC-funded services. They are at or below 125 percent of the federal poverty guidelines, an income of $27,563 a year for a family of four.[41]

The data in this report shows that:

- There is still a substantial justice gap. For every client served by an LSC-funded program, one person who seeks help is turned down because of insufficient resources. That was the conclusion of the 2005 Justice Gap Report, and the research for this report reaffirms that finding.
- There is now a substantial body of knowledge demonstrating that only a fraction of the legal problems experienced by low-income individuals is addressed with the help of an attorney. State studies, sponsored by equal justice commissions, state bar associations and legal aid programs, have drawn this conclusion, contribute to a body of work building since 1994, and reinforce a key finding of the 2005 Justice Gap Report.
- Nationally, on average, only one legal aid attorney is available to serve 6,415 low-income people. In comparison, there is one private attorney providing personal legal services for every 429 individuals in the general population.

- Most people who appear in state courts without an attorney do so because they cannot afford one, and the vast majority are low-income individuals who qualify for legal aid. The number of unrepresented litigants, particularly in family and housing courts, is increasing—a critical issue for courts and for LSC as it strives to ensure equal access to justice for all Americans.

As part of its mission, LSC has a responsibility to communicate to the public and the Congress on what is required to secure *necessary access to civil legal assistance.*

Accomplishing this goal will require a multifaceted approach which will include partnerships among federal and state governments, the organized bar, individual lawyers, private funders and concerned private parties. LSC adopted an action plan in 2007—"Help Close the Justice Gap, Unleash the Power of Pro Bono"—to encourage greater private attorney involvement in the delivery of civil legal assistance. The LSC Board of Directors approved a resolution in support of enhanced private attorney involvement and urged LSC-funded programs to adopt similar local resolutions to encourage pro bono services by the bar. More than 100 programs have done so. Across the nation, the creation of Access to Justice Commissions has energized efforts to increase state funding and pro bono support for civil legal aid. LSC has encouraged justices of state Supreme Courts and leaders of state bar associations to support the provision of high-quality civil legal services to low-income populations. LSC also has encouraged its grantees to help close the justice gap by carrying out their duties in the most efficient and economical way. In addition, LSC has urged grantees to enhance the services supported by federal funding through the use of technology and increased collaborations with courts, law schools and community group. Legal services programs at the state and local levels have increased funding for civil legal aid as a result of monetary contributions from lawyers, the public, business entities and private foundations.

Since the 2005 Justice Gap Report, many state legislatures have recognized the need to help close the justice gap in their states. During this period, 25 states and the District of Columbia adopted new or increased funding for civil legal aid. Overall state legislative funding rose by 63 percent.[42] In 2005, seven states had no state legislative funding for civil legal aid; in mid-2009, there are only two. In addition, during these years, many state IOLTA programs also adopted new revenue enhancement measures that increased funding for civil legal aid.

However, these legislative and IOLTA increases only benefited the particular states involved. The current economic recession—and in particular, low interest rates and shortfalls in many state budgets—is placing many of these gains at risk.

The federal government plays a vital role in providing a pathway to equal justice for all, consistent with its role in maintaining the formal civil justice system and providing an orderly forum for the resolution of disputes. LSC serves as the primary conduit for the federal government's share of civil legal assistance. It establishes the federal funding baseline, supporting and ensuring a backbone of civil legal aid providers throughout the country.

The findings in this report suggest a phased approach to addressing the unmet need. As a first, critical goal, there must be enough funding to serve all of those *currently* seeking help from LSC-funded programs. This requires a doubling of LSC funds and a doubling of the state, local and private funds that also support LSC grantees.

The long-term goal must be to develop resources sufficient to meet the civil legal needs of all eligible low-income persons. Pro bono efforts need to be expanded substantially in the years ahead, but even expanded pro bono contributions will not be enough to address a major portion of the unmet need. As we observed in our 2005 report, to fund these needs, the federal share must grow to be five times greater than it is now, or $1.6 billion. IOLTA and other state, local and private funding sources also will have to grow to address the overall needs.

In order to keep faith with our national commitment to equal access to justice, it is essential that the nation move toward the necessary funding levels and a renewed commitment to pro bono efforts in firm, measured strides that are designed to close the justice gap as quickly as possible. Without such meaningful steps, the nation's promise of equal justice for all will ring hollow for the nation's poor.

APPENDICES

Appendix A
Other State Studies of the Legal Needs of Low-Income People
Excerpts: Estimates of Unmet Legal Needs

***Achieving Access to Justice for Hawai'i's People* (2007)**
A Report of the Access to Justice Hui, Hawai'i Justice Foundation, Hawai'i State Bar Association, and the Judiciary of the State of Hawai'i, with the American Civil Liberties Union of Hawai'i, Domestic Violence Action Center, Legal Aid Society of Hawai'i, Na Loio – Immigrant Rights and Public Policy Center, Native Hawaiian Legal Corporation, University of Hawai'i Elder Law Program, Volunteer Legal Services Hawai'i, and William S. Richardson School of Law

To calculate the percentage of legal needs that were being met, results from two surveys were utilized.

- The first survey was one completed by twenty-nine social service providers who serve over 550,000 people in the state each year. They were asked to estimate the number of their clients who had problems in thirteen legal areas and estimate what percentage had their legal needs met. According to social service providers, the average of met legal needs was 14.68 percent.

- The second survey was conducted with seventy-eight potential clients who contacted the Legal Aid Society of Hawai'i and Volunteer Legal Services Hawai'i. The average of met legal needs was 31 percent.

These two figures were averaged together, for an estimate that one in five low- and moderate-income residents, or 22.84 percent, has his or her legal needs met.

Justice for All? An Examination of the Civil Legal Needs of the District of Columbia's Low-Income Community (2008)
District of Columbia Access to Justice Commission, with the assistance of DLA Piper LLP

Estimating the Magnitude of Unmet Legal Needs

It is extremely difficult to calculate the precise level of the low-income community's unmet legal needs.[546] Nationally, studies have indicated that about 80 percent of low-income residents' legal needs are unmet.[547] Prior studies in the District have estimated that the figure in the District is closer to 90 percent.[548] Whatever the actual figure, it is clear that the unmet need is substantial. The DC Courts' *pro se* statistics provide one snapshot of the unmet need. For example, in 2005:

• Almost 45 percent of formal probate matters, 98 percent of the small estate matters and 60 percent of the trust matters before the Probate Division of DC Superior Court involved *pro se* plaintiffs.

• About 98 percent of both petitioners and respondents in the Domestic Violence Unit of the DC Superior Court proceeded *pro se*.
• Approximately 77 percent of plaintiffs in divorce/custody/miscellaneous cases in Family Court were *pro se*.
• More than 98 percent of respondents in paternity and child support cases were *pro se*.
• About 97 percent of defendants who had to appear in Landlord/Tenant Court were *pro se*.[549]

We recognize that not everyone wants or needs full representation to address his or her legal problems. Many issues presumably could be resolved through brief advice or by giving the person materials relevant to the issue. Nonetheless, the *pro se* statistics from the DC Superior Court, which take into account representation from legal services providers, government attorneys and pro bono lawyers, indicate that thousands of people enter the DC Courts every year without a lawyer at their side. It is difficult to imagine a person of means making the same decision if given the choice.

Furthermore, it is likely that the matters that actually make it into court represent only a fraction of the existing legal needs in the community. As our study found, community-based organizations almost universally felt that the low-income community lacks knowledge about their legal rights, and an understanding of how to vindicate those rights. It is unlikely that those who do not know about their rights will ever go to court to seek resolution of a legal matter. Even those people who know about their rights and legal resources may be reluctant to bring matters to court without the advice or presence of counsel.[550]

546 Several other states have attempted to calculate the legal needs of the low-income community by relying on telephone surveys of low-income households. These studies found that low-income households have, on average, between 1.1 and 3.5 legal needs per year. *See* Echols, *supra* note 19, at 32.
547 *Id;* LSC, "Documenting the Justice Gap in America" (2005).
548 DC Bar Foundation, *supra* note 21; Cunningham, *supra* note 70.
549 *See* Appendix H.
550 *See supra* Section IV.C. to D.

Unequal Access to Justice: A Comprehensive Study of the Civil Legal Needs of the Poor in Indiana
A Report by Indiana Legal Services, Indiana Bar Foundation, Indiana State Bar Association (2008)

Of survey respondents with incomes below 125 percent of the federal poverty level, 86 percent reported having at least one legal problem in 2008.

The ratio of attorneys to Hoosiers living below 125 percent of the federal poverty level (FPL) is approximately *one attorney per 8,850 potential clients*. If Hoosiers with incomes between 125 percent of FPL and 200 percent of FPL are also considered, the ratio increases to approximately *one attorney per 16,100 potential clients*. In contrast, the ratio of private attorneys providing paid civil legal services to the general Indiana population was found to be about *one attorney per 688 potential clients*.

Information gathered from pro bono plan administrators and by Indiana Legal Services during preparation of this Final Report corroborates this discrepancy, suggesting that as many as 62 percent of those income-eligible applicants applying to plan administrators, and 75 percent of those income-eligible applicants applying to Indiana Legal Services, were unable to receive attorney representation necessary to fully meet their legal needs.

The insufficient number of pro bono and public service attorneys representing the poor in comparison to the need for legal assistance was a theme throughout the responses to the various surveys, questionnaires, and focus groups making up the Study.

The report also compares certain demographic data from 2008 and 1999—the last year a similar study was done—and found that Indiana's poverty population has grown by 35 percent over the time period.

APPENDIX B

Table: Methodological Variations in State Legal Needs Studies 2006-2009

	Sample Size (low-income)[1]	Primary survey type	Phone interviews supplemented with in-person?	Definition of low-income (as percentage of poverty)	Household or individual
Virginia	1043	phone	no	125 125-184	household
Utah	1185	cluster sampling	n/a	125[2]	household
Wisconsin	1122	phone	no	125 125-200	household
Nevada	1000	phone	yes (focus groups)	125 125-200	household
Alabama	500	phone	no	125	household
Georgia	1027[3]	phone	Yes (204 supplemental field interviews)	150	household
New Jersey	2412[4]	phone	no	200	individual

Explanation of Survey Types

- **Random telephone survey**: This methodology employs Random Digit Dialing (RDD) to place telephone calls. Parties who agree to participate in the survey are asked questions about their income to determine if they are low-income. Low-income respondents are interviewed. The sample will not reflect the responses of low-income people who do not have telephones or are not willing to respond to questions by telephone. The telephone survey is often supplemented by in-person interviews with low-income people likely to be in these categories.

- **"Cluster sampling" survey**: This methodology uses census data and other sources of information to identify the principal sub-populations of low-income people in the state according to demographic categories and characteristics (e.g., immigrants, homeless people, senior citizens, disabled people, African-Americans, Native Americans, Latinos, migrants, etc.). A sufficient number of people within each cluster group is interviewed to ensure reasonable levels of reliability. Within cluster groups, interviewees are selected as randomly as possible. Interviews are generally conducted in person. In addition to the cluster groups, other respondents in the general low-income population are also surveyed. The results from the various cluster groups are weighted to reflect their proportion of the low-income population as a whole. The survey is deemed to achieve maximum reliability at about 1,500 interviews.

---

[1] When generalizing sample estimates to a large or unknown population, the larger the sample size the more confidence can be attributed to the survey findings as representative of the population as a whole. The statistical rule of thumb is that 400 surveys provide a confidence interval of less than +/- 5 at a 95 percent confidence level, meaning that 95 percent of samples of the same size would generate an estimate within 5 percent of the estimate produced by the given sample, for estimates that are proportions or percentages.

[2] Text says 129 percent, but this can be presumed to be a typographical error.

[3] An additional 516 moderate-income people (incomes 150-300 percent of poverty) were also surveyed.

[4] An additional 400+ moderate-income people (incomes 200-400 percent of poverty) were also surveyed.

APPENDIX C

Table: Reasons Given for Not Getting an Attorney[5]	
Virginia	Reasons for taking no action, by percentage of respondents with a problem who took no action: • Not a problem (just the way things are): 20.5 • Don't know: 17.9 • Nothing could be done: 16.8 • Didn't want hassle: 15.1 • Didn't know who could help: 5.5
Utah	Reasons for not seeking legal help, by percentage of respondents with a problem who did not seek legal assistance: • Didn't know who could help: 32.8 • Too much hassle: 22.1 • Worried about cost: 20.6 • Thought nothing could be done: 18.7 • Not a legal problem (just the way things are): 17.3 • Afraid/intimidated (feared retaliation): 6.4 • Help not needed yet (wait and see): 5.3
Georgia	Reasons given for not seeking legal help, by percentage of respondents with a problem who did nothing: • Didn't know the problem was legal in nature: 18 • Believed nothing could be done about the problem: 16.7 • Didn't want the hassle: 7.5 • Didn't know where to go for help: 7.1 Of households with a legal problem, 73 percent did not know that the problem was legal in nature.
New Jersey	Major reasons given for not seeking legal assistance (no percentages reported): • Didn't think I needed a lawyer • Couldn't afford a lawyer • Tried to resolve on my own • Didn't think it was necessary • Problem not important enough • Didn't think there was anything to be done about the problem

APPENDIX D

Table: Awareness of Free Legal Aid/Lawyer Referral (**bold** figures represent data from most closely comparable questions)	
Utah	**23.6** percent were aware of a free legal assistance program; About 20 percent believed they were eligible for free legal assistance
Wisconsin	**37** percent were aware of free legal assistance 56 percent of people with income less than 125 percent of poverty guideline believed they were eligible for free legal services 28 percent of people with income between 125 and 200 percent of poverty guideline believed they were eligible for free legal services
Nevada	**33** percent are aware of free civil legal services
Alabama	**20** percent were aware of free legal assistance
Georgia	47.7 percent were *not* aware of legal services or attorney referral services

APPENDIX E

Tables from 2005 Justice Gap Study

Table 2005-1: Unable to Serve
(Table 1 in 2005 Justice Gap Report)

Type of Legal Problem Categories	Unable to Serve Twelve Month Projections	Calendar Year 2004 Cases Closed
Consumer	129,798	107,040
Education	12,234	6,830
Employment	46,122	18,986
Family	504,312	383,484
Juvenile	15,804	8,291
Health	24,660	27,780
Housing	143,904	218,688
Income	59,634	113,252
Individual	34,998	12,267
Miscellaneous	114,372	44,449
Total	**1,085,838**	**901,067**

Table 2005-2: State Legal Needs Studies Released 2000-2005
(Table 2 in 2005 Justice Gap Report)

State	Released	Sponsor/Funder	Survey/Analysis By
Oregon	2000	Oregon State Bar Judicial Department Office of the Governor	Sociology Department, Portland State University/D. Michael Dale
Vermont	2001	Committee on Equal Access to Justice	ORC Macro
New Jersey	2002	Legal Services of New Jersey	Schulman, Ronca, & Bucuvalas, Inc./ Poverty Research Institute of Legal Services of New Jersey
Massachusetts	2003	Massachusetts Legal Assistance Corporation	Schulman, Ronca, & Bucuvalas, Inc.
Connecticut	2003	Connecticut Bar Foundation	Institute for Survey and Research, University of Connecticut
Washington	2003	Supreme Court Civil Equal Justice Funding Task Force	Social and Economic Research Center, Washington State University/ Sociology Department, Portland State University/D. Michael Dale
Tennessee	2004	Tennessee Alliance for Legal Services	Office of Research and Public Service, University of Tennessee College of Social Work
Illinois	2005	Chicago Bar Association Illinois State Bar Association Chicago Bar Foundation Illinois Bar Foundation Lawyers Trust Fund of Illinois	Metro Chicago Information Center
Montana	2005	Montana State Bar Equal Justice Task Force	Sociology Department, Portland State University/D. Michael Dale

Table 2005-3: Legal Needs
(Table 3 in 2005 Justice Gap Report)

	Average number of legal needs in preceding year per low-income *household*
Oregon	3.2
Vermont	1.1
Connecticut	2.7
Washington	2.9
Massachusetts	2.4
Tennessee	3.3
Illinois	1.7
Montana	3.5
	Average number of *new* legal needs in preceding year per low-income *individual* experiencing at least one problem
New Jersey	1.8

Table 2005-4: Legal Help Received/Sought as a Percentage of Legal Need (Table 4 in 2005 Justice Gap Report)	
	***Received* legal help (by percentage of problems experienced by household)**
Oregon	18.1 percent of problems, help received from private bar or legal aid attorney
Washington	12 percent of problems, help received from private bar or legal aid attorney
Montana	16.4 percent of problems, help received from private bar or legal aid attorney
Vermont	9 percent of problems, help received from private bar, legal aid, courts, or other legal source
Illinois	16.4 percent of problems, legal assistance received
	***Received* legal help (by percentage of individuals with problems)**
New Jersey	16 percent of individuals with problems received legal help
	***Sought* legal help (by percentage of problems experienced by household)**
Connecticut	10 percent of problems, help sought from private bar, legal aid, family/friend, other
	***Sought* legal help (by percentage of problems experienced by individual)**
New Jersey (2002)	11 percent of problems, legal help sought
	***Sought* legal help (by percentage of households with problems)**
Massachusetts	16.4 percent of households (no more than; could be less) with a legal need sought legal help from private bar or legal aid
Tennessee	29.2 percent of households that identified their *biggest* legal problem sought legal help from private bar or legal aid

Table 2005-5: Methodological Differences in State Legal Needs Studies
(Appendix B in 2005 Justice Gap Report)

	Sample Size (low-income)	Primary survey type	Phone interviews supplemented with in-person?	Definition of low-income (as percentage of poverty)	Household or individual
Oregon	1011	cluster sampling	n/a	125 125+-200	household
Vermont	436	phone	yes, but results not incorporated with phone survey figure	187.5	household
New Jersey	1013	phone	no	200	individual
Massachusetts	1800 200	phone	yes	125 125+-184	household
Connecticut	400	phone	no	125	household
Washington	1333	cluster sampling	n/a	125	household
	427[5]	phone		125 125+-200	
Tennessee	824	phone	yes	125	household
Illinois	1645	phone	no	150	household
Montana	860	cluster sampling	n/a	125 125+-200	household

[5] The Washington study was based primarily on in-person interviews. However, a telephone sample was conducted for comparative purposes. In addition to the 427 low-income respondents, the telephone survey also included 383 respondents with incomes between 200 and 400 percent of poverty, to compare the responses of the low-income group to those with a slightly higher income level.

Table 2005-6: Importance of Problems as Ranked by Respondents (Data reported on p. 11 in 2005 Justice Gap Report)	
Montana	Respondents characterized 53 percent of the problems identified as "extremely important" and 91 percent as "important."
New Jersey (2002)	84 percent of people with a legal problem thought the problem was highly serious and important; 52 percent thought that they needed a lawyer to help with the problem.
Washington	Respondents characterized 56 percent of their legal problems as "extremely important" and 93 percent as "important."

Table 2005-7: Reasons Given for Not Getting an Attorney[7] (Appendix C in 2005 Justice Gap Report)	
Oregon	Reason for not getting a lawyer's help, by percentage of respondents with a problem who did not seek legal assistance: • Nothing can be done: 17 • Not a legal problem: 12 • Nowhere to get help: 12 • Too much hassle: 12 • Worried about cost • Afraid/intimidated 11 • Turned to other help: 7
New Jersey	Reason for not getting a lawyer's help, by percentage of respondents who perceived a need for legal help but did not seek it: • Could not afford: 56 • "Other reasons included the belief that the problem was not important enough to pursue, the fear of retaliation, and the belief that nothing could be done." No further breakdown given.
Connecticut	Reasons for not seeking legal assistance *from legal aid program*, by percentage of problems: • Did not know legal aid was available: 30 • Legal aid does not help with this problem: 10
Washington	Reason for not getting an attorney, as a percentage of households with a legal problem (more than one reason could be cited): • Thought nothing could be done: 27.9 • Didn't know who could help: 24.1 • Worried about cost: 22 • Not a legal problem just the way things are: 21 • Afraid or intimidated: 10 • Turned to someone else: 7.8
Massachusetts	Main reason did nothing, by percentage of all legal encounters for which households took no action: • Not a problem, just the way things are: 30 • Nothing could be done: 18 • Did not know who could help: 8
Tennessee	Reason for not taking action to resolve their most difficult legal problem, by percentage of households reporting no action: • Just the way things are: 17.6 • Nothing can be done: 16.8 • Didn't know where to go: 12 • Too much hassle: 12
Illinois	Reason for not having a lawyer, by percentage of household experiencing at least one problem: • Thought they could handle it on their own: 33 • Hiring a lawyer would be too expensive: 26 • A lawyer would not help resolve the situation: 9
Montana	Montana: Reasons for not seeking legal help, by percentage of respondents with a problem who did not seek legal assistance: • Thought nothing could be done: 19 • Did not see problem as legal: 23 • Didn't know who could help: 20 • Worried about cost: 19 • Too much hassle: 16 • Afraid: 10 • Didn't want public dispute: 9

[7] For some states, additional reasons with very small percentages are omitted in table.

Table 2005-8: Awareness of Free Legal Aid/Lawyer Referral
(Appendix D in 2005 Justice Gap Report)
(**bold** figures are most closely comparable)

New Jersey	**26** percent were aware of free legal services 8 percent were aware of lawyer referral services
Washington	**40.8** percent were aware of free legal services
Tennessee	**21.2** percent know of a place that gives free legal help 29 percent know of any place that helps you find a lawyer.
Illinois	**23** percent were aware of the availability of free legal assistance.
Montana	**48.5** percent were aware of free legal services 53.6 percent believe they are eligible for free legal services
Oregon	47 percent *not* aware of lawyer referral 39 percent *not* aware of legal aid 37 percent said *not* eligible for or didn't know if eligible for legal aid.
Connecticut	for 30 percent of cases, the reason that respondent gave for not taking action was that they did *not* know that legal aid was available (this figure is not comparable to others because it is linked to the problem and other options were given)

Board of Directors

End Notes

1 "Report on the Legal Needs of the Low-Income Public: Findings of the Comprehensive Legal Needs Study," American Bar Association, 1994.

2 "Income, Poverty, and Health Insurance Coverage in the United States: 2008," U.S. Census Bureau, September 10, 2009. The 2008 data reflect the initial effects of the recession and signal even larger increases for 2009 because of high unemployment rates.

3 The Justice Gap Advisory Committee members were Jonathan Asher, executive director, Colorado Legal Services; Terry Brooks, legal counsel to SCLAID; Bob Echols, state support consultant at the ABA Resource Center for Access to Justice Initiatives; Deborah Hankinson, former chair of SCLAID; Melville D. Miller, Jr., president, Legal Services of New Jersey; Don Saunders, Civil Director, NLADA; Lois Wood, executive director, Land of Lincoln Legal Assistance Foundation; and Anthony Young, executive director, Southern Arizona Legal Aid.

4 LSC is required by law to establish maximum income levels for persons eligible for civil legal assistance. Under LSC regulations, the maximum level is equivalent to 125 percent of the federal poverty guidelines, which are issued annually by the U.S. Department of Health and Human Services.

5 As in 2005, data from LSC-funded programs in the District of Columbia, Puerto Rico, Virgin Islands, Guam and Micronesia is also included.

6 The count did not include people who were denied services because they were financially or otherwise ineligible, because services were prohibited by LSC restrictions, or because their case was determined to have insufficient legal merit to proceed. Nor were cases in which a program made a referral to another program with

an expectation that the other program would provide substantial representation included in the count. The instructions provided by LSC to its grantees on completing the survey and other related documents can be viewed on-line at
https://grants s.pdf

7 In some places, other organizations do intake and do not send cases to the LSC-funded program when they know the program is not able to handle them.

8 As part of the research for this report, LSC grantees were asked to capture the number of clients that they assisted in a limited fashion where full extended representation would have been more likely to enable the client to obtain a satisfactory outcome. LSC grantees counted 82,500 such cases in the two-month period. This figure does not include cases where the programs judged that the advice and brief service provided was sufficient to resolve the problem presented. Programs estimated that, during the two-month study period, 46,000 cases were resolved in this manner.

9 For example, Pine Tree Legal Assistance, Maine's LSC grantee, asked people contacting the program in person (rather than by telephone) during the March-May period in which it collected "unable to serve" data whether they had other legal problems. It found that 66 percent of the people contacting the program in person had at least one legal problem beyond the one for which they were seeking immediate help, with an average of three additional problems.

10 The Virginia legal needs study considered under Methodology #2 reported that the average number of legal needs among households with at least one legal need was 3.62. The Alabama study reported that the average number of legal needs among households with at least one legal need was 3.6. The New Jersey study reported that 51.5 percent of those respondents who experienced at least one problem experienced more than one problem.

11 Programs typically make legal information available in ways that are not dependent on talking directly with an advocate, such as through their websites, brochures, clinics, and other community education media.

12 There is one way in which this data may be slightly over-inclusive, in that eligibility for LSC services was documented in most, but not all, cases. Eligibility was established for all cases in which the intake process was completed. People who were determined to be ineligible were not included in the count. However, the count of people who were turned away does include some applicants for whom eligibility information was not collected because, before doing screening, the program ascertained and informed the applicant that the type of case presented was not within the program's case-handling priorities. Nevertheless, programs report that it is their experience that an overwhelming majority of those who contact legal services offices are eligible for their services

13 The hypothesis that this two-month count is approximately equal to one-sixth of a year's intake was tested in 2005 by asking 10 percent of LSC grantee programs to compare their 2004 April and May intake numbers with their total intake for 2004. The 2004 April and May intake for these programs yielded a count of 19,926 cases. A 12-month extrapolation from this figure would be 119,556 cases. The combined full-year 2004 totals for these programs was 119,166, almost identical to the extrapolation. This confirms that the sample period in 2005 was likely to reflect accurately one-sixth of a full-year total. The Justice Gap Committee did not repeat this test in 2009, relying on the assumption that the same results would hold true.

14 Case data from 2008 was used for comparison because 2009 data will not be available until March 2010. Past experience suggests that 2009 case totals will be within a few percentage points of those for 2008.

15 Pro bono cases provided through programs' private attorney involvement (PAI) requirement are included in the count of clients served. Roughly 7 percent of all cases closed by LSC-funded programs in 2008 were provided by pro bono attorneys. Total PAI cases were more than 10 percent of LSC cases in 2008, with the additional cases being other PAI cases where private attorneys provide services at reduced fees paid by LSC programs.

16 Hawaii (2007) and the District of Columbia (2008) also conducted studies of legal needs and the extent to which they were being met; while these studies were based upon data from a variety of sources, those sources did not include a random survey of low-income people. In addition, Indiana (2008) conducted a survey-based study of legal needs, but the questionnaire used did not solicit data about unmet legal needs . For this reason, these three studies cannot be compared directly to the other seven studies considered in this section. However, the findings on unmet legal needs from these studies are reported in Appendix A. All of the studies discussed in this report, as well as all other state studies of the legal needs of low-income people released in 2000 and later and a list of studies released before 2000, are available online at
http://www.abanet.org/legalservices/sclaid/atjresourcecenter/compublicawareness.html
(under "Public Awareness and Communications").

17 The one study using the "cluster sampling" methodology (Utah) is based on a sample of 1,185, somewhat smaller than the 1,500 which is deemed to achieve maximum reliability. See Appendix B. However, the consistency of its findings with those in other states indicates that these findings can also be considered reliable.

18 The most common types of problems reported in the seven studies were in the areas of housing (such as evictions, foreclosure, utility issues, unsafe housing conditions and homelessness), consumer (such as abusive debt collection, oppressive contract terms, bankruptcy, and consumer scams), family (such as divorce, domestic violence, child custody, visitation, and support), employment (such as wage claims, unemployment, discrimination), health care (such as disputes over charges, access to services, and nursing home problems),

and government benefits (such as difficulty in applying and denials). Although the distribution of problem types varied somewhat from state to state, these problem types appeared in all seven states. Other problem types reported at relatively high levels in at least one of the studies (but not a majority) were education, municipal services, and disability.

[19] The Utah study notes that this figure conservatively understates the number of problems experienced by low-income Utahns each year, since detailed information was only recorded for five legal problems per household. Research from other states has shown that more than five problems occur with some frequency.

[20] The Wisconsin study reports that for the 45 percent of respondents who indicated that they or a household member had experienced at least one legal problem in the past year, the mean number of categories (out of thirteen) for which the household faced a problem or issue was 2.1. However, if a respondent experienced more than one problem within a particular category, only one problem was counted.

[21] The Nevada study reports that for the 68 percent of respondents who indicated that they or a household member had experienced at least one legal problem in the past year, the mean number of categories (out of nine) for which the household faced a problem or issue was 2.4. However, if a respondent experienced more than one problem within a particular category, only one problem was counted.

[22] The New Jersey study reported that 32.5 percent of lower-income respondents reported at least one new legal problem during the preceding year.

[23] Several studies explored the reasons that many people did not seek legal help for their problems. See Appendix C; on the related issue of the lack of awareness of civil legal aid, see Appendix D. For comparable findings in the 2005 Justice Gap Report, see Appendix E, Tables 2005-7 and 2005-8. Of the state studies analyzed there, several report a finding only for legal help *sought*, not *received*.

[24] The general population as used in this report excludes people at or below 125 percent of the federal poverty guidelines, which makes them eligible for LSC-funded legal services.

[25] This was calculated as follows: The American Bar Association periodically conducts a census of lawyers by polling state bar associations or licensing agencies for a count of resident, active attorneys. Figures for 2007 indicate that there were a total of 1,130,136 attorneys in the 50 states that year. The American Bar Foundation (ABF) collects statistics indicating the percentage of lawyers in each type of employment – private practice, federal judiciary, federal government, state judiciary and state government, etc. In 2005 (the most recent year for which such calculations are available) 75.2% of lawyers were in private practice.

[26] Calculated as follows: ABF calculated that in 2005 (the most recent year for which figures are available), 48.4% of the lawyers in private practice were solo, and that 38.8% of the lawyers in firms were in firms of 2-10 lawyers. Thus, of the estimated 849,862 lawyers in private practice, about 581,482, or 68%, were in firms of 1-10 lawyers.

[27] If all 849,862 attorneys in private practice are considered, not just those providing personal legal services, the ratio becomes 1:292.

[28] Pro bono services have been taken into consideration in the other two methodologies in this report. The contribution of pro bono attorneys is reflected in Methodology #1, at note 15, and Methodology #2 takes into consideration legal help provided by *all* attorneys, legal aid and private, pro bono and paid.

[29] "Guidance to LSC Programs for the Development of Enhanced Private Attorney Involvement," LSC Program Letter 07-2, December 20, 2007. See: www.lsc.gov/program

[30] In 1985, LSC adopted 45 CFR 1614, which requires each recipient of LSC funds to devote an amount equal to at least 12.5 percent of those funds to involving members of the private bar in providing services to eligible clients. Some of these funds go toward supporting pro bono programs either directly or through sub-grants with third-party organizations, such as bar associations. The infrastructure supported with these funds leverages public funding to involve thousands of private lawyers nationwide who donate pro bono services to address the legal problems of the poor.

[31] "Self-Represented Pro Se Statistics Memorandum," September 25, 2006, National Center for State Courts, http://www.ncsconline.org/wc/publications/memos/prosestatsmemo.htm#other. The states from which lower state court data was reported (the most relevant data for the purposes of this report, as noted above), were California, Florida, Iowa, New Hampshire, Massachusetts, Utah, Washington, and Wisconsin.

[32] Surveys of judges and self-help programs were distributed by e-mail to contacts of the Self-Represented Litigation Network. Contacts included judges and others who had attended the Harvard Judicial Conference on the Self- Represented in 2007, the key contacts in every state of the Network, and those included in a national directory of self-help centers. There were approximately 100 responses for each of the two surveys. For additional information on the Self-Represented Litigation Network, see www.srln.org.

[33] Indeed, some people who represent themselves have received advice or written information about how to do so from a legal aid program; in many instances, these people actually need an attorney, but the legal aid program is able to provide them only with these limited services. See discussion above at note 8.

[34] "Self-Represented Litigants: Characteristics, Needs, Services: the Results of Two Surveys," Office of the Deputy Chief Administrative Judge for Judicial Initiatives, December, 2005, Table 4, p. 4.

[35] "A Report to the California Legislature: Family Law Information Centers: An Evaluation Of Three Pilot Programs," Judicial Council of California; Administrative Office of the Courts, 2003.

[36] Self-Represented Pro Se Statistics Memorandum, September 25, 2006, National Center for State Courts, http://www.ncsconline.org/wc/publications/memos/prosestatsmemo.htm#other.

[37] "Assessing the Needs of Self-Represented Litigants in Our Courts, Final Report and Recommendations," Massachusetts Supreme Judicial Court Steering Committee on Self-Represented Litigants, November 2008.

[38] "Justice for All? An Examination of the Civil Legal Needs of the District of Columbia's Low-Income Community," District of Columbia Access to Justice Commission, with the assistance of DLA Piper LLP, 2008.

[39] For a compilation of these studies, see Russell Engler, *Connecting Self-Representation to Civil Gideon: What Existing Data Reveal About When Counsel is Most Needed*, Fordham Urb. L.J. (forthcoming 2009).

[40] Specifically, key areas for potential research are: national figures on self-represented/unrepresented litigants, by state, court and case type, distinguishing between those who receive support services and those who receive none; the consequences of not having the full representation of an attorney and how these consequences vary by case type; and the additional cost necessary to address the needs of the currently under-represented.

[41] Federal Register, Vol. 74, No. 19, January 30, 2009, page 5620.

[42] Based on resource data from the ABA Project to Expand Resources for Legal Services (PERLS), an initiative of the ABA Standing Committee on Legal Aid and Indigent Defendants.

In: Legal Aid for the Poor and the Legal Services Corporation ISBN: 978-1-61668-939-1
Editor: Carl T. Donovan

Chapter 5

LEGAL SERVICES CORPORATION FACT BOOK - 2008

Carl T. Donovan

LEGAL SERVICES CORPORATION 2008 AT A GLANCE

Amount of LSC Funding and Related Support	$354,647,367
Number of Programs Receiving Grants	137
Number of Offices	918
Number of Service Areas[1]	206
Local LSC-Funded Programs	
Amount of Non-LSC Funding and Related Support	$526,322,522
Number of Full-time Staff as of December 31, 2008	
Attorneys	4,144[2]
Paralegals	1,582
Other Staff	3,166
Total	**8,892**
Number of Cases Closed	
Basic Field - General (Program Staff Only)	781,501
Private Attorney Involvement	93,174
Basic Field - Native American	9,552
Basic Field - Migrant Farmworkers	4,928
Total	**889,155**
Number of Cases Open on December 31, 2008	234,812
Total Number of Individual Clients Served During the Year	887,704[3]

Source: LSC Funding Tables and Grant Activity Reports – 2008

FUNDING

1976 – 2008 Annual LSC Appropriations

Grant Year	Annual LSC Appropriations[4] ($)	Percentage Change from Prior Year [5]
1976	116,960,000	
1977	125,000,000	6.9%
1978	205,000,000	64.0%
1979	270,000,000	31.7%
1980	300,000,000	11.1%
1981	321,300,000	7.1%
1982	241,000,000	-25.0%
1983	241,000,000	0.0%
1984	275,000,000	14.1%
1985	305,000,000	10.9%
1986	292,363,000	-4.1%
1987	305,500,000	4.5%
1988	305,500,000	0.0%
1989	308,555,000	1.0%
1990	316,525,000	2.6%
1991	328,182,000	3.7%
1992	350,000,000	6.6%
1993	357,000,000	2.0%
1994	400,000,000	12.0%
1995	400,000,000	0.0%
1996	278,000,000	-30.5%
1997	283,000,000	1.8%
1998	283,000,000	0.0%
1999	300,000,000	6.0%
2000	303,841,000	1.3%
2001	329,274,000	8.4%
2002	329,300,000	0.0%
2003	336,645,488	2.2%
2004	335,282,450	-0.4%
2005	330,803,705	-1.3%
2006	326,577,984	-1.3%
2007	348,578,000	5.4%
2008	350,490,000	0.5%

Source: LSC Historical Data as of 2008

2008 Poverty Population and LSC Funding Summary by State

State*	Total Poverty Population	Basic Field General Poverty Population	Basic Field Migrant Poverty Population	Basic Field General Amount ($)	Basic Field Migrant Amount ($)	Basic Field Nat. American Amount ($) [6]	Basic Field Total ($)
Alabama	698,097	694,540	3,557	6,224,674	0	0	6,224,674
Alaska	80,405	80,405	0	720,614	0	525,140	1,245,754
Arizona	698,669	682,618	16,051	6,117,826	143,854	3,152,763	9,414,443
Arkansas	411,777	403,232	8,545	3,613,885	0	0	3,613,885
California	4,706,130	4,420,741	285,389	39,619,998	2,557,741	857,881	43,035,620
Colorado	388,952	372,896	16,056	3,342,005	143,899	93,252	3,579,156
Connecticut	259,514	257,713	1,801	2,309,701	0	0	2,309,701
Delaware	69,901	67,217	2,684	602,419	0	0	602,419
District of Columbia	109,500	109,500	0	981,372	0	0	981,372
Florida	1,952,629	1,855,536	97,093	16,629,866	870,176	0	17,500,042
Georgia	1,033,793	991,407	42,386	8,885,285	379,876	0	9,265,161
Guam	34,792	34,792	0	311,816	0	0	311,816
Hawaii	150,439	142,989	7,450	1,331,580	16,699	222,428	1,570,707
Idaho	148,732	128,525	20,207	1,151,879	181,101	63,085	1,396,065
Illinois	1,291,958	1,264,971	26,987	11,337,047	241,866	0	11,578,913
Indiana	559,484	547,192	12,292	4,904,098	110,165	0	5,014,263
Iowa	258,008	253,929	4,079	2,275,787	36,557	0	2,312,344
Kansas	257,829	256,544	1,285	2,299,224	11,517	0	2,310,741
Kentucky	621,096	616,495	4,601	5,525,211	0	0	5,525,211
Louisiana	851,113	848,136	2,977	7,601,248	0	0	7,601,248
Maine	135,501	127,741	7,760	1,144,853	121,009	77,787	1,343,649
Maryland	438,676	428,847	9,829	3,843,455	112,145	0	3,955,600
Massachusetts	573,421	571,622	1,799	5,123,047	0	0	5,123,047
Michigan	1,021,605	956,530	65,075	8,572,707	583,222	159,845	9,315,774
Micronesia	178,317	178,317	0	1,598,130	0	0	1,598,130
Minnesota	380,476	358,846	21,630	3,216,085	306,161	232,054	3,754,300
Mississippi	548,079	541,909	6,170	4,856,750	0	80,718	4,937,468

(Continued)

State*	Total Poverty Population	Basic Field General Poverty Population	Basic Field Migrant Poverty Population	Basic Field General Amount ($)	Basic Field Migrant Amount ($)	Basic Field Nat. American Amount ($) [6]	Basic Field Total ($)
Missouri	637,891	629,084	8,807	5,638,038	78,931	0	5,716,969
Montana	128,355	122,454	5,901	1,097,469	52,886	154,612	1,304,967
Nebraska	161,269	156,698	4,571	1,404,374	40,967	32,097	1,477,438
Nevada	205,685	205,413	272	1,840,972	2,438	129,120	1,972,530
New Hampshire	78,530	77,455	1,075	694,175	0	0	694,175
New Jersey	699,668	686,623	13,045	6,153,720	116,913	0	6,270,633
New Mexico	328,933	319,491	9,442	2,863,373	84,622	473,232	3,421,227
New York	2,692,202	2,662,277	29,925	23,860,121	268,197	0	24,128,318
North Carolina	958,667	900,725	57,942	8,072,566	519,293	211,921	8,803,780
North Dakota	73,457	60,926	12,531	546,037	0	261,564	807,601
Ohio	1,170,698	1,157,080	13,618	10,370,096	122,049	0	10,492,145
Oklahoma	491,235	484,470	6,765	4,341,964	60,630	795,057	5,197,651
Oregon	388,740	328,520	60,220	2,944,294	539,710	179,250	3,663,254
Pennsylvania	1,304,117	1,286,199	17,918	11,527,297	160,586	0	11,687,883
Puerto Rico	1,818,687	1,787,255	31,432	16,017,912	281,703	0	16,299,615
Rhode Island	120,548	120,357	191	1,078,675	0	0	1,078,675
South Carolina	547,869	526,485	21,384	4,718,515	191,650	0	4,910,165
South Dakota	95,900	95,471	429	855,640	3,845	906,639	1,766,124
Tennessee	746,789	739,932	6,857	6,631,492	0	0	6,631,492
Texas	3,117,609	2,967,441	150,168	26,595,091	1,638,979	30,390	28,264,460
Utah	206,328	198,995	7,333	1,783,452	65,720	79,886	1,929,058
Vermont	55,506	54,630	876	489,610	0	0	489,610
Virgin Islands	34,931	34,931	0	313,062	0	0	313,062
Virginia	656,641	639,590	17,051	5,732,195	152,816	0	5,885,011
Washington	612,370	533,459	78,911	4,781,018	707,224	276,611	5,764,853
West Virginia	315,794	311,842	3,952	2,794,821	35,419	0	2,830,240
Wisconsin	451,538	441,695	9,843	3,958,602	88,216	150,626	4,197,444
Wyoming	54,777	53,432	1,345	478,874	12,054	167,794	658,722
	36,013,627	34,776,120	1,237,507	311,724,017	11,040,836	9,313,752	332,078,605

*State includes territories and other jurisdictions.

2008 LSC and Non-LSC Funding Received by LSC-Funded Programs by State[7]

	LSC Basic Field Grants	LSC Derivative Income	Other LSC Funds	LSC Total	Other Federal Grants	State and Local Grants	IOLTA	Private Grants	Non-LSC Derivative Income	Other Non-LSC Funds	Non-LSC Total	LSC & Non-LSC Total	Non-LSC %
Alabama	6,256,553	7,132	127,384	6,391,069	612,982	15,000	200,000	55,000	0	121,565	1,004,547	7,395,616	13.6
Alaska	1,245,754	64,045	0	1,309,799	372,660	620,865	61,063	1,852	57,819	448,131	1,562,390	2,872,189	54.4
Arizona	9,414,443	381,455	206,848	10,002,746	494,128	1,724,413	1,073,275	771,914	567,137	415,998	5,046,865	15,049,611	33.5
Arkansas	3,690,468	126,321	148,640	3,965,429	155,984	680,326	567,728	99,429	115,464	338,414	1,957,345	5,922,774	33.0
California	43,035,620	2,434,270	502,249	45,972,139	6,444,580	14,853,527	6,730,827	8,232,538	2,061,313	5,781,485	44,104,270	90,076,409	49.0
Colorado	3,579,156	3,204	70,000	3,652,360	1,206,760	994,066	2,593,213	1,429,350	3,266,663	122,881	9,612,933	13,265,293	72.5
Connecticut	2,324,902	178,486	7,000	2,510,388	0	20,268	650,004	0	0	68,676	738,948	3,249,336	22.7
Delaware	626,474	3,277	15,812	645,563	46,146	0	353,500	0	0	182,918	582,564	1,228,127	47.4
District of Columbia	981,372	17,878	0	999,250	0	0	86,250	0	628,954	735,048	1,450,252	2,449,502	59.2
Florida	17,500,042	1,092,670	545,612	19,138,324	3,125,387	6,233,809	5,550,177	516,935	2,069,606	2,148,590	19,644,504	38,782,828	50.7
Georgia	9,265,161	30,556	51,027	9,346,744	2,807,378	3,467,206	3,500,000	2,838,750	81,319	1,467,541	14,162,194	23,508,938	60.2
Guam	311,816	255	62	312,133	613,087	0	0	0	0	1,091	614,178	926,311	66.3
Hawaii	1,570,707	0	44,298	1,615,005	1,399,393	3,212,136	110,000	1,071	280,000	514,778	5,517,378	7,132,383	77.4
Idaho	1,396,065	0	10,100	1,406,165	505,018	12,037	190,130	68,500	155,000	24,000	954,685	2,360,850	40.4
Illinois	11,578,913	540,167	75,028	12,194,108	3,619,680	3,831,135	4,729,508	4,116,061	0	2,732,882	19,029,266	31,223,374	60.9
Indiana	5,014,263	454,131	185	5,468,579	577,953	945,517	0	338,903	526,970	704,123	3,093,466	8,562,045	36.1
Iowa	2,312,344	77,850	0	2,390,194	941,135	2,310,254	866,471	1,279,002	0	425,826	5,822,688	8,212,882	70.9
Kansas	2,310,741	8,989	0	2,319,730	1,277,974	3,959,989	120,688	528,621	0	140,373	6,027,645	8,347,375	72.2
Kentucky	5,566,446	617,802	83,263	6,267,511	1,473,127	4,967,331	1,099,397	984,346	2,206,018	869,923	11,600,142	17,867,653	64.9
Louisiana	7,627,929	438,996	107,821	8,174,746	1,343,144	1,173,366	1,073,381	629,919	854,719	432,354	5,506,883	13,681,629	40.3
Maine	1,328,448	0	46,774	1,375,222	436,179	1,293,668	523,879	496,342	1,541,521	539,954	4,831,543	6,206,765	77.8
Maryland	3,931,545	14,662	27,500	3,973,707	432,191	7,959,352	8,658,763	862,088	0	529,672	18,442,066	22,415,773	82.3
Massachusetts	5,123,047	296,689	46,966	5,466,702	91,357	59,808	447,485	155,556	494,121	518,287	1,766,614	7,233,316	24.4
Michigan	9,315,774	404,473	50,903	9,771,150	1,255,717	2,592,439	1,049,720	6,747,576	1,387,895	903,025	13,936,372	23,707,522	58.8
Micronesia	1,598,130	11,618	15,000	1,624,748	0	663,866	0	7,400	0	23,984	695,250	2,319,998	30.0
Minnesota	3,641,993	57,381	5,857	3,705,231	1,157,307	8,518,134	1,307,520	1,046,257	908,382	1,426,526	14,364,126	18,069,357	79.5
Mississippi	4,992,765	328,562	5,050	5,326,377	593,559	810,843	1,465,119	69,670	114,934	5,030	3,059,155	8,385,532	36.5

(Continued)

	LSC Basic Field Grants	LSC Derivative Income	Other LSC Funds	LSC Total	Other Federal Grants	State and Local Grants	IOLTA	Private Grants	Non-LSC Derivative Income	Other Non-LSC Funds	Non-LSC Total	LSC & Non-LSC Total	Non-LSC %
Missouri	5,716,969	48,432	27,657	5,793,058	1,248,913	4,657,291	1,330,967	2,842,464	641,691	1,460,749	12,182,075	17,975,133	67.8
Montana	1,304,967	7,412	92,000	1,404,379	937,201	6,822	593,000	89,440	0	336,209	1,962,672	3,367,051	58.3
Nebraska	1,477,438	0	0	1,477,438	0	606,918	200,000	0	0	0	806,918	2,284,356	35.3
Nevada	1,972,530	80,841	750	2,054,121	164,967	339,984	120,000	22,144	0	45,331	692,426	2,746,547	25.2
New Hampshire	694,175	166	12,500	706,841	40,000	0	60,000	0	0	72,530	172,530	879,371	19.6
New Jersey	6,270,633	734,931	0	7,005,564	2,311,477	17,691,780	16,014,544	288,944	3,478,874	2,224,458	42,010,077	49,015,641	85.7
New Mexico	3,421,227	692,699	28,460	4,142,386	135,224	2,002,438	0	223,851	0	19,953	2,381,466	6,523,852	36.5
New York	24,128,318	1,502,463	197,873	25,828,654	5,319,680	31,909,925	9,162,755	5,758,013	11,066,359	1,774,992	64,991,724	90,820,378	71.6
North Carolina	8,803,780	970,347	182,108	9,956,235	804,348	6,054,705	2,230,000	1,246,161	1,081,128	1,120,095	12,536,437	22,492,672	55.7
North Dakota	919,908	70,035	20,753	1,010,696	308,600	424,214	53,500	187,671	0	4,100	978,085	1,988,781	49.2
Ohio	10,492,145	10,979	267,352	10,770,476	3,288,806	5,308,149	19,793,065	2,860,726	14,257,870	2,275,985	47,784,601	58,555,077	81.6
Oklahoma	5,197,651	452,433	20,113	5,670,197	677,194	1,868,969	514,250	749,655	1,583,113	465,115	5,858,296	11,528,493	50.8
Oregon	3,663,254	22,302	0	3,685,556	553,052	2,608,729	704,439	416,837	322	481,449	4,764,828	8,450,384	56.4
Pennsylvania	11,687,883	1,002,535	22,044	12,712,462	5,108,071	10,621,672	4,133,662	1,186,889	3,601,333	1,606,932	26,258,559	38,971,021	67.4
Puerto Rico	16,299,615	45,807	409,541	16,754,963	230,027	3,662,937	0	0	185,316	15,229	4,093,509	20,848,472	19.6
Rhode Island	1,078,675	0	0	1,078,675	465,568	1,169,803	975,680	46,000	0	113,052	2,770,103	3,848,778	72.0
South Carolina	4,910,165	390,005	358,902	5,659,072	354,788	1,769,971	2,332,691	115,960	310,323	72,941	4,956,674	10,615,746	46.7
South Dakota	1,766,124	113,357	21,426	1,900,907	373,920	10,729	31,000	185,202	14,981	197,906	813,738	2,714,645	30.0
Tennessee	6,692,946	179,383	478,453	7,350,782	4,192,201	4,538,495	677,600	618,258	650,444	1,666,511	12,343,509	19,694,291	62.7
Texas	27,971,331	2,056,677	133,856	30,161,864	1,507,150	4,450,753	6,396,201	1,418,123	1,414,036	7,176,031	22,362,294	52,524,158	42.6
Utah	1,929,058	43,616	22,500	1,995,174	567,808	350,914	60,000	408,220	537,069	13,889	1,937,900	3,933,074	49.3
Vermont	489,610	53,250	64,315	607,175	0	0	54,000	5,000	0	5,567	64,567	671,742	9.6
Virgin Islands	313,062	0	0	313,062	263,718	902,915	112,500	57,500	0	10,500	1,347,133	1,660,195	81.1
Virginia	5,885,011	201,755	7,206	6,093,972	583,522	5,592,126	1,431,221	559,476	2,409,776	432,773	11,008,894	17,102,866	64.4
Washington	5,764,853	582,117	301,418	6,648,388	550,979	12,393,297	378,750	107,107	1,895,281	108,382	15,433,796	22,082,184	69.9
West Virginia	2,830,240	4,455	55,515	2,890,210	281,199	3,617,609	325,124	249,243	0	186,779	4,659,954	7,550,164	61.7
Wisconsin	4,197,444	790,956	2,819	4,991,219	1,614,633	658,532	1,104,683	208,179	1,467,703	967,758	6,021,488	11,012,707	54.7
Wyoming	658,722	0	0	658,722	0	0	0	0	0	0	0	658,722	0.0
	332,078,605	17,647,822	4,920,940	354,647,367	62,865,872	194,139,032	111,797,730	51,128,143	61,913,454	44,478,291	526,322,522	880,969,889	59.7

Source: LSC Funding Tables and Grant Activity Reports - 2008

2008 LSC and Non-LSC Funding Summary

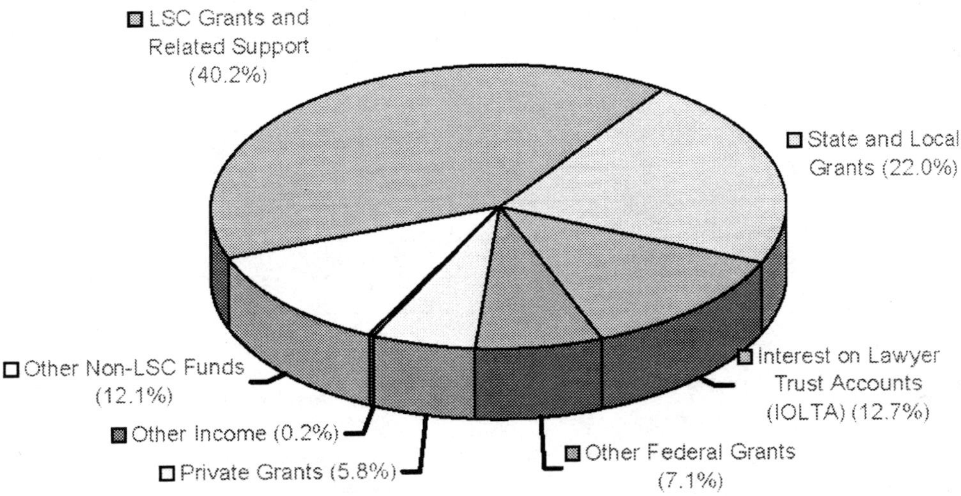

Funding Type[8]	Amount ($)	Percent*
LSC Grants and Related Support	354,647,367	40.2%
State and Local Grants	194,139,032	22.0%
Interest on Lawyer Trust Accounts (IOLTA)	111,797,730	12.7%
Other Federal Grants	62,865,872	7.1%
Private Grants	51,128,143	5.8%
Other Non-LSC Funds	106,391,745	12.1%
Other Income	1,743,518	0.2%
Total	882,713,407	100.0%

*Percentages do not total exactly because of rounding.

Source: LSC Funding Tables and Grant Activity Reports – 2008

2008 LSC and Non-LSC Funding Summary

	Amount $	Percent of Programs' Total Funding*
LSC FUNDING SOURCES:		
Basic Field Grants	332,078,605	37.6%
LSC Derivative Income		
Interest/Investment Income	1,171,956	0.1%
Attorney Fee Awards - LSC Case(s)[9]	22,400	0.0%
Publication Income	9,023	0.0%
Carryover Funds	16,444,443	1.9%
Other LSC Funds	4,920,940	0.6%
Subtotal LSC Sources:	**354,647,367**	**40.2%**

(Continued)

	Amount $	Percent of Programs' Total Funding*
Non - Lsc Funding Sources:		
Other Federal Grants		
Title XX of Social Security Act	4,742,101	0.5%
Older Americans Act	19,830,063	2.2%
Violence Against Women Act	11,311,064	1.3%
Other Federal Grants	22,910,430	2.6%
Community Development Block Grants	4,072,214	0.5%
State and Local Grants		
State Grants	145,930,991	16.5%
Local Grants	48,208,041	5.5%
Private Grants		
United Way	13,886,526	1.6%
Foundation Grants	31,355,429	3.6%
Bar Association Grants	5,886,188	0.7%
IOLTA	111,797,730	12.7%
Non-LSC Derivative Income		
Attorney Fee Awards[9]	253,824	0.0%
Publication Income	309,099	0.0%
Carryover Funds	61,350,531	7.0%
Other Non-LSC Funds	44,478,291	5.0%
Subtotal NON-LSC Sources:	526,322,522	59.6%
OTHER INCOME:		
Fees & Receipts from Client Services	1,431,009	0.2%
Other Income	312,509	0.0%
Subtotal Client Service Income:	1,743,518	0.2%
TOTAL CASH RESOURCES:	882,713,407	100.0%

*Percentages do not total exactly because of rounding.
Source: Grant Activity Reports – 2008

Client Services

2000 - 2008 Total LSC-Eligible Cases Closed by LSC-Funded Programs

	Basic Field - General						
	Program Staff	Private Attorneys	Totals	Basic Field Nat. American	Basic Field Migrant	Totals	Change From Prior Year
2000	873,199	121,030	994,229	11,481	6,658	1,012,368	
2001	877,492	118,749	996,241	10,334	7,538	1,014,113	0.2%
2002	847,642	114,632	962,274	10,053	6,507	978,834	-3.5%
2003	806,735	112,300	919,035	9,986	6,772	935,793	-4.4%

	Basic Field - General						
	Program Staff	Private Attorneys	Totals	Basic Field Nat. American	Basic Field Migrant	Totals	Change From Prior Year
2004	782,793	102,256	885,049	10,527	5,491	901,067	-3.7%
2005	792,644	97,493	890,137	10,967	5,234	906,338	0.6%
2006	786,923	93,922	880,845	9,796	4,847	895,488	-1.2%
2007	793,997	97,531	891,528	9,716	5,263	906,507	1.2%
2008	781,501	93,174	874,675	9,552	4,928	889,155	-1.9%

Source: Grant Activity Reports- 2008

2008 LSC-Eligible Case Services Summary by Reason for Closure

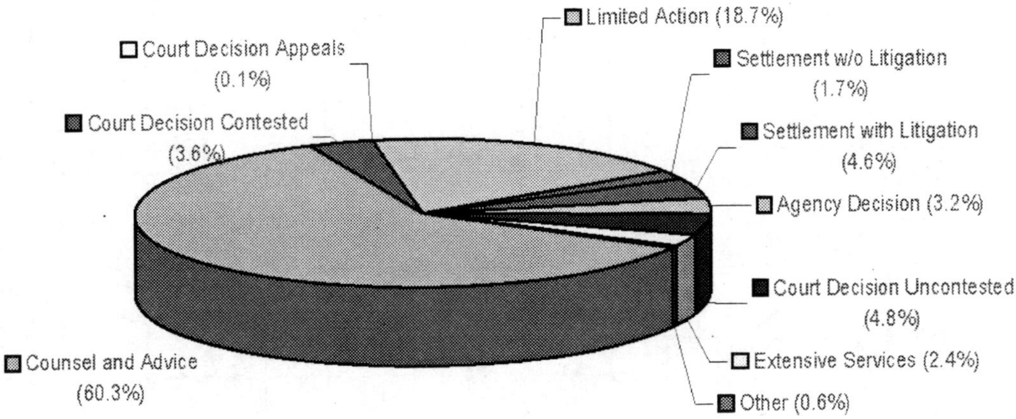

Reason for Closure[10]	Total Closed Cases	Percent
Counsel and Advice (60.3%)	535,783	60.3%
Limited Action (18.7%)	166,306	18.7%
Settlement w/o Litigation (1.7%)	15,409	1.7%
Settlement with Litigation (4.6%)	41,282	4.6%
Agency Decision (3.2%)	28,574	3.2%
Court Decision Uncontested (4.8%)	42,552	4.8%
Court Decision Contested (3.6%)	31,668	3.6%
Court Decision Appeals (0.1%)	452	0.1%
Extensive Services (2.4%)	21,516	2.4%
Other Closure Method (0.6%)	5,613	0.6%
Total	**889,155**	**100.0%**

Source: Grant Activity Reports - 2008

2008 LSC-Eligible Cases Closed by Case Type and Reason for Closure

	Counsel and Advice	Limited Action	Negotiated Settlement w/o Litig.	Negotiated Settlement with Litig.	Admin Agency Decision	Uncontested Court Decision	Contested Court Decision	Appeals	Other	Extensive Service	Total	Percent*
Consumer/Finance												
01 – Bankruptcy/Debtor Relief	24,358	1,857	70	122	50	3,675	570	1	311	639	31,653	3.6%
02 – Collection (Including Repossession/ Deficiency/Garnishment)	35,703	7,430	1,000	2,283	62	1,067	1,522	12	399	941	50,419	5.7%
03 – Contracts/Warranties	6,344	1,017	253	167	15	78	114	3	41	126	8,158	0.9%
04 – Collection Practices/Creditor Harassment	2,326	897	115	53	7	40	36	0	12	47	3,533	0.4%
05 – Predatory Lending Practices (Not Mortgages)	138	33	12	4	1	1	4	0	0	1	194	0.0%
06 – Loans/Installment Purchase (Not Collections)	891	256	37	22	10	7	11	2	11	31	1,278	0.1%
07 – Public Utilities	2,760	1,304	221	25	24	13	16	0	16	103	4,482	0.5%
08 – Unfair and Deceptive Sales & Practices (Not Real Property)	1,093	199	55	26	0	7	13	0	3	20	1,416	0.2%
09 – Other Consumer/Finance	5,322	1,238	156	136	33	64	71	2	59	190	7,271	0.8%
	78,935	14,231	1,919	2,838	202	4,952	2,357	20	852	2,098	108,404	12.2%
Education												
12 – Discipline (Including Expulsion and Suspension)	532	149	119	37	137	1	7	1	7	36	1,026	0.1%
13 – Special Education/Learning Disabilities	703	246	365	78	102	2	5	3	8	117	1,629	0.2%
14 – Access (Including Bilingual, Residency, Testing)	194	392	63	5	12	5	3	1	4	20	699	0.1%
15 – Vocational Education	44	110	3	6	8	5	0	0	1	9	186	0.0%
16 – Student Financial Aid	312	400	10	2	47	0	2	0	2	9	784	0.1%
19 – Other Education	792	1,483	93	20	27	14	5	1	40	40	2,515	0.3%
	2,577	2,780	653	148	333	27	22	6	62	231	6,839	0.8%

	Counsel and Advice	Limited Action	Negotiated Settlement w/o Litig.	Negotiated Settlement with Litig.	Admin Agency Decision	Uncontested Court Decision	Contested Court Decision	Appeals	Other	Extensive Service	Total	Percent*
Employment												
21 – Employment Discrimination	2,761	192	51	56	38	16	14	14	7	77	3,226	0.4%
22 – Wage Claims and other FLSA Issues	1,976	720	288	508	142	88	98	1	49	51	3,921	0.4%
23 – EITC (Earned Income Tax Credit)	644	956	33	14	62	10	2	2	6	198	1,927	0.2%
24 – Taxes (Not EITC)	1,577	1,279	122	22	246	14	10	0	43	343	3,656	0.4%
25 – Employee Rights	2,641	195	12	41	45	1	0	1	11	7	2,954	0.3%
26 – Agricultural Worker Issues (Not Wage Claims/FLSA Issues)	118	128	21	25	8	1	24	0	8	8	341	0.0%
29 – Other Employment	7,285	2,449	130	145	239	327	79	5	88	124	10,871	1.2%
	17,002	5,919	657	811	780	457	227	23	212	808	26,896	3.0%
Family												
30 Adoption	1,666	163	9	24	5	821	83	3	51	75	2,900	0.3%
31 Custody/Visitation	65,344	9,024	396	4,451	41	3,185	4,638	27	474	1,476	89,056	10.0%
32 Divorce/Separation	74,727	13,046	435	4,473	66	15,686	5,415	25	1,115	4,427	119,415	13.4%
33 Guardianship	3,436	1,381	43	86	9	1,186	231	1	103	146	6,622	0.7%
34 Name Change	1,819	910	4	5	10	802	42	0	22	40	3,654	0.4%
35 Parental Rights Termination	1,381	83	1	27	5	53	69	2	5	17	1,643	0.2%
36 Paternity	4,215	1,021	16	142	34	305	338	3	26	145	6,245	0.7%
37 Domestic Abuse	16,256	4,059	318	6,799	23	7,797	6,972	34	206	2,255	44,719	5.0%
38 Support	21,235	2,428	137	1,055	104	706	1,976	14	132	454	28,241	3.2%
39 Other Family	6,518	1,884	87	197	44	328	288	26	55	124	9,551	1.1%
	196,597	33,999	1,446	17,259	341	30,869	20,052	135	2,189	9,159	312,046	35.1%
Juvenile												
41 – Delinquent	395	29	73	822	3	266	893	1	2	45	2,529	0.3%
42 – Neglected/Abused/Dependent	1,564	153	21	331	27	958	1,117	10	40	113	4,334	0.5%
43 – Emancipation	779	502	5	1	12	165	9	0	4	67	1,544	0.2%
44 – Minor Guardian/Conservatorship	3,156	1,095	14	66	1	747	146	1	14	337	5,577	0.6%
49 – Other Juvenile	790	57	17	96	18	62	102	2	5	10	1,159	0.1%

(Continued)

	Counsel and Advice	Limited Action	Negotiated Settlement w/o Litig.	Negotiated Settlement with Litig.	Admin Agency Decision	Uncontested Court Decision	Contested Court Decision	Appeals	Other	Extensive Service	Total	Percent
Health												
52 – Medicare	881	1,057	54	8	63	0	0	1	10	55	2,129	0.2%
53 – Government Children's Health Insurance Prog.	143	191	34	17	21	0	1	2	0	8	417	0.0%
54 – Home and Community Based Care	197	159	14	17	42	5	8	0	2	29	473	0.1%
55 – Private Health Insurance	177	72	9	4	3	0	2	0	2	5	274	0.0%
56 – Long Term Health Care Facilities	207	116	18	14	28	0	3	0	3	16	405	0.0%
57 – State and Local Health	1,480	826	12	9	15	1	1	1	2	12	2,359	0.3%
59 – Other Health	2,035	3,062	125	90	149	10	13	4	45	137	5,670	0.6%
	13,773	11,749	1,195	707	2,170	43	62	24	174	905	30,802	3.5%
Housing												
61 – Federally Subsidized Housing	22,592	11,729	2,250	4,133	1,614	457	1,311	36	154	614	44,890	5.0%
62 – Homeownership/Real Property (Not Foreclosure)	7,891	2,552	409	472	68	196	349	5	118	513	12,573	1.4%
63 – Private Landlord/Tenant	86,353	17,014	1,898	9,582	142	1,125	3,337	37	385	746	120,619	13.6%
64 – Public Housing	6,650	13,561	683	1,089	534	161	391	8	54	176	23,307	2.6%
65 – Mobile Homes	2,040	382	82	172	6	22	72	1	11	45	2,833	0.3%
66 – Housing Discrimination	431	107	72	25	16	1	7	0	9	26	694	0.1%
67 – Mortgage Foreclosures (Not Predatory Lending/Practices)	7,506	1,374	192	323	7	64	168	4	42	240	9,920	1.1%
68 – Mortgage Predatory Lending/Practices	891	160	42	72	1	6	13	1	13	54	1,253	0.1%
69 – Other Housing	7,856	3,937	399	343	117	191	240	4	59	277	13,423	1.5%
	142,210	50,816	6,027	16,211	2,505	2,223	5,888	96	845	2,691	229,512	25.8%
Income												
71 – TANF	5,375	3,189	1,015	735	1,256	11	20	9	77	307	11,994	1.3%
72 – Social Security (Not SSDI)	1,846	657	53	6	335	64	32	0	15	83	3,091	0.3%
73 – Food Stamps	6,964	4,248	692	347	545	7	2	4	36	173	13,018	1.5%
74 – SSDI	7,387	1,598	161	35	2,097	18	21	5	77	330	11,729	1.3%

	Counsel and Advice	Limited Action	Negotiated Settlement w/o Litig.	Negotiated Settlement with Litig.	Admin Agency Decision	Uncontested Court Decision	Contested Court Decision	Appeals	Other	Extensive Service	Total	Percent
75 – SSI	15,063	4,361	304	71	11,386	34	56	37	252	1,809	33,373	3.8%
76 – Unemployment Compensation	9,080	1,374	70	40	4,160	48	204	38	38	102	15,154	1.7%
78 – State and Local Income Maintenance	1,669	1,249	175	180	179	1	4	1	11	59	3,528	0.4%
79 – Other Income Maintenance	2,628	2,273	310	95	262	84	25	2	15	118	5,812	0.7%
	50,392	19,054	2,785	1,512	20,258	270	364	96	524	3,002	98,257	11.1%
Individual												
81 – Immigration/Naturalization	1,664	1,466	28	13	1,502	24	17	5	74	322	5,115	0.6%
82 – Mental Health	304	123	64	3	6	4	7	1	7	6	525	0.1%
84 – Disability Rights	226	106	20	5	26	1	1	1	3	17	406	0.0%
85 – Civil Rights	456	280	6	2	2	6	2	0	1	4	759	0.1%
86 – Human Trafficking	9	6	0	0	59	0	0	0	0	0	74	0.0%
89 – Other Individual Rights	3,816	1,920	95	28	50	219	125	4	29	85	6,371	0.7%
	6,475	3,901	213	51	1,645	254	152	11	114	434	13,250	1.5%
MISC												
91 – Legal Assistance to Non-Profit Org or Group (Incl Incorp/ Dissolution)	135	93	8	8	29	2	0	0	9	115	399	0.0%
92 – Indian/Tribal Law	552	269	23	182	26	83	55	2	8	111	1,311	0.1%
93 – Licenses (Drivers, Occupational, and Others)	1,852	3,188	31	36	31	45	15	3	33	53	5,287	0.6%
94 – Torts	2,649	312	34	78	2	40	68	1	37	35	3,256	0.4%
95 – Wills/Estates	8,117	7,461	90	42	23	924	70	9	219	943	17,898	2.0%
96 – Advance Directives/Powers of Attorney	1,783	7,264	102	2	2	6	3	0	110	240	9,512	1.1%
97 – Municipal Legal Needs	74	28	2	4	4	0	0	0	0	1	113	0.0%
99 – Other Miscellaneous	5,976	3,406	94	77	162	159	66	12	160	118	10,230	1.2%
	21,138	22,021	384	429	279	1,259	277	27	576	1,616	48,006	5.4%
Totals	535,783	166,306	15,409	41,282	28,574	42,552	31,668	452	5,613	21,516	889,155	
Percentages	60.3%	18.7%	1.7%	4.6%	3.2%	4.8%	3.6%	0.1%	0.6%	2.4%	100.0%	

*Percentages do not total exactly because of rounding. Source: Grant Activity Reports – 2008

2008 LSC-Eligible Case Services Summary by Case Type

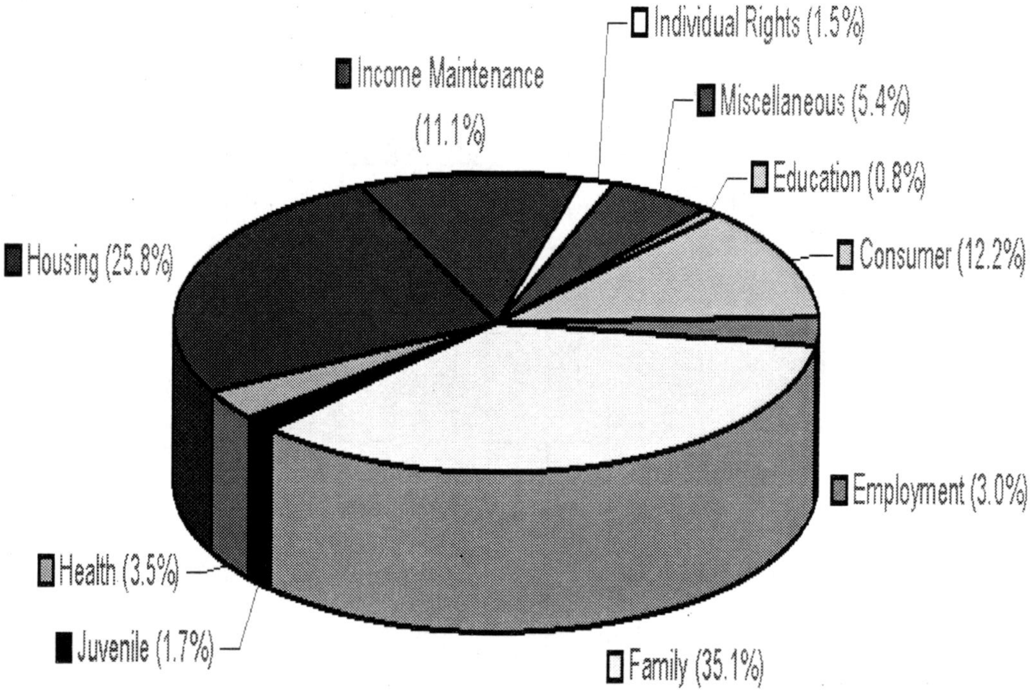

Type of Case	Total Closed Cases	Percent*
Consumer	108,404	12.2%
Education	6,839	0.8%
Employment	26,896	3.0%
Family	312,046	35.1%
Juvenile	15,143	1.7%
Health	30,802	3.5%
Housing	229,512	25.8%
Income Maintenance	98,257	11.1%
Individual Rights	13,250	1.5%
Miscellaneous	48,006	5.4%
Total	**889,15**	**100.00%**

* Percentages do not total exactly because of rounding.
Source: Grant Activity Reports – 2008

2008 LSC-Eligible Cases Closed by Case Type

Consumer/Finance	Number of Cases	Percent*
Bankruptcy/Debtor Relief	31,653	3.6%
Collection (Incl Repossession/Deficiency/Garnishment)	50,419	5.7%
Contracts/Warranties	8,158	0.9%
Collection Practices/Creditor Harassment	3,533	0.4%
Predatory Lending Practices (Not Mortgages)	194	0.0%
Loans/Installment Purchase (Not Collections)	1,278	0.1%
Public Utilities	4,482	0.5%
Unfair & Deceptive Sales & Prac (Not Real Property)	1,416	0.2%
Other Consumer/Finance	7,271	0.8%
	108,404	**12.2%**

Education	Number of Cases	Percent*
Discipline (Incl Expulsion and Suspension)	1,026	0.1%
Special Education/Learning Disabilities	1,629	0.2%
Access (Including Bilingual, Residency, Testing)	699	0.1%
Vocational Education	186	0.0%
Student Financial Aid	784	0.1%
Other Education	2,515	0.3%
	6,839	**0.8%**

Health	Number of Cases	Percent*
Medicaid	19,075	2.1%
Medicare	2,129	0.2%
Government Children's Health Insurance Programs	417	0.0%
Home and Community Based Care	473	0.1%
Private Health Insurance	274	0.0%
Long Term Health Care Facilities	405	0.0%
State and Local Health	2,359	0.3%
Other Health	5,670	0.6%
	30,802	**3.5%**

Housing	Number of Cases	Percent*
Federally Subsidized Housing	44,890	5.0%
Homeownership/Real Property (Not Foreclosure)	12,573	1.4%
Private Landlord/Tenant	120,619	13.6%
Public Housing	23,307	2.6%
Mobile Homes	2,833	0.3%
Housing Discrimination	694	0.1%
Mortgage Foreclosures (Not Predatory Lending/Practices	9,920	1.1%
Mortgage Predatory Lending/Practices	1,253	0.1%
Other Housing	13,423	1.5%
	229,512	**25.8%**

(Continued)

Employment		
Employment Discrimination	3,226	0.4%
Wage Claims and other FLSA Issues	3,921	0.4%
EITC (Earned Income Tax Credit)	1,927	0.2%
Taxes (Not EITC)	3,656	0.4%
Employee Rights	2,954	0.3%
Agricultural Worker Issues (Not Wage Claims/FLSA)	341	0.0%
Other Employment	10,871	1.2%
	26,896	**3.0%**

Family		
Adoption	2,900	0.3%
Custody/Visitation	89,056	10.0%
Divorce/Separation	119,415	13.4%
Guardianship	6,622	0.7%
Name Change	3,654	0.4%
Parental Rights Termination	1,643	0.2%
Paternity	6,245	0.7%
Domestic Abuse	44,719	5.0%
Support	28,241	3.2%
Other Family	9,551	1.1%
	312,046	**35.1%**

Juvenile		
Delinquent	2,529	0.3%
Neglected/Abused/Dependent	4,334	0.5%
Emancipation	1,544	0.2%
Minor Guardian/Conservatorship	5,577	0.6%
Other Juvenile	1,159	0.1%
	15,143	**1.7%**

Income Maintenance		
TANF	11,994	1.3%
Social Security (Not SSDI)	3,091	0.3%
Food Stamps	13,018	1.5%
SSDI	11,729	1.3%
SSI	33,373	3.8%
Unemployment Compensation	15,154	1.7%
Veterans Benefits	558	0.1%
State and Local Income Maintenance	3,528	0.4%
Other Income Maintenance	5,812	0.7%
	98,257	**11.1%**

Individual Rights		
Immigration/Naturalization	5,115	0.6%
Mental Health	525	0.1%
Disability Rights	406	0.0%
Civil Rights	759	0.1%
Human Trafficking	74	0.0%
Other Individual Rights	6,371	0.7%
	13,250	**1.5%**

Miscellaneous		
Lgl Assist to Non-Profit Org or Grp (Incl Incorp/Dissol)	399	0.0%
Indian/Tribal Law	1,311	0.1%
Licenses (Drivers, Occupational, and Others)	5,287	0.6%
Torts	3,256	0.4%
Wills/Estates	17,898	2.0%
Advance Directives/Powers of Attorney	9,512	1.1%
Municipal Legal Needs	113	0.0%
Other Miscellaneous	10,230	1.2%
	48,006	**5.4%**

Total	**889,155**	**100.0%**

* Percentages do not total exactly because of rounding.
Source: Grant Activity Reports – 2008

CLIENT DEMOGRAPHICS

2008 Ethnicity of LSC Clients

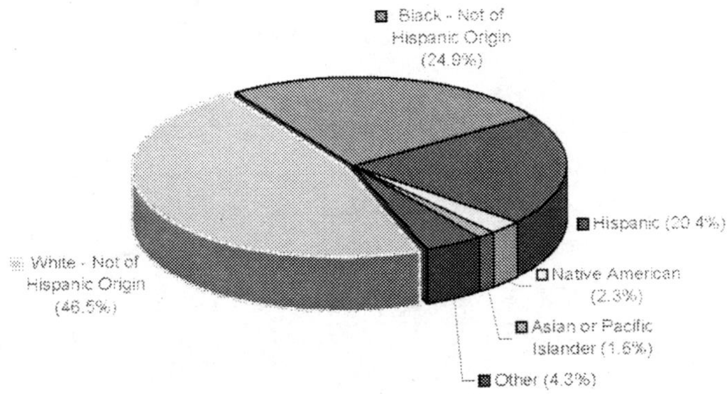

Ethnic Group	Total Individual Clients	Percent*
White - Not of Hispanic Origin	409,210	46.5%
Black - Not of Hispanic Origin	218,981	24.9%
Hispanic	179,692	20.4%
Native American	20,599	2.3%
Asian or Pacific Islander	14,031	1.6%
Other	38,008	4.3%
Total	**880,521**	**100.0%**

* Percentages do not total exactly because of rounding.

Source: Grant Activity Reports – 2008

2008 Age and Gender of LSC Clients[11]

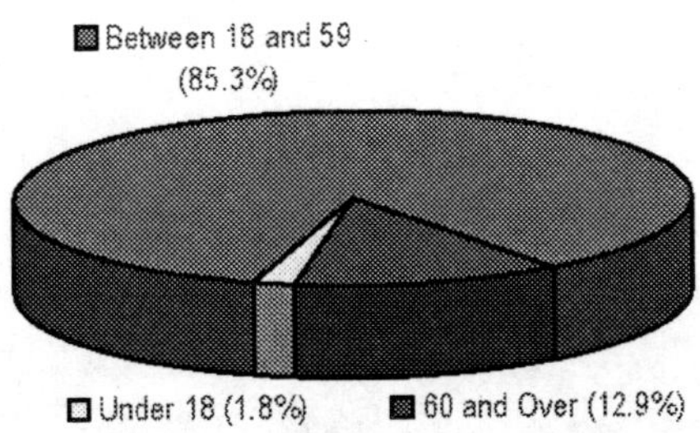

Age Group	Total Individual Clients	Percent
Under 18	16,194	1.8%
Between 18 and 59	750,976	85.3%
60 and Over	113,351	12.9%
Total	**880,521**	**100.0%**

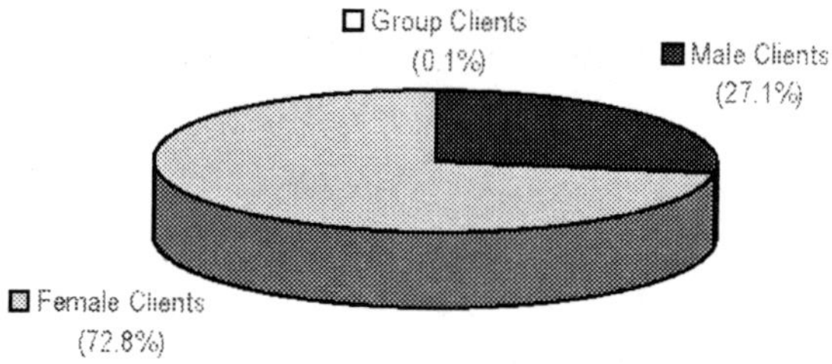

Gender/Type	Total Clients	Percent
Male Clients	240,773	27.1%
Female Clients	646,325	72.8%
Group Clients	606	0.1%
Total	**887,704**	**100.0%**

Source: Grant Activity Reports – 2008

2008 Age, Ethnicity and Gender of LSC Clients[12]

	Under Age 18	Ages 18 through 59	Age 60 and Over	Total Individual Clients
White - Not of Hispanic Origin	4,544	348,098	56,568	409,210
Black - Not of Hispanic Origin	3,650	190,840	24,491	218,981
Hispanic Origin	6,171	152,731	20,790	179,692
Native American	585	16,444	3,570	20,599
Asian or Pacific Islander	237	11,311	2,483	14,031
Other	1,007	31,552	5,449	38,008
Total	**16,194**	**750,976**	**113,351**	**880,521**

Men	240,773
Women	646,325
Groups	606
Total	**887,704**

Source: Grant Activity Reports – 2008

PRIVATE ATTORNEY INVOLVEMENT

2008 Private Attorney Involvement (PAI) for LSC Programs[13]

Component Type[14]	Cases Referred	Cases Closed	Attorneys Accepting Referrals
Pro Bono	58,791	57,719	26,749
Contract/Judicare	32,781	31,052	4,942
Other PAT	19,134	4,397	4,027
Total	**110,706**	**93,168**	**35,718**

Source: Grant Activity Reports - 2008

2007 - 2008 PAI with Percentage Change for LSC Programs

Pro Bono

	Cases Closed	Attorneys Accepting Referrals
2007	64,494	23,631
2008	57,719	26,749
Percentage Change	-10.5%	13.2%

Contract/Judicare

	Cases Closed	Attorneys Accepting Referrals
2007	28,457	2,708
2008	31,052	4,942
Percentage Change	9.1%	82.5%

Other PAI

	Cases Closed	Attorneys Accepting Referrals
2007	4,580	4,847
2008	4,397	4,027
Percentage Change	-4.0%	-16.9%

Source: Grant Activity Reports - 2008

STAFFING

2008 Staffing Level with Average Salary and Experience for LSC Programs*

Position	Full-time	Attorneys	Women	Men	Average Years in Profession	Average Salary
Executive Director	138	133	44	94	29.5	107,168
Deputy Director	88	77	44	44	27.7	96,939
Director of Litigation	76	76	25	51	27.5	87,912
Managing Attorney	669	669	361	308	20.9	70,330
Supervising Attorney	431	431	259	172	18.3	70,796
Staff Attorney	2,758	2,753	1,847	911	10.2	53,494
Paralegal	1,582	15	1,298	284	15.6	38,122
Information Technology Staff	122	11	32	90	13.4	53,274
PAI Coordinator	117	38	104	13	17.8	48,701
Training Responsible Person	6	2	6	0	15.7	51,476
Financial Professional	246	4	187	59	22.9	56,511
Management Professional	250	21	200	50	21.1	61,443

(Continued)

Law Clerk	102	5	66	36	0.8	24,046
Senior Aide	2	0	1	1	12.5	23,574
Administrative Assistant	352	0	337	15	21.1	39,097
Secretarial/Clerical	1,632	5	1,583	49	16.9	31,704
Other Position/Job	321	29	249	72	13.3	38,147
Total / Average	8,892	4,269	6,643	2,249	15.5	49,193

* Figures include all full-time (90% and above) staff members who were employed for over 6 months in 2008 even if terminated prior to 12/31/08. Figures do not include sub-recipient staffing.

Source: Grant Activity Reports – 2008

2008 Staff Ethnicity and Gender for LSC Programs*

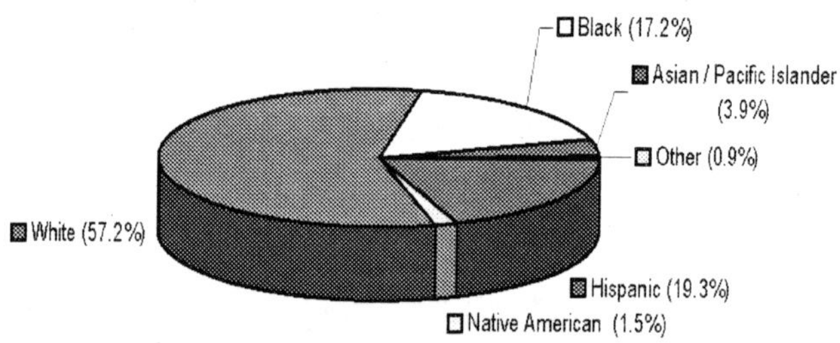

Ethnic Group	Number of Staff	Percent
White	5,089	57.2%
Black	1,531	17.2%
Hispanic	1,716	19.3%
Native American	130	1.5%
Asian / Pacific Islander	343	3.9%
Other	83	0.9%
Total	**8,892**	**100.0%**

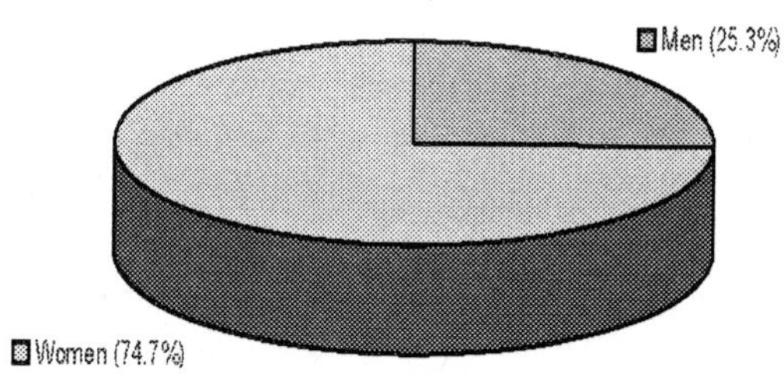

Gender	Number of Staff	Percent
Men	2,249	25.3%
Women	6,643	74.7%
Total	**8,892**	**100.0%**

* Figures include all full-time (90% and above) staff members who were employed for over 6 months in 2008 even if terminated prior to 12/31/08. Figures do not include sub-recipient staffing.

Source: Grant Activity Reports – 2008

2008 Summary of Staff Positions by Job Classification, Ethnicity and Gender for LSC Programs*

	White		Black		Hispanic		Native American		Asian/Pac		Other		Total		
	Male	Female	Male	Female	Male	Female	Male	Female	Male	Female	Male	Female	Male	Female	Total
01-Executive Director	74	25	11	10	6	5	1	2	2	2	0	0	94	44	138
03-Deputy Director	35	33	5	4	4	4	0	0	0	2	0	1	44	44	88
05-Director of Litigation	45	19	3	2	0	3	1	1	2	0	0	0	51	25	76
07-Managing Attorney	229	253	26	57	43	40	3	3	7	6	0	2	308	361	669
09-Supervising Attorney	133	184	18	42	14	22	1	2	6	6	0	3	172	259	431
11-Staff Attorney	687	1,237	71	248	101	200	3	25	37	107	12	30	911	1,847	2,758
13-Paralegal	120	576	55	312	84	338	0	24	23	35	2	13	284	1,298	1,582
14-Information Technology Staff	56	20	11	5	10	5	1	2	10	0	2	0	90	32	122
15-PAI Coordinator	10	67	0	23	3	13	0	0	0	1	0	0	13	104	117
17-Training Responsible Person	0	3	0	2	0	1	0	0	0	0	0	0	0	6	6
18-Financial Professional	32	110	10	34	9	19	0	6	7	16	1	2	59	187	246
19-Management Professional	29	101	5	61	14	29	1	0	0	8	1	1	50	200	250
21-Law Clerk	18	35	5	13	11	13	0	2	2	2	0	1	36	66	102
23-Senior Aide	1	0	0	1	0	0	0	0	0	0	0	0	1	1	2
25-Administrative Assistant	8	142	3	78	1	104	0	7	2	5	1	1	15	337	352
27-Secretarial/Clerical	14	639	9	353	24	508	0	39	1	38	1	6	49	1,583	1,632
99-Other Position/Job	26	128	14	40	25	63	1	5	6	10	0	3	72	249	321
Total	1,517	3,572	246	1,285	349	1,367	12	118	105	238	20	63	2,249	6,643	8,892

* Figures include all full-time (90% and above) staff members who were employed for over 6 months in 2008 even if terminated prior to 12/31/08. Figures do not include sub-recipient staffing.

Source: Grant Activity Reports - 2008

2008 Summary of LSC Program Staffing Levels by Job Classification, Years of Experience and Average Salary[15]

	Director		Deputy Director		Director Litigation Of		Managing Attorney	
Years of Experience	# O Positions	Average	# of Positions	Average Salary	# of Positions	Average Salary	# of Positions	Average Salary
0-1 YEAR	0	0	0	0	0	0	3	46,597
2 YEARS	0	0	0	0	0	0	4	45,975
3 YEARS	0	0	0	0	0	0	3	39,036
4 YEARS	0	0	0	0	0	0	14	46,940
5 YEARS	0	0	0	0	1	51,650	15	56,150
6-7 YEARS	0	0	0	0	1	51,650	24	54,277
8-9 YEARS	1	120,046	0	0	2	57,500	39	60,230
10-14 YEARS	4	86,835	7	66,232	2	67,410	84	64,821
15-19 YEARS	11	102,144	7	88,329	6	81,092	114	70,860
20 OR MORE YEARS	122	108,183	74	100,658	64	91,276	369	75,707
Total Count / Avg. Salary	**138**	**107,168**	**88**	**96,939**	**76**	**87,912**	**669**	**70,330**

	Supervising Attorney		Staff Attorney		PARALEGAL		Information Technology Staff	
Years of Experience	# O Positions	Average	# of Positions	Average Salary	# of Positions	Average Salary	# of Positions	Average Salary
0-1 YEAR	2	72,500	291	43,661	136	28,056	7	36,161
2 YEARS	6	46,616	314	44,137	83	30,004	4	37,648
3 YEARS	9	54,986	284	44,258	75	31,568	5	46,941
4 YEARS	11	52,540	210	46,413	64	31,445	6	43,739
5 YEARS	15	56,510	148	48,760	40	32,762	4	39,913
6-7 YEARS	30	59,037	237	51,120	102	34,055	17	47,657
8-9 YEARS	22	63,787	181	53,090	95	35,668	8	45,764
10-14 YEARS	68	64,345	319	58,298	200	37,760	26	55,222
15-19 YEARS	77	71,484	255	63,556	191	40,289	14	59,427
20 OR MORE YEARS	191	79,130	511	67,611	590	44,071	31	64,351
Total Count / Avg. Salary	**431**	**70,796**	**2,750**	**53,518**	**1,576**	**38,139**	**122**	**53,274**

Source: Grant Activity Reports – 2008

Years of Experience	Pai Coordinator # O Positions	Pai Coordinator Average Salary	Training Person Responsible # of Positions	Training Person Responsible Average Salary	Professional Financial # of Positions	Professional Financial Average Salary	Professional Management # of Positions	Professional Management Average Salary	Law Clerk # of Positions	Law Clerk Average Salary
0-1 YEAR	6	33,484	0	0	4	45,447	8	48,933	89	21,752
2 YEARS	0	0	0	0	3	39,176	5	42,774	7	40,821
3 YEARS	7	42,854	0	0	3	42,147	4	41,990	3	36,592
4 YEARS	2	36,023	0	0	4	31,873	7	47,265	0	0
5 YEARS	5	38,621	0	0	3	63,024	10	52,349	0	0
6-7 YEARS	9	48,180	0	0	11	47,878	6	55,805	0	0
8-9 YEARS	7	39,811	2	51,200	5	51,357	13	57,215	0	0
10-14 YEARS	12	49,176	2	33,234	24	56,667	27	60,733	0	0
15-19 YEARS	15	47,521	0	0	37	54,845	31	61,260	2	50,244
20 OR MORE YEARS	54	54,014	2	69,993	152	59,124	139	65,580	0	0
Total Count / Avg. Salary	**117**	**48,701**	**6**	**51,476**	**246**	**56,511**	**250**	**61,443**	**101**	**23,696**

Years of Experience	Senior Aide # of Positions	Senior Aide Average Salary	Administrative Assistant # of Positions	Administrative Assistant Average Salary	Secretarial/ Clerical # of Positions	Secretarial/ Clerical Average Salary	Other # of Positions	Other Average Salary
0-1 YEAR	0	0	8	28,916	99	24,545	19	29,260
2 YEARS	0	0	6	32,372	80	24,830	23	28,654
3 YEARS	0	0	6	33,254	68	26,584	27	31,627
4 YEARS	0	0	9	30,752	54	28,099	7	45,163
5 YEARS	0	0	6	28,706	55	27,360	10	34,789
6-7 YEARS	0	0	23	33,579	114	27,344	30	36,989
8-9 YEARS	0	0	26	37,345	108	30,356	23	40,296
10-14 YEARS	2	23,574	31	38,477	227	31,332	64	41,968
15-19 YEARS	0	0	41	42,075	165	33,772	27	40,341
20 OR MORE YEARS	0	0	195	40,826	661	35,385	88	41,096
Total Count / Avg. Salary	**2**	**23,574**	**351**	**39,021**	**1,631**	**31,708**	**318**	**38,242**

Source: Grant Activity Reports – 2008

2007 - 2008 Staffing Levels for LSC Programs

*Numbers of Full-time Staff**

Position	2007	2008	Percentage Change From 2007
Attorneys[16]	3,920	4,144	5.7%
Paralegals	1,526	1,582	3.7%
Other Staff Members	3,082	3,166	2.7%
Total	8,528	8,892	4.3%

* Figures include all full-time (90% and above) staff members who were employed for over 6 months in 2008 even if terminated prior to 12/31/08. Figures do not include sub-recipient staffing.

2008 Full-Time Equivalents (FTE's) - As of 12/31/08

Attorneys	4418
Paralegals	1693
Other	3452
Total	9563

LSC ORGANIZATIONAL CHART (AS OF JULY 2009)

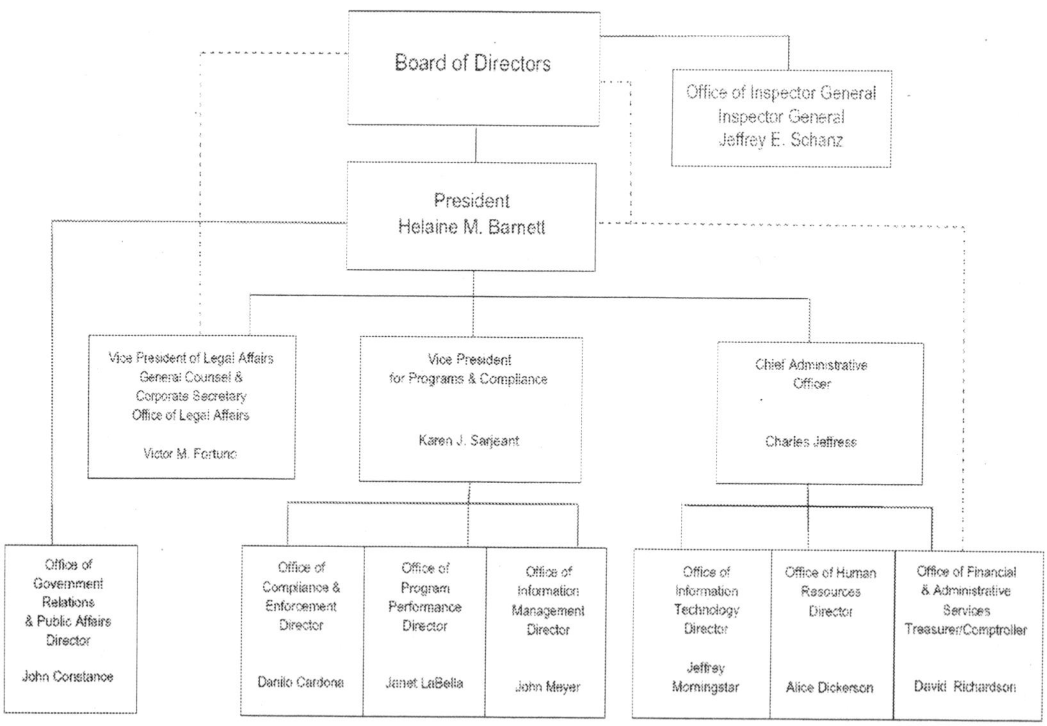

End Notes

[1] There are three types of service areas: Basic Field – General, which are geographical areas that are States and other political jurisdictions or portions thereof, collectively covering all of the United States and serving all client-eligible persons therein; Basic Field – Migrant, which are entire States or political jurisdictions, but are limited to serving eligible Migrant Farmworkers therein; and Basic Field – Native American, which are descriptive and only approximately geographical and serve only Native Americans therein. Grantee programs may, and often do, serve more than one service area.

[2] The computation of the number of attorneys includes all Job Codes 5 to 11 (Litigation Director to Staff Attorney) and all Directors and Deputy Directors who are attorneys. It does not include the small number of attorneys serving in non-attorney positions – e.g. Management Professionals who are attorneys.

[3] This number is less than the number of cases closed because some clients have more than one case.

[4] Not including special supplemental emergency funds, and Veterans Court funds.

[5] The 1976 figure includes $24,630,000 supplemental appropriations due to the Fiscal Year change from July 1 to October 1 and therefore includes five quarters' funding.

[6] Funding for Basic Field – Native American service areas is not calculated by Native American poverty population. In many instances, accurate Native American poverty population figures are not available. Native American service areas are not always by county or other political subdivision. These service areas are sometimes described by language such as: Native Americans living in or near the ___ Reservation and members of the _____ Tribe living off reservation who have cases which require litigation in the Tribal Court.

[7] LSC Derivative Income includes LSC interest/investment income, publication income, and carryover funds.
Other LSC Funds includes LSC funding other than Basic Field, such as Technology Initiative Grants (TIG) and Emergency Grants
Other Federal Grants includes Title XX, Older Americans Act, Violence Against Women Act, other federal and community development block grants
IOLTA also includes filing fees distributed to LSC programs through State IOLTA funders
Private Grants includes United Way, private foundation and bar association grants.
Non-LSC Derivative Income includes publication income and carryover funds.

[8] LSC Grants and Related Support includes LSC Basic Field grants, interest/investment income, publication income, carryover funds, and other LSC funds.
IOLTA also includes filing fees distributed to LSC programs through State IOLTA funders
Other Federal Grants includes Title XX, Older Americans Act, Violence Against Women Act, other federal and community development block grants.
Private Grants includes United Way, private foundation and bar association grants.
Other Non-LSC Funds includes publication income, carryover and other non-LSC funds.
Other Income includes gross fees and receipts from client services.

[9] Refers to cases on which work was performed prior to 4/24/96.

[10] LSC significantly revised/updated the criteria for case reporting/closure in the 2008 CSR Handbook. Four categories -- C-Referred After Legal Assessment, D-Insufficient Merit, E-Client Withdrew, J-Change in Eligibility -- were discontinued. One, L-Extensive Service, was added, and the title of one, B-Brief Service, was changed to Limited Action. See descriptions below of these two and of Counsel and Advice.
Counsel and Advice -A case closed in which the program provided legal advice to an eligible client should be closed as Counsel and Advice (e.g., the advocate ascertained and reviewed relevant facts, exercised judgment in interpreting the particular facts presented by the client and in applying the relevant law to the facts presented, and counseled the client concerning his or her legal problem).
Limited Action - A case closed in which the program took limited action(s) on behalf of an eligible client that addressed the client's legal problem that is not so complex or extended as to meet the requirements for CSR Category L should be closed as Limited Action. Examples include, communications by letter, telephone or other means to a third party; preparation of a simple legal document such as a routine will or power of attorney
Extensive Service - A case closed in which the program undertook extensive research, preparation of complex legal documents, extensive interaction with third parties on behalf of an eligible client, or extensive on-going assistance to clients who are proceeding pro se should be closed as Extensive Service. Some examples of extensive service include preparation of complex advance directives, wills, contracts, real estate documents or other legal documents, or the provision of extensive transactional work.

[11] Totals by age are not equal to the totals by gender because a few programs were not able to provide complete information.

[12] Totals by age and ethnicity are not equal to the totals by gender because a few programs were not able to provide complete information.

[13] Private Attorney Involvement (PAI) is an LSC program to involve private attorneys (those not working for an LSC grantee) in the delivery of legal services to low-income clients eligible for LSC-funded legal assistance.

As provided in 45 C.F.R. 1614, LSC grantees are required to devote at least 12.5% of the amount of their LSC Basic Field-General funding to this method of delivery of legal services.

[14] Pro Bono – PAI programs in which attorneys are recruited and assisted to provide legal services to eligible clients without compensation.

Contract/Judicare – PAI programs in which attorneys are compensated at a reduced rate to provide legal services to eligible clients, either

(1) Under a contract with the grantee program under which an attorney receives a reduced fee either for a single case or for a set number of cases.

(2) As a member of a "Judicare" panel where all private attorneys who practice in the service area are invited to participate. Attorneys may elect on a case-by-case basis whether to take a client. Under some models clients may choose among panel attorneys while under others, panel attorneys are assigned to a client by rotation.

Other PAI – Any PAI program not falling into the pro bono or contract/Judicare category, such as co-counseling arrangements with individual attorneys or law firms.

[15] Years of Experience rounded to the nearest year. Figures include all full-time (90% and above) staff members who were employed for over 6 months in 2008, even if terminated prior to 12/31/08. Figures do not include sub-recipient staffing.

[16] The computation of the number of attorneys includes all Job Codes 5 to 11 (Litigation Director to Staff Attorney) and all Directors and Deputy Directors who are attorneys. It does not include the small number of attorneys serving in non- attorney positions – e.g. Management Professionals who are attorneys.

In: Legal Aid for the Poor and the Legal Services Corporation ISBN: 978-1-61668-939-1
Editor: Carl T. Donovan

Chapter 6

WHAT IS THE LEGAL SERVICES CORPORATION?

Carl T. Donovan

LSC is the single largest provider of civil legal aid for the poor in the nation. Established by Congress in 1974, LSC operates as an independent 501(c)(3) nonprofit corporation that promotes equal access to justice and provides grants for high-quality civil legal assistance to low-income Americans. LSC distributes more than 95 percent of its total funding to 137 independent nonprofit legal aid programs with 918 offices that provide legal assistance to low-income individuals and families throughout the nation.

LSC promotes equal access to justice by awarding grants to legal services providers through a competitive grants process; conducting compliance reviews and program visits to oversee program quality and compliance with statutory and regulatory requirements as well as restrictions that accompany LSC funding; and by providing training and technical assistance to programs. LSC encourages programs to leverage limited resources by partnering and collaborating with other funders of civil legal aid, including state and local governments, IOLTA, access to justice commissions, the private bar, philanthropic foundations, and the business community.

The Corporation is headed by a bipartisan board of directors whose 11 members are appointed by the President and confirmed by the Senate. The board is chaired by Frank B. Strickland. Helaine M. Barnett, a career legal aid lawyer, has served as president of LSC since January 2004.

WHO ARE HELPED BY LSC-FUNDED PROGRAMS?

Three out of four clients are women—many of whom are struggling to keep their children safe and their families together. Overall, the clients are the most vulnerable among us and are as diverse as our nation, encompassing all races, ethnic groups and ages, including the working poor, veterans, homeowners and renters facing foreclosure or evictions, families with children, farmers, people with disabilities, victims of domestic violence, the elderly and victims of natural disasters.

WHAT KIND OF HELP IS AVAILABLE?

LSC grantees provide a wide range of civil legal assistance to their clients. The most frequent cases involve:

- **Family law:** LSC grantees continue to help victims of domestic violence by obtaining protective and restraining orders, helping parents obtain and keep custody of their children, helping family members obtain guardianship for children without parents, and other family law matters. More than a third of all cases closed by the local programs are family law cases.
- **Housing & Foreclosure Cases:** More than 25 percent of cases involve helping to resolve landlord-tenant disputes, helping homeowners prevent foreclosures or renegotiate their loans, assisting renters with eviction notices whose landlords are being foreclosed on, and helping people maintain federal housing subsidies when appropriate.
- **Consumer Issues:** Twelve percent of cases involve protecting the elderly and other vulnerable groups from being victimized by unscrupulous lenders, helping people file for bankruptcy when appropriate and helping people manage their debts.
- **Income Maintenance:** Approximately 11 percent of cases involve helping working Americans obtain promised compensation from private employers, helping people obtain and retain government benefits such as disability benefits to which they are entitled.

HOW MANY ARE HELPED?

About 54 million people—including 18.5 million children—are eligible for LSC-funded services. LSC-funded programs close nearly one million cases per year nationwide and provide other legal assistance to more than five million people. The clients served are at or below 125 percent of the federal poverty level threshold, an income of $27,563 a year for a family of four.

THE GROWING JUSTICE GAP

An overwhelming demand exists for civil legal services. In 2005, LSC's Justice Gap Report, the first comprehensive national statistical study of unmet civil legal needs, established that for every client who received service, one eligible applicant was turned away. Fifty percent of eligible potential clients requesting assistance from LSC grantees were turned away for lack of adequate program resources. Those findings were reaffirmed in an updated and expanded Justice Gap Report released in 2009. Using different methodologies, state studies also have found that less than 20 percent of the legal problems experienced by the poor were addressed with the help of a private lawyer or legal aid staff attorney. At a time when poor Americans are struggling to keep their jobs, homes and basic necessities for their families, it is crucial for the federal government to address the civil legal needs of these vulnerable people as a national priority.

In: Legal Aid for the Poor and the Legal Services Corporation ISBN: 978-1-61668-939-1
Editor: Carl T. Donovan

Chapter 7

TESTIMONY OF HELAINE M. BARNETT, PRESIDENT, LEGAL SERVICES CORPORATION, BEFORE THE SUBCOMMITTEE ON COMMERCIAL AND ADMINISTRATIVE LAW

Helaine M. Barnett

Good morning, Chairman Cohen, Congressman Franks and other members of the Subcommittee. I am Helaine Barnett, in my sixth year as president of the Legal Services Corporation (LSC), and it is my pleasure to be with you today.

I am joined by Mike McKay of Seattle, the distinguished Vice Chairman of the LSC Board of Directors. Mike has served on the Board since 2003, and he chairs the Finance Committee of the Board. LSC benefits from his deep knowledge of the judicial system, both from his service as the U.S. Attorney for the Western District of Washington (1989-1 993) and from his years as an attorney providing *pro bono* services to the poor in the Seattle area and years of volunteer work with the state Equal Justice Coalition. Mike and his brother, John, a former LSC president, were honored by the Legal Foundation of Washington in 2008, with the 22nd annual Charles A. Goldmark Distinguished Service Award. We are most fortunate to have Mike as one of our leaders.

I would like to begin by thanking you, Chairman Cohen, and the other Subcommittee members for your continuing support of civil legal aid programs around the nation and for giving us an opportunity to discuss the legal services that LSC-funded programs provide to the nation's poor. A part of my testimony will summarize the Corporation's recently released report that contains updated and expanded information on the "justice gap," an urgent and complex challenge to our nation and its promise of ensuring equal access to justice for all.

The Legal Services Corporation

My entire legal career has been devoted to providing legal assistance to low- income individuals and families. I have been privileged to be the longest-serving president of the Legal Services Corporation in its 35-year history. Prior to my appointment in January 2004, I spent 37 years at the Legal Aid Society of New York City, with three decades of service in the management of its Civil Division and as its Attorney In Charge from 1994 to the end of 2003. I know first hand what our mission means to the lives of our clients and have a deep personal commitment to the mission of providing high-quality civil legal assistance to eligible low-income Americans.

The clients of LSC-funded programs are the most vulnerable among us. They live at or below 125 percent of the federal poverty guideline—an income of $27,563 for a family of four. Three out of four clients are women, and many are mothers struggling to keep their families together and their children safe, fed and housed. Program clients are all races and ethnicities, young and old, and include the working poor, people with disabilities, victims of domestic violence, victims of natural disasters, families with children, veterans and military families.

LSC-funded programs closed 889,155 cases in 2008, our most recent data. Family law cases accounted for 35 percent of these cases, the largest category of casework. Housing was the next largest category, representing about 26 percent of total cases closed. LSC has funded the development of statewide websites, which allows ever-increasing numbers to access legal information and download legal forms via the Internet. According to LSC data, web-based services that offer access to legal education materials, legal forms and self-help materials have grown from 8 million in 2004 to nearly 13 million in 2008. LSCfunded programs expect to receive increasing numbers of requests for help in coming months because of the continuing effects of the recession—from people who have lost jobs, lost health care and are at risk of losing their homes through foreclosure.

The Legal Services Corporation, established by Congress as an independent 501(c)(3) nonprofit organization, is the single largest source of funding for civil legal aid for low-income Americans. LSC provides grants to 137 independent nonprofit programs with 918 offices that serve every Congressional District.

The Corporation marked its 35th anniversary in July, and I want to thank you Chairman Cohen for honoring us with a commemorative statement in the Congressional Record. The White House also honored us with a Presidential Proclamation in July. Just weeks earlier, the House rejected an amendment to eliminate LSC, on a 323-to-1 05 vote. We are most appreciative of the bipartisan support for equal access to justice for all Americans.

The Corporation's Fiscal Year 2009 appropriation is $390 million. The House has approved a FY2010 appropriation that would provide $440 million for LSC. The Senate Appropriations Committee has approved a $400 million appropriation. For the first time in several years, the White House has proposed to increase funding for LSC, requesting $435 million for FY2010.

LSC distributes more than 95 percent of its annual appropriation directly to the nonprofit programs that deliver civil legal services. The Corporation provides guidance and oversight to ensure that the programs provide high-quality services and comply with Congressional requirements, funding restrictions, LSC rules and regulations. Administrative expenses are less than 4 percent of our budget—low by any standard.

The Corporation's challenge is great. About 54 million people—including 18.5 million children—are eligible for LSC-funded services, according to Census Bureau data released last month. That represents an increase of almost three million people from 2007 to 2008. This is the highest number of people eligible for civil legal assistance in LSC's history. Although there are reports that the recession appears to be ending, the Office of Management and Budget projects that unemployment will remain high, peaking at a rate above 10 percent. LSC will likely see another increase in the number of people eligible for legal services when the Census issues a new count next year.

These are harsh economic times. Millions of Americans are falling deeper into poverty and millions more are slipping into poverty for the first time. Clients come to civil legal aid programs when they need a lawyer to help them escape an abusive relationship; to gain access to health care, food, subsistence income and disability benefits, and to prevent foreclosure and eviction that may lead to homelessness. LSC-funded programs save lives and save taxpayer dollars by averting more costly interventions by state and local social services and public assistance agencies.

Legal aid can help prevent the downward spiral of the poor into costly public support. It greatly improves their chances of keeping their home rather than moving into a shelter, holding a job rather than going onto public assistance, retaining custody and support of their children rather than losing them to foster care, receiving early medical care rather than costly hospitalization, and escaping an abusive relationship rather than suffering further injury or even death. Civil legal assistance saves both lives and money.

In these troubled economic times, legal aid can facilitate solutions and help clients who have nowhere else to turn. Ensuring that the poor are adequately represented in the civil judicial system greatly improves their chances of keeping or securing basic necessities—the keys to stability and self-sufficiency. It also helps keep communities healthy. The work of LSC and its programs are more critical than ever before.

The Justice Gap

Last month, LSC released an updated and expanded report on the "justice gap"—the difference between the level of civil legal assistance available to low- income Americans and the level that is necessary to meet their needs. This 2009 report, "Documenting the Justice Gap in America: The Current Unmet Civil Legal Needs of Low-Income Americans," updates the first Justice Gap Report released by the Corporation in 2005.

The program data collected in 2009 confirmed the conclusion of the 2005 Justice Gap Report—that there continues to be a major gap between the civil legal needs of low-income people and the legal help that they receive.

For every client served by an LSC-funded program, one person who sought help is turned down because of insufficient resources, the 2009 data show. In one category—foreclosures—LSC-funded programs are turning away two people for every client served. Programs also are meeting less than half of the requests for assistance with employment and family law matters, according to the program data.

The report used three different methodologies to examine the extent of unmet civil legal needs. First, LSC asked programs to document the number of people actually seeking assistance from the program who could not be served due to insufficient program resources. Programs collected the data from March to May 2009, the same time period used in 2005 for data collection. Second, LSC analyzed civil legal needs studies from seven states that were conducted since the 2005 report. Those findings were compared to nine state studies conducted during 2000-2005 that were discussed in the 2005 report. In addition, the report took into account the Comprehensive Legal Needs Study funded by the American Bar Association and released in 1994. In the third methodology, the report counted the number of legal aid attorneys (working in LSC and in non-LSC programs) available to low-income Americans and compared that to the total number of private attorneys providing personal legal services to the general population of the nation.

The first methodology documented again for 2009 that 50 percent of the potential clients requesting assistance from LSC-funded programs were turned away for lack of adequate resources.

The new state legal needs studies add to a body of social science knowledge that shows only a small fraction of the legal problems experienced by low-income people (less than one in five) are addressed with the assistance of either a private attorney or a legal aid lawyer.

The report's analysis of the most recent available figures on numbers of attorneys shows that nationally, on average, only one legal aid attorney is available for every 6,415 low-income people. By comparison, there is one private attorney providing personal legal services for every 429 persons in the general population who are above the LSC poverty threshold.

In addition, the 2009 report included new data indicating that lower state courts, particularly housing and family courts, are facing significantly increased numbers of unrepresented litigants. Studies show that the vast majority who appear without representation are unable to afford an attorney, and a large percentage of them are low-income people who qualify for legal aid. A growing body of research indicates that outcomes for unrepresented litigants are less favorable than those for represented litigants.

Despite increases in funding for civil legal assistance over the past four years by the Congress, by 25 states and the District of Columbia, the nation continues to confront a substantial justice gap. As an initial, critical goal, as a nation, we must provide enough funding to serve at least all those currently seeking help from LSC programs. The 2009 Justice Gap Report found that this would require a doubling of LSC funds and a doubling of the state, local and private funds that also support LSC programs.

The long-term goal must be to develop resources sufficient to meet the civil legal needs of all eligible low-income people, and that would require the federal, state, local and private funding to grow by five times. *Pro bono* efforts need to be expanded substantially in the years ahead, but even expanded *pro bono* contributions will not be enough to address a major portion of the unmet need.

Too often we summarize by using numbers, but I want to emphasize that LSC programs are focused on people and their pressing civil legal needs. Legal aid lawyers help the poor with shelter, protection from domestic violence, access to health care and income maintenance. Families, and especially children, depend on legal aid lawyers daily to help them achieve safety, security and a path to self- sufficiency.

STRATEGIES TO CLOSE THE JUSTICE GAP

Closing the justice gap and securing necessary access to civil legal assistance requires a multifaceted approach built around increased federal, state and local government funding and an array of public-private partnerships that include individual lawyers, the organized bar, foundations, charitable donors and other concerned private parties.

Pro bono services and private attorney involvement (PAI) are important elements in LSC's efforts to close the justice gap. In 2008, private attorneys closed approximately 10 percent of LSC cases on behalf of LSC programs.

Since the 2005 Justice Gap Report, LSC has undertaken a major initiative to increase the involvement of private attorneys in LSC-funded programs. The LSC Board of Directors adopted a PAI action plan, "Help Close the Justice Gap, Unleash the Power of Pro Bono," which included a call to programs to adopt resolutions that recognize and celebrate the involvement of private attorneys in the delivery of civil legal services, and 107 programs have done so to date.

LSC also in 2007 provided guidance to programs on resources and innovative approaches available to more effectively integrate private attorneys into the delivery of civil legal aid. LSC has recommended that programs develop longterm relationships with large law firms, corporate and government attorneys, and offer support to small law firms, solo practitioners and judicare attorneys so that they may more effectively assist low-income clients. Just as importantly, the American Bar Association and various state and local bar associations have sought to encourage and support *pro bono* contributions by private lawyers.

Across the nation, the creation of state Access to Justice Commissions has energized efforts to increase state funding and *pro bono* support for civil legal aid. Justices of state Supreme Courts and the heads of state bar associations are leaders in these efforts, and LSC has encouraged the creation of commissions, highlighted the importance of integrated statewide delivery systems, and urged the involvement of local legal aid programs in setting goals for the commissions. Twenty-four states and the District of Columbia now have such commissions.

In your state, Mr. Chairman, the Tennessee Supreme Court announced the creation of a statewide Access to Justice Commission in April 2009 to help address the unmet civil legal needs of low-income individuals in Tennessee. Congressman Franks, the State Bar of Arizona created the Arizona Foundation for Legal Services & Education in 1978, as the Interest on Lawyers' Trust Accounts (IOLTA) funder with a mission of promoting access to justice for all Arizonans. State-based initiatives like these are invaluable in raising awareness about the justice gap in America and in setting priorities that help low-income families, especially during economic downturns when the poor more than others are at risk of losing their job, health insurance and even their home.

To expand the reach of their services, many LSC-funded programs are joining in partnerships. Programs have joined with local and state groups to address the foreclosure crisis and related housing issues, including partnering with lenders and banks to explore workouts that keep families in their homes and help others write down loans. In an effort to improve overall health outcomes for low-income children and families, more than 35 LSC-funded programs are participating in medical-legal partnerships, where legal aid attorneys and *pro bono* attorneys are trained to work as part of health-care teams to enforce the laws and regulations in place to protect health. In California, Illinois and Tennessee, programs are addressing challenges facing military veterans, including homelessness, reemployment rights and improved coordination of services with local military commands.

Technology is increasingly an important tool for improving access to justice and in providing self-help options for those that we are unable to directly serve. LSC's Technology Initiative Grants (TIG) use past successes as a guide to expand intake through online systems; expand assistance for *pro se* litigants through the development of more automated forms; explore innovative uses of new technologies, and provide support for replication of other technologies that have been demonstrated to both improve and expand client services. In rural areas, technology can help deliver services more efficiently.

LSC is committed to exploring ways of using technology to expand access to justice. This is essential in a good economy, imperative in a weak economy, and vital in a natural disaster or other local emergency.

Although *pro bono* efforts and technology projects need to be expanded substantially in the years ahead, these endeavors will not be enough to address a major portion of the unmet need for legal services. Federal, state, local and private funding also will have to grow to address the overall need.

Since the 2005 Justice Gap Report, many state legislatures have recognized the need to help close the justice gap in their states. Twenty-five states and the District of Columbia have adopted new or increased funding for civil legal aid. In addition, many state Interest on Lawyers' Trust Accounts (IOLTA) programs also adopted new revenue measures. But these state legislative and IOLTA increases only benefited the particular states taking action to increase legal aid funding, and the economic recession is placing many of these gains at risk.

IOLTA revenue—the second-largest single source of funding (12.7 percent in 2008) for LSC programs—has decreased significantly because the short-term interest rate has dropped to almost zero. The National Association of IOLTA Programs reports that projected IOLTA revenue will be about $93 million this year, a dramatic 67 percent decline from 2008, when IOLTA revenue was nearly $284 million. The impact of the IOLTA erosion varies state by state, but numerous LSC programs project they will receive significantly less IOLTA funding in the coming year and will struggle to maintain staff and services to clients.

Many states may not be able to make up IOLTA losses, in part because of overall state and local budget shortfalls. Charitable organizations also will be unlikely to contribute as much to legal aid as in the past because of the impact of the recession on the stock market and other revenue sources for private giving.

The weak economy has created stresses for legal aid programs. The recent federal funding increases provided by the Congress may help programs to avert layoffs and offset drops in IOLTA, state funding and charitable donations. With limited resources, many programs have limited intake capacity—they can only accept so many requests for assistance each day or answer so many telephone calls. One development we see is a growth in Internet use at LSC-funded programs and at LSC-funded statewide websites. Technology can provide clients with videos and information on dozens of areas of law, including foreclosures and military and veterans' issues, and provide resources to legal aid staffs, volunteers and courts. Technology permits programs to overcome distance, share information in multiple languages and expand access to legal information.

Going forward, the federal government must continue to play a vital role in providing a pathway to equal justice for all, consistent with its role in maintaining the formal civil justice system and providing an orderly forum for the resolution of disputes.

CHARTING NEW DIRECTIONS

Our nation's commitment to equal access to justice is far from being fulfilled, and will be achieved only through bipartisan support in the Congress, strategic partnerships with business and community groups and the dedicated work of LSC-funded staff attorneys and private lawyers rendering *pro bono* assistance to clients.

In 2004, LSC launched a Quality Initiative—the Corporation's vision for supporting, building and institutionalizing strategies within legal services programs to increase the capacity for the delivery of high-quality legal services. The centerpiece of the Quality Initiative is the revised LSC Performance Criteria, distributed to programs in 2007. It reflects a collective view of best practices to promote the delivery of high-quality legal services. LSC convened a conference of all program executive directors in 2008 to focus on quality as a value, as essential to the provision of legal services and as a vital ingredient of leadership.

Importantly, members of Congress have introduced bills that would reauthorize the Corporation and enhance efforts to increase the LSC budget by authorizing $750 million as a new, annual funding level. The LSC Board of Directors has called for strong, measured strides to help close the justice gap, and the House and Senate reauthorization bills would accelerate LSC efforts to meet that goal. LSC is deeply appreciative of these efforts to strengthen funding for the delivery of civil legal assistance to low-income individuals and families across the nation.

LSC also wants to take this opportunity to express support for provisions in the reauthorization bills that would improve oversight of the Corporation's grants management.

LSC is committed to holding itself and its 137 programs to the highest standards—which will ensure the most effective and efficient delivery of civil legal assistance to clients and will reinforce the importance of providing high-quality services.

The Corporation receives LSC Inspector General Management Information Memoranda, which are timely reports that offer opportunities to take appropriate action where necessary to improve operations. LSC responds to the Inspector General memoranda and acts on findings from Inspector General audits and investigations.

LSC also accepts and acts on recommendations from the Government Accountability Office, and during the last two years has implemented more than a dozen major actions to improve Board governance, financial and grants oversight and management practices.

LSC has revised and updated written guidelines for the Corporation's two oversight offices, and fully reviewed and updated the procedures for on-site program visits.

When conducting on-site visits, LSC's Office of Compliance and Enforcement (OCE) performs regulatory and fiscal compliance reviews. These OCE reviews include oversight on prohibited political activities, proper use of non-LSC funds, transfers of funds, program integrity, private attorney involvement, use of sub- grants in legal services delivery, proper payment of membership fees or dues, timekeeping, attorney fees and internal controls associated with program accounting practices. LSC also has sent advisories to all LSC-funded programs reminding them about important fiscal internal control requirements and regulatory compliance requirements.

LSC's Office of Program Performance (OPP) administers the competitive grants system, engages in program quality assessments, and promotes the development and implementation of strategies to support and improve the delivery of high quality legal services. Through on-site visits, LSC identifies areas of programs' operations that would benefit from additional review, support and technical assistance. The on-site program assessment reviews are patterned on the LSC Performance Criteria, look at issues such as: the quality of board governance and oversight of programs' operations; the processes used to target priority legal needs and allocate program resources; how effectively potential clients are able to access the legal services programs; the quality of the legal work provided; and a range of program management and administration issues focusing on programs' use and implementation of acknowledged best practices for the operation of legal services programs. A critical component of the work of OPP is the sharing of innovations and best practices in legal services delivery among recipients.

In addition, LSC has:

- Enhanced coordination of program visits by OCE and OPP staff.
- Performed follow-up on each of the improper uses of grant funds involving nine programs identified in a December 2007 GAO report (GAO-08 37).
- Completed or has proceedings underway to complete actions to strengthen internal controls at LSC-funded programs, as recommended by the Inspector General.
- Strengthened internal controls over contracts for consultants on program visits.

Oversight and emphasis on proper financial management practices and provisions of law and regulation are priorities of the LSC Board, management and staff. In particular, the Board and LSC management are focusing on the oversight responsibilities of the individual boards of the nonprofit organizations that receive LSC funding. Local boards, which best understand the priorities and needs of their communities, are the linchpins in ensuring that LSC-funded programs provide high-quality civil legal assistance in compliance with all laws, regulations and best governance practices. Training is an essential component in ensuring effective oversight, particularly in the areas of board governance and fiscal compliance, and in the delivery of high-quality civil legal assistance. In fiscal years 2010 and 2011, LSC will focus on making training a priority in these areas.

Conclusion

The people who come to LSC-funded programs are truly among the most vulnerable in our society. They are in search of fair treatment and solutions to pressing legal problems.

Every day, legal aid attorneys help low-income clients avoid unlawful eviction and the prospect of homelessness, escape domestic violence and maintain custody of their children. These lawyers not only open the doors to justice, in many cases they help prevent the downward spiral of the poor into costly public support.

The Domestic Violence Project at Memphis Area Legal Services represented a mother of three children who was locked in a power struggle with her estranged husband. Although she had left him, he stalked her, harassed her, and vandalized her property. After being convicted for aggravated assault and burglary, but before sentencing, the husband taunted the legal aid client by claiming he could deny her a divorce. With the assistance of the Memphis program, the woman was able to obtain a divorce and is raising her children in a stable home, free of abuse and violence.

Many LSC-funded programs are increasingly involved in foreclosure cases, and they often involve allegations of predatory lending. The Legal Aid Society of Cleveland participates in "Save the Dream," a statewide response in Ohio to the foreclosure crisis there led by the state's chief justice and governor. Cleveland legal aid trained and mentored 300 volunteer attorneys in Northeast Ohio, and these *pro bono* attorneys work with legal aid staff to prevent foreclosures. Community Legal Services in Phoenix has established a foreclosure law project to help homeowners and participates in a volunteer lawyers program, which recruits and trains *pro bono* attorneys to help low-income homeowners at risk of losing their homes. Other programs—such as Atlanta Legal Aid, West Tennessee Legal Services, Iowa Legal Aid and the Legal Aid Foundation of Los Angeles—have created similar foreclosure projects.

One couple with two children came to the Cleveland legal aid program for help because of a rise in their mortgage rate, which had an initial rate of 9.75 percent with a cap of 15.75 percent. As the date approached for the interest rate to reset, medical expenses and the loss of a job by the husband created financial problems, which led the lender to file a foreclosure action. Unable to keep up their payments under a forbearance agreement, the couple turned to housing authorities, the state of Ohio and the Cleveland legal aid program for help. Legal aid lawyers assisted the couple through mediation, which ended with a loan modification, ensuring a 6 percent fixed rate for 30 years.

In Tucson, staff attorneys at Southern Arizona Legal Aid helped stop the eviction of a woman who was accused of not paying her rent. The case began when the woman received a letter from a law firm representing a creditor indicating that the landlord was involved in a bankruptcy case and that the woman must begin paying her rent to the law firm. The woman did, but then received a nonpayment of rent notice from the landlord, who began an eviction suit. Legal aid lawyers looked into the matter and got the creditor's attorney to contact the landlord. The eviction effort was dropped.

The Legal Aid Foundation of Los Angeles sponsors a Homeless Veterans Project. It helped an honorably discharged Army veteran who had served in Vietnam and lived with the ravages of war. Every day was a quest for food and shelter. The Los Angeles project filed a claim for benefits with the Veterans Affairs Department, pointing out that their client had physical limitations, an inability to work and was homeless. The VA granted pension, medical and housing benefits, and this veteran is reunited with his once-estranged son and lives in an apartment.

As these examples show, civil legal assistance saves lives and makes communities stronger. Telling people who come to our offices that we are unable to assist them is by far the hardest task of the day, because we know that they often have nowhere else to turn. With the help of this Congress, with the support of the organized bar and private attorneys providing *pro bono* services, with partnerships in business and community groups, with the involvement of courts and law schools, we can make progress toward achieving the goal of equal access to justice.

As U.S. Supreme Court Justice Lewis Powell Jr. said, "Equal justice under law is not merely a caption on the façade of the Supreme Court building. It is perhaps the most inspiring ideal of our society . . . it is fundamental that justice should be the same, in substance and availability, without regard to economic status.

Thank you. I am happy to respond to your questions.

In: Legal Aid for the Poor and the Legal Services Corporation ISBN: 978-1-61668-939-1
Editor: Carl T. Donovan

Chapter 8

TESTIMONY OF HARRISON D. MCIVER, III, EXECUTIVE DIRECTOR/CEO, MEMPHIS AREA LEGAL SERVICES, INC., BEFORE THE COMMERCIAL AND ADMINISTRATIVE LAW SUBCOMMITTEE OF THE HOUSE JUDICIARY COMMITTEE

Harrison D. Mciver

Chairman Cohen, Ranking Member Franks, and other members of the Subcommittee, my name is Harrison D. McIver, III, Executive Director/CEO of Memphis Area Legal Services, Inc. (MALS), a position I have held for more than eleven (11) years. As my short bio indicates, I would be considered a legal aid lifer having spent my entire career (32 years) in legal aid law firms or related organizations. I am indeed honored to be invited and have the opportunity to testify at this hearing and share the wonderful work that MALS and its dedicated staff do on a daily basis in a community where nearly 200,000 people qualify for our services. I am not testifying for my firm alone, but for 137 legal aid law firms, with thousands of dedicated legal aid workers, from across this country. All are here with me in spirit. I am also giving voice to the plight of the millions of potentially eligible clients. But for the efforts of legal aid law firms, with the assistance of volunteer attorneys, paralegals and others, access to justice would be even less of a reality than it is today.

MEMPHIS AREA LEGAL SERVICES HISTORY

The Memphis Area Legal Services, Inc. story began in response to a profound tragedy for our nation. In 1968 in the wake of the death of Dr. Martin Luther King, Jr., the commitment and resolve of thirty members of the legal profession in the Memphis area, led by W. J. Michael "Mike" Cody, honored Dr. King's memory by advancing the dream of the dreamer. Though these lawyers and law students initially faced staunch opposition from the local bar, they nevertheless persevered until their dreams were realized when, on June 15, 1968, the Neighborhood Legal Services Project (NLSP) was established. When they were twice denied funding by the Office of Economic Opportunity (OEO), the NLSP founders pooled their own funds to support and organize the project and volunteered their time after normal work hours, with law students and a secretary staffing the office. Two years later, OEO funded Memphis and Shelby County Legal Services (MSCLS), due in no small part to many of the unsung heroes who helped establish the original NLSP. In 1974, when Congress passed the Legal Services Corporation (LSC) Act, Memphis and other legal aid programs received additional funding. Subsequently, Memphis and Shelby County Legal Services' name was changed to Memphis Area Legal Services, Inc. (MALS) to better reflect the expansion of services to the three rural counties of Fayette, Lauderdale, and Tipton. MALS is one of four LSC-funded law firms in Tennessee.

Today, MALS, which will celebrate its official 40th Anniversary in 2010, is a multi-faceted law firm guided by values and principles that embody its commitment to "equal justice under law." Through its well-trained, dedicated and capable staff, [1] complemented by the volunteerism of the private bar, MALS continues to provide free legal assistance through advice and counsel, court and administrative representation, and community education and outreach to the low- income and elderly residents in Shelby, Fayette, Lauderdale, and Tipton counties, in accordance with board approved substantive priorities.

Delivery of Legal Assistance Faces Enormous Challenges

LSC's "Documenting the Justice Gap in America" accurately depicts the growing challenges legal aid firms are facing in our efforts to address the critical needs of our client population. This challenge is exacerbated by our struggling economy. While I believe that closing the justice gap will require multiple strategies and the collective efforts of all key stakeholders, we must start with a substantial increase in funding from Congress for LSC. Additionally, other federal grant opportunities, significant expansion and innovations in private attorney involvement/pro bono programs, and increased support from state and local governments, as well as the private sector will be needed.

MALS, like other legal aid law firms across this country as well as many private law firms, is feeling the brunt of a severe recession. But unlike private law firms, MALS's challenges arose as more and more low-income individuals and families experienced legal problems that were exacerbated by the bad economy. Notably, the unemployment number nationally is close to 10%, but in the four counties served by MALS the average rate is 13.3 %. Legal aid firms have always had more clients than they could ever serve, but nothing like what we have experienced over the past year. Bringing it close to home, MALS this year was forced to turn away nearly 65 % of the poor people who needed us, simply because we did not have the resources available that were necessary to meet their legal needs.

To put it bluntly: the Justice Gap in West Tennessee grew even wider this year. More than 200,000 people now live below the poverty line in our four county service area. That number represents an increase of 45,000 or a 23 % increase over the 2000 census figures. Things are not likely to improve in light of these staggering figures, and next year threatens to be the worse. We have 20 attorneys on staff, which means there is only one attorney for every

10,000 eligible clients in our community, compared to the one-to-300 attorney-client ratio for the general population. MALS expects 15,000 requests from low-income individuals for legal services in 2010. That's an overwhelmingly disheartening figure. Yet the lack of legal resources is not limited to MALS. As reported in the "Justice Gap", studies of legal needs throughout the nation conducted over a 15-year period show that less than one in five low-income persons actually receives the legal help they need. The mission of MALS and other legal aid organizations is to work hard every day to fulfill this nation's promise of "equal justice under law."

The demand for our services is best demonstrated by the number of applications that we receive for our services. When that number increases, it generally signals some combination of an increase in the number of individuals eligible for our services and in the level of hardship being faced by those who are eligible. Using that barometer, in 2006, we received 6631 applications for our services. By 2008, that number had increased by nearly 29% to 8552 applications. Using the first three quarters as a guide, in 2009, we will receive 10,694 applications. While the number has increased substantially each year, the greatest spike is from the 8552 applications that we received in 2008 to the 10,694 that we are projected to receive this year. That is a 25 % increase in just the past year, the approximate increase in the poverty population.

To show the impact that the economy is having on our client base, in 2006, fewer than 1500 applicants reported that they were either receiving unemployment benefits or had no income at all. In 2009, we have already had over 2000 applicants in that category and are expecting over 2800 by year's end. In 2006, we completed 2984 cases on behalf of our clients. By 2008, that number was up over 22%, to 3650 cases. And, in 2009, we are well ahead of where we were a year ago.

The 3650 cases completed in 2008 breakdown as follows: Consumer 14%, Education 1%, Employment 2%, Family 9%, Health 4%, Housing 27%, Income Maintenance 29%, Juvenile 1%, and other 14%.

RESOURCES HAVE NOT KEPT PACE WITH DEMAND

While MALS relies heavily on its Legal Services Corporation grant, the core funding to sustain its delivery model, we have also aggressively pursued non-LSC funding in order to meet the ever-growing demand for legal assistance in our service area. MALS' total budget for 2008 was \$3,504,578 of which \$1,383,092 or 39% was from the LSC, and the other 61% included \$150,495 in IOLTA funds, \$240,294 in grants/contracts with the City of Memphis, \$793,765 in State of Tennessee dedicated funds, \$367,102 in other federal grants, \$148,651 in foundation funds, and \$421,179 in private contributions and cy pres awards.

MALS' total budget for 2009 is \$3,541,705, of which \$1,515,836 or 42% will come from the Legal Services Corporation, and the other 58% from other sources, including \$150,295 from IOLTA funds, \$285,000 from the City of Memphis, \$797,698 from the State of Tennessee, \$417,876 from other federal awards, \$175,000 from foundations, and \$300,000 from private contributions.

Despite our proactive efforts to increase revenues, we still fall far short in our capacity to respond to the widening of the justice gap.

MALS Work on Behalf of Low-Income Clients

We at MALS are extremely proud of the work we do for our clients. We have a reputation as an excellent law firm, staffed with highly skilled and experienced attorneys who are dedicated advocates for their clients. Our attorneys and support staff help people faced with foreclosures and other housing issues such as evictions, landlord and tenant disputes and housing discrimination, domestic violence and other family law matters, healthcare issues, and issues relating to social security and veteran benefits. Without access to a lawyer, for people faced with these devastating legal problems, equal justice under the law would be meaningless.

The following stories are but a few examples of the thousands of clients who have received high quality assistance from our dedicated staff. The vignettes are factual but the names are changed to maintain confidentiality.

- **"Dorothy"** suffered from extensive memory lapses and lost her ability to write, much less work. Doctors found a massive brain tumor. Yet, she was denied SSI benefits. She turned to MALS for help, and our paralegal advocated for her before the Social Security Administration. She now receives SSI benefits as well as health coverage.
- **"Julie"** was married for twenty years to a controlling and abusive husband. She tried to leave with her son, but due to her economic situation and lack of affordable legal assistance, she was forced to stay with her husband. Eventually, she turned to our Family/Domestic Violence Unit when his abusive outbursts became more frequent and more violent. MALS was able to obtain an order of protection, possession of the marital home, and custody of their son.
- **"Carolyn,"** a 70-year client, refinanced her home for $75,000, at an APR of 14.83% on a 30-year mortgage with a variable interest rate and a balloon payment. Our appraiser found the property was worth only $49,000. Over the life of the loan, Carolyn would have paid total of $337,734.00. After filing suit in federal court, MALS reached a settlement, with the principal lowered to $39,000, at 6% fixed interest. The term of the loan stayed the same but the balloon payment provision was removed, and all arrearages were forgiven. Now the total repaid will be $84,175. This representation saved our client $253,559.
- **"Alicia"** had lived in her home for 30 years. She owed $4,942 on the mortgage and had an A-1 credit rating. She was persuaded to obtain an equity loan for home improvements and to "pay off some bills," for a total amount of $19,057 at an 18% interest rate. Part of the amount that was financed was for credit life insurance for the lender. A year later our client was persuaded to refinance again at a similar rate and fees in excess of 15%, negatively amortizing the loan. Our Fair Housing Center attorney reached settlement after threatening the lender with litigation. The interest rate on the new loan was 6%. All outstanding property taxes were paid by lender, the principal was reduced to $20,935, and the 30- year term was reduced to 10 years. Our client would have paid a total of $189,378 over the course of the original loans. We saved her $161,488, and in addition she received a settlement of $27,890.

- **"Sara"** requires the use of a wheelchair. A women's regional clothing store not far from her home required Sara and others using wheelchairs to enter the store through a rear service entrance in an alley. Many times Sara had to wait for long periods of time in the alley before someone opened the door for her. Once, she was completely denied entry. MALS sued on her behalf in federal court under the Americans with Disabilities Act and filed an administrative complaint with the United States Department of Justice. Through our combined efforts, we reached a consent judgment where the store will make modifications for wheelchair access through the front door and other modifications to become ADA compliant.

Volunteer Opportunities for Attorneys & Volunteers at MALS

MALS is fortunate to have a large group of dedicated pro bono attorneys and other volunteers who are interested in our work and are willing to give their time in a variety of ways to supplement the work of our small but dedicated staff. Among our numerous pro bono programs are the following:

Traditional Case Referral: The longest running of MALS' volunteer lawyers' efforts is a basic pro bono program in which attorneys enroll and agree to take a certain number of a specific type of cases and provide individual representation or co-counsel with a MALS attorney.

The Bankruptcy Alternatives and Pro Bono Project was initiated because of a developing consensus among members of the Access to Justice Committee, bankruptcies judges and the MemphisDEBT Collaborative that our community was reaching a crisis point as consumers and debtors used the bankruptcy courts as their number one choice for resolving consumer and debt-related problems. Under the project, applicants for a bankruptcy are enrolled in a bankruptcy class conducted by MALS volunteer attorneys to ensure that applicants only use the bankruptcy options as a last resort, while determining which applicants truly are in need of additional assistance. The applicants who complete the class and need to file a Chapter 7bankruptcy are referred to pro bono bankruptcy attorneys.

Atticus Referral Network: Originally conceived of by young lawyers, this program was specifically designed to facilitate a faster referral process using technology. The focus was recruitment at the bigger law firms to enlist associates to join in this network by designating a firm attorney in-house to serve a 'gatekeeper' function. The gatekeeper then forwards the requests from MALS' staff on to firm members who can select a case for pro bono representation.

MBA Business Section /Corporate Counsel Pro Bono Initiative (CCPBI): The most recent initiative creates a partnership between CCPBI, the Memphis Bar Association Business Section and MALS to provide a variety of services. Additionally, the CCPBI and the Business Section plan to work with the Memphis Small Business Chamber of Commerce, the

Memphis Music Foundation and the Alliance for Nonprofit Excellence to match attorneys with small businesses, small business entrepreneurs, and non-profit entities.

Low Income Taxpayer Clinic (LITC): MALS has been awarded a grant from the IRS to create a LITC with a pro bono component to assist individuals with problems involving personal income taxes.

Law School Clinic: Third year law students at the University of Memphis School of Law under the supervision of clinical faculty provide legal assistance to eligible clients referred by the MALS Pro Bono Project. Currently the clinical program is housed at MALS.

In addition to these projects, our pro bono volunteers staff MALS's In-house Telephone Advice, Screening and Referral Project; Attorney of the Day, Courthouse (Pro SE) Project; Advice and Counsel Clinics; Saturday Legal Clinics; Advance Directives Panel; Conservatorship Panel; and Volunteer Mediation Panel.

MALS' Responsiveness to Specific Crises

Disaster response: In 2005, when Hurricanes Katrina and Rita devastated the Gulf Coast; an estimated 20,000-25,000 displaced individuals arrived in the Memphis, Shelby County with a myriad of needs including legal assistance. The legal community came together to formulate a strategy to respond. MALS was called upon to coordinate and implement the strategy, first by organizing volunteers and staff to be on-site at Red Cross designated centers. MALS then successfully acquired additional resources to establish a more long-term response. With United Way and Presbyterian Church grants, MALS hired additional personnel to staff an outreach center which focused primarily on FEMA-related matters.

Domestic violence (DV) is an epidemic in the city of Memphis and the surrounding suburbs. In 2007 and 2008, the Memphis metropolitan area had the second highest rate of violent crime in the country, and in 2008 more than 58% percent of all local violent crime was domestic violence-related. In 2008, a record number of 35 domestic homicides created what local leaders pronounced a "public safety emergency." In response to this crisis, MALS successfully sought a Legal Assistance for Victims of Domestic Violence grant from the US Department of Justice (DOJ). That funding complemented an earlier grant that had established a collaboration involving the city and county governments, law enforcement, victims' assistance, the YWCA and MALS as the administrative agent.

With a new Legal Assistance for Victims grant and a supporting grant from the Women's Foundation for Greater Memphis, MALS sought to address both the legal and other issues that impede the victims from freeing themselves from the abusive relations while achieving a level of self-sufficiency. Thus, the Opportunity Plus Project was created to enhance the well-being of domestic violence survivors and their families by empowering them to become economically and emotionally self-sufficient. Research indicates that financial independence, self- sufficiency and self-confidence are factors that enable victims of violence to leave their abusers and live free of violence. Economic independence is the primary factor that enables victims of violence to live independent from their abusers. This is one of the primary reasons that the Domestic Violence Project places emphasis on obtaining orders of financial support.

Foreclosure: Another crisis that has engulfed our country in recent years has been the continuing foreclosure saga. The foreclosure crisis in Shelby County continues to worsen. In 2008, we experienced a record breaking number of foreclosures (more than 12,000), and the number of foreclosure sales actually exceeded the number of arms length sales for the first time in history. Through the end of August, there have been 9,104 foreclosures initiated in Shelby County as compared to 8,494 for the same period in 2008. This is a 7% increase.

Our Home Preservation Project continues to help more than 1,000 clients each year with foreclosure issues. However, one new issue that is becoming more and more common relates to tenants who are facing eviction because the home in which they are living has been sold at foreclosure. In many instances the tenant has continued to pay rent and had no knowledge of the foreclosure until a Sheriff's Deputy or process server appeared at their door with a foreclosure warrant. In that situation, the tenant often was faced with having their belongings set out on the street within thirty days of learning of the foreclosure. In some ways, a tenant in this position is in a worse position than a homeowner who loses his or her home to foreclosure.

In 2008, as a part of our Memphis Fair Housing Center, MALS established the Home Preservation Project (HPP) to target these compelling and systematic housing problems. The HPP was a natural outgrowth of effective advocacy in addition to fair housing and predatory mortgage lending in the Memphis area.

LIFTING THE ATTORNEYS' FEES AND CLASS ACTION RESTRICTIONS WOULD EXPAND RESOURCES TO SERVE CLIENTS

In 1996, Congress imposed on LSC grantees a wide variety of restrictions that have had a major impact on the ability of MALS and other legal aid programs to fully serve the low-income client community. Two of the most significant of these are the restrictions on seeking attorneys' fees and participating in class actions. Not only have these restrictions significantly limited the tools that MALS is able to use in representing its clients, but they have also substantially limited the resources that we have available to serve the eligible clients who need our help. This is but one example of the impact of these restrictions on the client community served by MALS.

By the year 2000, it had become clear that thousands of Memphians were at risk of losing their homes as a result of the proliferation of predatory mortgage loans, particularly in identifiably African-American communities in Memphis. MALS had become actively engaged in litigating individual predatory lending cases by that time and had developed a great deal of expertise in the area. A pattern of extremely exploitative lending activity had emerged that involved a group of real estate agents, home improvement companies, closing agents, mortgage brokers, appraisers, and national mortgage lenders. A team of MALS attorneys began working on a series of cases that involved allegations of reverse redlining in violation of the Fair Housing Act; the civil RICO laws; the Home Ownership Equity Protection Act; the federal Truth-InLending Act, and a large number of other legal theories.

Ultimately federal lawsuits were filed on behalf of 17 plaintiffs against more than 30 defendants. MALS was able to bring these cases because it receives substantial resources from sources other than Legal Services Corporation to do fair housing litigation.

The litigation went on for 7 years before settlements were reached against all defendants. By that time, MALS attorneys had invested 10,435 hours in the case. The settlements involved restructured mortgages, which saved the plaintiffs $1,678, 401 in mortgage payments over the life of the loans. The plaintiffs also involved monetary damages of $1,298,000, for a total benefit of $2,976,401. In addition, MALS was able to recover $86,500 in actual costs and expenses it had invested in the case.

Although MALS was able to recover its out-of–pocket costs, it was not able to get reimbursed for any of the time its attorneys and staff spent on the case. Had MALS been able to recover attorneys' fees, even at the modest rate of $175 per hour, it could have recouped $1,826,125 from the defendants for its work on the cases. This would have enabled MALS to serve between 2,500 and 3,000 additional clients in the years since 2007. In addition, based upon information obtained through discovery it appears that, had the cases been consolidated and certified as a class action, there may have been as many as 1,800 class members who could have received relief through the litigation.

MALS continues to be the only law firm in the Memphis area that does significant litigation regarding predatory mortgage lending and mortgage foreclosures and there continues to be an extraordinary need to help the approximate 15,000 families who will be faced with foreclosures in Shelby County this year.

CONCLUSION

I would like to thank the Subcommittee, Chairman Cohen, and Ranking Member Franks for holding these hearings and providing me with the opportunity to champion the essential contributions that Memphis Area Legal Services and legal aid organizations around the country are making to make "equal justice under law" more of a reality. As Judge Learned Hand stated, "if we are to keep our democracy, there must be one commandment, thou shalt not ration justice." Beginning to close the justice gap will be major step in our effort to ensure that we are not "rationing justice."

End Notes

[1] MALS' employs a staff of 53 composed of 20 attorneys, 12 paralegals/housing counselors, 5 intake counselors, and 16 other administrative and support staff.

In: Legal Aid for the Poor and the Legal Services Corporation ISBN: 978-1-61668-939-1
Editor: Carl T. Donovan

Chapter 9

TESTIMONY OF MICHAEL D. MCKAY, VICE-CHAIRMAN, BOARD OF DIRECTORS, LEGAL SERVICES CORPORATION, BEFORE THE SUBCOMMITTEE ON COMMERCIAL AND ADMINISTRATIVE LAW OF THE HOUSE JUDICIARY COMMITTEE

Michael D. McKay

Chairman Cohen, Congressman Franks, members of the Subcommittee, I am Michael McKay, Vice Chairman of the Board of Directors of the Legal Services Corporation, and it is my privilege to be with you today. Mr. Chairman, I thank you for holding this hearing and for your interest in LSC and the provision of civil legal assistance to low-income Americans. Mr. Chairman, as you and Mr. Franks know, the Legal Services Corporation is the largest funder of civil legal assistance in the country. The Corporation makes competitive grants to 137 independent 501 (c) 3 corporations for the provision of civil legal aid to clients who are at or below 125 percent of the federal poverty guideline.

I bring you greetings today from Chairman Frank Strickland and our entire bipartisan Board. Each Board member is eager to do the right thing by the people we serve, and we listen to and respect one another's viewpoints about how best to fulfill LSC's mission. Providing civil legal assistance to individual indigent clients has never been more important.

As you will note from the resume that I have provided to the Committee, I was honored to be the United States Attorney for the Western District of Washington under President George H. W. Bush, and currently have an active commercial and criminal practice of law as a partner with McKay Chadwell in Seattle. However, some of my most rewarding cases have been the least publicized. I had the opportunity to represent a low-income public housing tenant from the Middle East whose case I took through Volunteer Lawyer Services many years ago. She endured harassment, broken windows, and physical violence at the hands of her neighbors. When the police came to investigate, language barriers caused them to believe her attackers, and she was evicted and brought up on criminal charges. I took her case pro bono, the charges were ultimately dropped, and the tenant was moved into another housing-authority unit far from her attackers. Without legal aid and pro bono, women like her would be high and dry. An evicted person would be out in the street.

Mr. Chairman, I believe so strongly in the obligation of all attorneys to contribute to equal justice efforts that I continued to take cases pro bono while I was U.S. Attorney, and I have recruited members of my firm and my local bar to do the same virtually my entire professional career. Those of us who have fulfilled that obligation know just how rewarding it is, but we also know how great the need is in our society for legal aid. Government clearly has a role. Funding, leadership, and oversight are in part a federal obligation and a necessity if we are to address the serious ills in our society and ensure equal access to justice for all Americans. That is why I am honored to be a member of this Board and proud of the work that we have done to strengthen LSC.

The recently released report on the Justice Gap in America, which we will be speaking about today, makes clear that legal aid has never been more in need of resources both from government and private sources. Equally important, of course, is the proper use of the funds that the Congress has entrusted to our stewardship. We consider that stewardship to be a central mission of our Board and the Corporation, and before President Barnett speaks to you about the Justice Gap this morning, I would like to say a few words about what our Board and LSC have done to improve and ensure that vital responsibility.

Our Board, prompted by two Government Accountability Office (GAO) reports, has concentrated its efforts over the last two years to improve our governance practices, to bring our Board's governance practices into alignment with Sarbanes/Oxley requirements, to improve the Board's oversight of the Corporation's financial and compliance responsibilities, and to focus the Corporation's attention on improved internal cooperation and good management practices. In making these efforts, the Board has had the assistance of and complete cooperation from the Corporation's management. We have made great progress and I'd like to outline those results for you today.

Established a New Code of Conduct and Ethics

LSC management researched codes of conduct for corporations and boards similar in size and structure to LSC, drafted a Code of Ethics and Conduct for directors, officers and employees of the Corporation and presented it to the Board early last year. The Board adopted the Code on March 24, 2008, and the Corporation has conducted training for all employees, officers, and directors. In addition, training in compliance with the Code is now an important part of new employee orientation.

Modernized Board Governance

An Ad Hoc Committee of the Board researched corporate audit committee options and charters, recommended the establishment of a separate Audit Committee, and proposed a charter for the new Committee. The Board approved the new committee and its charter. The

Audit Committee held its first meeting at the Oklahoma City Board meeting in April 2008, at which time it adopted a work plan for the coming year. The Board has drafted and approved charters for all its standing committees. A charter for a newly constituted Governance and Performance Review Committee was adopted at the August 2008 meeting of the Board. At its first meeting, the committee affirmed the importance of establishing a comprehensive training and transition plan for the next Board, and agreed on a board member self-assessment tool for Board approval and implementation. We completed the Board self-assessment and an evaluation of the full Board at our annual Board meeting in January 2009. The Committee's newly approved charter includes an annual review cycle.

The Board has established Board training and transition as a priority for 2009. We want to do everything that we can to facilitate a fully oriented and functioning Board in the shortest possible interval after the President appoints and the Senate confirms the new Board's members. To ensure that our efforts to improve Board governance are sustained, future Boards need to know not only the rules and procedures that have been established but also the background and history of our actions and the benefits that the new policies and procedures provide in fulfilling the mission of LSC.

STRENGTHENED FINANCIAL ACCOUNTABILITY PROCEDURES

LSC management evaluated the use of financial standards for LSC's annual financial statements, and with the LSC Board of Directors' approval, decided to continue to use the Government Accounting Standards Board guidelines for LSC's financial reports. The Board took the steps necessary to receive the LSC annual audit report from LSC's independent public accountant in a timelier manner. Accordingly, we have been able to act on the previous year's report at the end of January for each of the last two fiscal years.

In addition, LSC has revised and updated written guidelines for the fiscal component of the Corporation's Office of Compliance and Enforcement (OCE)'s regulatory compliance reviews and established written guidance for following up on grantee interviews. When reviewing programs on-site, OCE is now conducting expanded financial reviews that are designed specifically to address issues raised by GAO. These include review of prohibited political activities, proper use of non-LSC funds, transfers of funds, program integrity, private attorney involvement, sub-grants, membership fees or dues, timekeeping, attorney fees, and internal controls associated with the programs' accounting practices.

An advisory was sent to all LSC-funded programs on March 20, 2008, reminding Executive Directors of the need for appropriate documentation of expenditures of LSC funds and of the regulations regarding unallowable costs. The advisory specifically stressed the prohibition of expenditures of LSC funds for alcohol and lobbying, of the need for the grantees to adopt written policies governing salary advances, and of the regulation governing derivative income.

I am also pleased to report that for the fifth consecutive year, LSC received an opinion from outside auditors that LSC's financial statements present fairly, in all material respects, the financial position of LSC.

Established a Risk Management Program

LSC management has this year established a formal and rigorous risk management program at the Corporation. Management researched a variety of risk management programs and best practices, identified the risk environment for the corporation, and performed an office-by-office risk assessment process. The final Risk Management Plan for LSC includes a full listing of the risks to LSC's strategic objectives, a delineation of the strategies to be followed to mitigate those risks, a list of the offices responsible for each of those strategies, and the dates of annual review. The completed program was presented to the Board at its January 2009 meeting and unanimously approved. One of the key annual duties of our new Audit Committee will be to review processes for risk assessment and mitigation, and the status of ongoing implementation of the plan.

To mitigate the risk of an interruption in grant payments or support to our 137 grantees, LSC management developed and implemented an emergency continuity of operations plan (COOP) for the Corporation, including notification protocols and procedures for each individual LSC office. As a part of the readiness aspect of the plan, LSC has established a remote computer facility and is using it as a backup for its computer operations. A test of the COOP, including the telephone tree initiation of the plan, was performed last September. Both announced and unannounced testing will be conducted on a regular schedule.

In a related area, LSC has reviewed and expanded the current risk factors for selection of grantees for program visits. The Corporation is updating procedures included in the Office of Program Performance (OPP) and OCE manuals. OCE and OPP will each apply the risk factors-such as date of last LSC visit, issues identified by the OIG, any change in grantee leadership, and issues related to program size (large or small). Together they will discuss their conclusions and make decisions about which programs to visit for compliance and programmatic oversight.

In addition, LSC has updated procedures to ensure that they reflect our current practice of using information and results from oversight and audit activities and other risk criteria in planning internal control and compliance reviews.

Tightened Turnaround Times on Reports and Guidance to Grantees

In fulfillment of a commitment to go beyond the GAO recommendations to make related improvements, LSC suspended routine on-site program visits in February and March 2008 to complete all outstanding reports to LSC programs. In addition, LSC has set firm goals for report preparation following program visits, such that reports will be provided to the grantees within 90 days of on-site program visits (for the large, statewide programs with multiple offices, the goal is 120 days). These and other procedures all have been laid out in writing in manuals.

Improved Coordination and Communication between Program, Compliance, And Inspector General Offices

LSC management developed and implemented policies and procedures for information sharing among the OIG, OCE, and OPP and coordination of OCE and OPP on-site visits. LSC worked with an Ad Hoc Committee of the Board to establish working groups and held many hours of joint staff meetings to work on the roles and responsibilities of the various oversight offices. New information sharing and coordination of site visits, where appropriate, among OCE, OPP, and the OIG, is now proceeding. Care is being taken to ensure the OIG's independence. New training of LSC's oversight staff has now been completed and quarterly staff meetings to continue coordination of work efforts are being conducted.

Continued Emphasis on Oversight

Oversight and emphasis on compliance with proper financial management practices and provisions of law and regulation will continue to be a priority of the Board this year. President Barnett issued an advisory letter to all grantees in December on the subject of compliance guidance, and indicated that this will be an annual alert on issues that have surfaced in the year's compliance reviews. The Board recently initiated an effort with LSC management to focus on the oversight responsibilities of the individual grantee boards. They are vital partners in ensuring that the programs provide high-quality civil legal services in compliance with all laws, regulations, and best governance practices.

Conclusion

Mr. Chairman and members of the Subcommittee, let me say again in closing what an honor it is to be here today. It has also been a privilege to work with my Board colleagues to support the mission of the Legal Services Corporation. I would be happy to answer any questions that you might have at the appropriate time.

In: Legal Aid for the Poor and the Legal Services Corporation ISBN: 978-1-61668-939-1
Editor: Carl T. Donovan

Chapter 10

TESTIMONY OF DONALD SAUNDERS, DIRECTOR OF CIVIL LEGAL SERVICES ON BEHALF OF THE NATIONAL LEGAL AID AND DEFENDER ASSOCIATION, BEFORE THE COMMERCIAL AND ADMINISTRATIVE LAW COMMITTEE OF THE HOUSE JUDICIARY COMMITTEE

Donald Saunders

Good afternoon, Mr. Chairman. My name is Donald Saunders, and I am the Director of the Civil Division of the National Legal Aid & Defender Association ("NLADA"). I submit this testimony at the request of Chairman Cohen, and I would like to thank him and the members of the Subcommittee for giving NLADA the opportunity to voice its support for the Legal Services Corporation ("LSC") and to comment on the provisions of the Civil Access to Justice Act of 2009 ("House Bill") that was recently introduced by Subcommittee member Scott and numerous co-sponsors, including Chairman Cohen and Subcommittee Members Watt, Delahunt, Johnson and Conyers.

NLADA, founded in 1911, is the oldest and largest national, nonprofit membership organization devoting all of its resources to advocating for equal access to justice for all people. For almost a century, NLADA has championed effective legal assistance for people who cannot afford counsel. We serve as a collective voice for both civil legal services and public defense services throughout the nation, and provide a wide range of services and benefits to its individual and organizational members. Among NLADA's 700 program members and 15,000 attorney members are most of the 137 recipients of LSC funds. I am proud to be here on their behalf and on behalf of the legal services community as a whole.

FRAMEWORK FOR THE FEDERAL LEGAL SERVICES PROGRAM

In the Preamble to the Constitution, our forefathers stated clearly and forcefully the purpose of the government they were creating:

> *We, the people of the United States, in order to form a more perfect union, establish justice, insure domestic tranquility, provide for the common defense…*

and so on. It is noteworthy that "establish justice" comes before and is the basis for "domestic tranquility" and that both come before "provide for the common defense." I think the sequence and those priorities are not accidental and we need to constantly bear them in mind.

Until passage and implementation of the Economic Opportunity Act of 1964 ("OEO"), the federal government had not sought to "establish justice" for poor people and had not provided any support for their representation in civil legal matters. With the passage of the OEO, the federal government began its efforts to fill this void. Ten years later, in 1974, Congress passed and the President signed the Legal Services Corporation Act ("LSC Act"), the comprehensive legislation to make permanent the vital legal services program started under the OEO.

The findings and declaration of purpose to the original LSC Act set out the appropriate framework for considering how to once again move forward on establishing justice for poor people.[1] Congress found that

1. "there is a need to provide equal access to the system of justice in our Nation for individuals who seek redress of grievances;
2. "there is a need to provide high quality legal assistance to those who would be otherwise unable to afford adequate legal counsel...[;]
3. "[there is a need] to continue the present vital legal services program;
4. "providing legal assistance to those who face an economic barrier to adequate legal counsel will serve best the ends of justice and assist in improving opportunities for low-income persons consistent with the purposes of [the Act];
5. "for many of our citizens, the availability of legal services has reaffirmed faith in our government of laws;
6. "to preserve its strength, the legal services program must be kept free from the influence of or use by it of political pressures; and
7. "attorneys providing legal assistance must have full freedom to protect the best interests of their clients in keeping with the [Model Rules of Professional Responsibility] ...and the high standards of the legal profession."

It is important to keep in mind these critical principles, which are as salient today as they were when the LSC Act was first passed, and to evaluate where we are at present and where we should go in the future.

What we have today is a fundamentally sound legal services delivery system. Although it is woefully underfunded, unfairly restricted and continually besieged by its critics, the legal services delivery system continues to work extraordinarily well for those of our clients that it does serve. Of course, it can be made to work better. There is no enterprise, whether in government or in the private sector, that cannot benefit from efforts to enhance and improve it. That certainly includes the delivery of legal services to poor people in this country which has been evolving in form and in scope now for more than a century. Nevertheless, the basic system established by the LSC Act has served us well for 35 years; it should be improved and enhanced, not undermined or limited.

The civil legal aid system should be funded adequately and strengthened to provide meaningful access to our system of justice for low-income persons residing in the United States. Currently, the system is severely underfunded and LSC funding has remained relatively stagnant for more than a decade. As we show later in our testimony, LSC funding has gone down in real dollar terms by more than 48% since its high water mark in 1980. Yet, civil legal aid is a federal responsibility. LSC continues to be the primary single funder for civil legal aid, provides the underpinning and sets the standards for the entire program. To achieve equal access to justice in our country, it is therefore essential to increase LSC funding to provide a firm foundation for the rest of the legal aid system.

Nevertheless, increasing LSC funding is not sufficient to guarantee equal access to justice. Equal access is not a reality when legal services attorneys are not able to use the same tools and strategies that other members of the legal profession are free to use on behalf of their clients. For example, the current appropriations act restriction on claiming attorneys' fees in those situations where other lawyers are permitted to seek them limits the leverage which legal aid attorneys can use in negotiations with defendants and undermines the fundamental policy goals of awarding attorneys' fees against losing parties which are to deter and punish illegal conduct. These and other similar restrictions on what legal services attorneys can do on behalf of eligible clients that were imposed by appropriations riders in 1996 are inconsistent with the purposes of the LSC Act and limit the ability of LSC-funded programs to provide effective and efficient legal assistance to the disadvantaged residents of the United States.

Restricting what LSC programs can do with non-LSC funds is particularly troubling. Even though such restrictions were inappropriate in our view regarding LSC funds, there was no justification whatsoever for also preventing LSC programs from receiving non-LSC funds that are provided for purposes that Congress does not want to fund with federal dollars. State legislatures and other public funders as well as private donors should have the same opportunity as Congress to determine the purposes for which their funds will be used and to select the institutions that can best carry out those purposes. Congress should not interfere in decisions by other public funders, including state controlled IOLTA programs, on how to allocate their funds and with whom to contract, nor should it intrude unnecessarily into the funding decisions of the private sector. Moreover, Congress should encourage, rather than discourage, the creation of alternative funding sources for civil legal services and should encourage public-private collaboration to ensure the provision of effective legal services and efficient use of resources, rather than stimulate wasteful duplication of programs that occurs when funders are forced to put their resources elsewhere in order to accomplish their purposes.

Legal Needs of the Disadvantaged

As the testimony from the Legal Services Corporation, the American Bar Association and Harrison McIver of Memphis Area Legal Services aptly demonstrates, low-income households experience large numbers of legal needs, and the resources that are available to meet those needs are wholly inadequate. Legal needs studies conducted by numerous states during the past several years found that the combined efforts of publicly-funded legal services providers and the private bar serve only a small portion of the legal needs reported by low-income households. The LSC *Justice Gap* report showed that 50% of the eligible applicants who actually found their way to an LSC-funded program were turned away for lack of resources. Since 2000, numerous legal needs studies have been completed, and they have found that in the states studied, only 9% to 29.4% of the legal needs of low-income households were being met by legal aid programs or members of the private bar.

New legal needs are constantly arising to challenge the ability of legal aid programs to serve the low-income community. Current Census data reveals that the number of people in the United States eligible for LSC-funded services has increased significantly over the last several years, and, with the current economic crisis, the numbers of unemployed and newly poor who are likely to be eligible for LSC-funded services is growing rapidly. Low-income people are increasingly losing their homes to foreclosure, including large numbers of tenants who are being evicted because their landlords are facing foreclosure on rental properties. Low-wage workers are facing major job losses as significant lay-offs continue. Instances of domestic violence are rising as individuals face significant stress caused by economic insecurity. Low-income consumers are experiencing mounting credit problems. As a result, the need for civil legal assistance is on the rise.

The current foreclosure crisis facing many thousands of low-income homeowners and tenants clearly illustrates the need for a strong legal services program. Families of limited means across the United States have turned to LSC-funded providers in increasing numbers to protect their vital interests in remaining in safe and affordable housing. LSC grantees in every region of the nation are reporting significant increases in the number of applicants needing legal assistance to prevent them from losing their homes to foreclosure. Many of these clients, both homeowners and tenants, have defenses that can only be raised by skilled and knowledgeable LSC attorneys. Otherwise, the legal system is hopelessly skewed in favor of lenders who fail to follow the law regarding interest rates, fees or other consumer protections.

The following stories from actual cases handled by legal services programs in the last several years amply underscore the fact that justice often turns on access to representation:

- Southern **Arizona** Legal Aid (SALA) helped a 55-year housecleaner stay in her home that had fallen prey to foreclosure. After living in her home for twenty years, she began struggling with her payments due to a 9.38 percent hike on the interest rate of her subprime loan. A SALA attorney assigned to her case sought a loan modification with her servicer to prevent her home from going into foreclosure. She was successful in negotiating a loan agreement that modified the interest rate to an amount that SALA's client could afford.
- Communities served by LSC grantee Neighborhood Legal Services of **Los Angeles County** are not only at the epicenter of the foreclosure crises, but are now looking at

unemployment rates of 15% or more. Jobs in the informal service sector of the economy that many low-income families depend upon for survival have virtually disappeared - leaving homeowners jobless while they struggle with unconscionable mortgage payments to protect homes that are more than $100,000 underwater. For these families threatened with homelessness LSC-funded legal services programs are the safety net of last resort.

Neighborhood Legal Services has responded decisively to meet this crisis by collaborating with community groups and local officials to develop creative pre-foreclosure solutions to keep families in their homes and maintain vibrant local communities. The City of Los Angeles has invested more than $1 million to pilot a model developed by NLS-LA and its partners in the Northeast San Fernando Valley that avoids foreclosures through a mortgage renegotiation framework that reduces principal and leaves homeowners with fixed-rate interest loans and affordable payments. NLS-LA is implementing similar models with the African- American middle class communities of South Los Angeles and in the multi-ethnic San Gabriel Valley City of El Monte. Next month the same model will be presented to HUD Secretary Donovan.

NLS-LA is also at the forefront of providing emergency help to families struggling to keep their lives together. In 2009 alone, NLS-LA's widely praised system of court-based Self-Help Legal Access Centers will assist more than *100,000 people* with family law and eviction problems. And, through $1.2 million of city and county grants from HUD's stimulus-funded Homeless Prevention and Rapid Re-Housing Program (HPRP), NLS-LA added 7 new staff to help the newly unemployed avoid homelessness.

- "Rhonda" had lived with her husband Samuel in Shelby County **Iowa** for almost ten years with their three children. In their rural home, he controlled what she wore, who she spoke to, and where she went. There was always emotional abuse, but as the years passed, Richard became physically abusive. She didn't know where to turn and felt like she could not reach out or he would find out. She lived through many assaults, many injuries-- even while she was pregnant with his children. Richard has even raped her.

  At the end of 2008, Richard strangled Rhonda until she blacked out then he held her hostage behind locked doors for two days. When he left the home, she escaped and was able to get to help. She made contact with Iowa Legal Aid to discuss what options were available to protect her and the children from his violence. Legal Aid attorney staff helped her get a protection order that restrained him from further abuse. Rhonda and her children were able to live without the daily fear and isolation that Richard imposed, though not entirely. Richard violated the order many times, and Iowa Legal Aid was there to help her with holding him in contempt of the protection order, and helping her contact law enforcement. Richard eventually spent time in jail for his many violations and Rhonda and the children are working toward healing.
- The Miller family of Central **Massachusetts** thought they had exhausted all of their options in trying to save their home. Then they called legal aid.

  Marine specialist Philip Miller, his wife Morgan, and their two young children were close to being evicted after the mortgage company foreclosed on their home. Philip had returned injured after an 18-month tour of duty in Iraq and was unable to work due to injuries. At the same time, the couple's adjustable rate mortgage jumped to almost 11 percent.

The Millers were unable to afford the inflated payments, and the mortgage company was unwilling to negotiate. Then, their legal aid attorney stepped in and got the mortgage company to dismiss the eviction. Now, more than a year later, the Millers are working with their attorney to renegotiate the terms of their loan, with the goal of buying back their home. Spc. Miller is healthy again and preparing to leave for his second tour of duty in Iraq.

- When Congress bailed out Fannie Mae, one provision included in the legislation instructed Fannie Mae not to evict tenants from foreclosed buildings, if the tenants were in good standing (paying their rent). The provision makes good sense -- in an economy in which foreclosed buildings sit empty, why should people be made homeless to create streets lined with empty buildings, when the current tenants want to stay and keep paying their rent? Fannie Mae was not complying with this requirement, however -- until lawyers at New Haven Legal Assistance (not an LSC grantee) representing families threatened with illegal eviction threatened to file a national class action to force Fannie Mae to comply. Officials at Fannie Mae reached a settlement instructing their national network to follow the law. Since then, legal aid programs **across the country** have been working on behalf of paying tenants to enforce individual compliance with the corrected national Fannie Mae policy.

Along with the growth in those low-income populations that have traditionally been served by legal aid programs and the newly poor suffering from the recession, other new legal needs are also arising with respect to returning veterans from Iraq and Afghanistan, many with limited income and severe physical and mental disabilities, including post traumatic stress disorder and traumatic brain injuries, have begun to further swell the ranks of the low-income population and strain existing legal aid resources. Nationally, 5.6% of all veterans live below the poverty line, and a disproportionately high number are among America's homeless population. Many of these veterans have unique legal needs associated with their military service as well as the more typical legal problems experienced by low-income populations.

Reauthorization of the Legal Services Corporation Act

For many years LSC has enjoyed the support of a strong bi-partisan majority in Congress. Both the House of Representatives and the Obama Administration have sought a significant increase in funding for LSC for FY2010. Nevertheless, the last time that Congress reauthorized LSC was 1977, and that reauthorization expired in 1980. Since 1980, LSC has been funded through annual appropriations that have often been encumbered by a series of riders that have been imposed, at least in part, because the LSC Act has not been revisited and thoughtfully revised through the reauthorizations process to take into account changing needs and circumstances.

Earlier this month, Representative Scott introduced the Civil Access to Justice Act of 2009 (H.R. 3764).[2] The House Bill represents a thoughtful reevaluation of and a significant improvement over the current LSC Act. The House Bill authorizes a significant increase in funding for LSC; it updates or eliminates numerous outdated LSC Act provisions; and eliminates or incorporates and improves upon a wide variety of provisions from the current appropriations act.

NLADA strongly supports the passage of the Civil Access to Justice Act of 2009.

The House Bill Responds to the Needs of the Low-Income Client Community

The House Bill includes numerous provisions that would, if enacted, assist LSC grantees to better respond to the legal needs of the low-income client community. The bill would authorize Congress to appropriate up to $750 million, which represents the inflation-adjusted amount that was appropriated for LSC in 1981, which was the high-water mark for LSC funding. That amount would go a long way toward filling the justice gap that exists.

The House bill would also eliminate the provision in the current appropriations act that restricts non-LSC funds to the same degree as LSC funds. The bill would permit grantees to use their non-LSC funds to serve categories of low-income clients who are not now permitted to be served by LSC grantees with any funds, including certain aliens and prisoners. The House Bill would still prohibit LSC funds from being used to represent these ineligible aliens and prisoners.

The House Bill also would eliminate the current restriction on attorneys' fees and class actions and would permit grantees to engage in legislative and administrative representation under a wider range of circumstances than is currently allowed, so that LSC funded advocates would be able to utilize the advocacy tools to represent their low- income clients that other lawyers are permitted to use on behalf of their paying clients.

While there are numerous restrictions and requirements that are included in the current appropriations act that NLADA has long opposed, since 1996 the appropriations acts have also added numerous positive improvements to the LSC system that have been incorporated into the House Bill which we support. The House Bill incorporates a system of competition for grants and census-based funding to help insure that LSC grantees provide high quality legal assistance and that limited LSC resources are fairly and appropriately distributed. The House Bill requires grantees' advocates to maintain timekeeping records to ensure the correct allocation of resources among funders and to improve accountability. And the House Bill continues to authorize funding for technology grants which have been crucial in grantees' efforts to improve the delivery of legal assistance.

The House Bill also includes a number of additional provisions to strengthen and improve LSC and its grantees. It contains a series of new LSC governance requirements recommended by the Government Accountability Office, including new requirements for LSC to improve its internal control structure and to protect against the impact of disasters. The bill also includes new restrictions on LSC's private fundraising and new requirements on LSC's use of funds for certain representational and other activities.

The House Bill requires LSC to develop new training standards on compliance and encourages training on domestic violence or other areas where grantee training is needed. In addition, the bill contains provisions that are intended to increase the participation of private attorneys in the delivery of legal assistance by encouraging pro bono services by private lawyers and requiring grantee boards to include pro bono liaisons to the State Bar. To promote the recruitment and retention of high quality recipient staff, the bill authorizes the continuation of LSC's pilot loan repayment assistance or initiation of other programs. To give grantees flexibility to include on their governing boards individuals who are able to assist in fundraising, development of relationships with the business community, and support from the public, the bill lowers the number of board members who are required to be lawyers.

In order to better protect the client privacy and confidentiality of client records, the House Bill limits LSC's access to client records that are confidential under applicable rules of professional responsibility. The bill eliminates the current appropriations act provision that undermines the authority of State courts and bar associations to enforce the rules of professional responsibility dealing with client confidentiality that apply to the lawyers practicing within their jurisdictions, and restores the original LSC Act provision that respects that authority. Despite arguments that have long been made by LSC's Inspector General, LSC does not need to have access to client names in order to ensure compliance with Congressional mandates and other requirements. LSC's Office of Compliance and Enforcement ("OCE") and numerous other grant making agencies have successfully used unique client identifiers to check grantee records for compliance with restrictions and requirements and to ensure that clients are appropriately served.

The House Bill's Approach to Restrictions

Since 1996, LSC grantees have been encumbered in their efforts to represent their clients by a significant number of restrictions and requirements that apply to a grantee's LSC funds as well as to funds received from other federal, state, local and private funds. The House Bill would eliminate most of these restrictions and requirements that have hampered LSC grantees in their ability to provide a full range of legal assistance to the low-income client community.

As noted above, the House Bill would eliminate the restriction on the use of non-LSC funds, as well as the attorneys' fee and class action restriction. In addition, the bill retains but modifies several of the appropriations act restrictions on use of LSC funds. The House Bill would expand the categories of aliens who could be represented with LSC funds to include most aliens who are in the US legally and several limited categories of undocumented aliens including disaster victims, certain groups of children, and some victims of torture. The bill would limit the restriction on representation of prisoners to litigation involving prison conditions, and specifically permit prisoner re-entry litigation. The bill would limit the restriction on eviction defense for public housing residents to those who have been convicted of certain drug related charges.

The original LSC Act, as it was amended in 1977, included a number of limitations on LSC recipients. The House Bill leaves in place most of these LSC Act restrictions and requirements including the restrictions on: legislative and administrative advocacy; public policy advocacy training; organizing; priorities; financial eligibility; outside practice of law; political activity; fee-generating cases; criminal representation; habeas corpus representation; desegregation; and representation in Selective Service cases. The House Bill also leaves in place the appropriations act restriction on the use of both LSC and non-LSC funds for representation in abortion litigation.

Additional Needed Improvements

While we are very supportive of the House Bill as it is currently drafted, we think there may be areas where there could be additional improvements. For example, we believe it would be helpful if the bill made it clear that LSC grantees are subject to the OMB Circular A-133 ("A-133") and that grantee audits should be done using Government Auditing Standards ("GAS"). We also think that the bill should make it clear that LSC funds are to be considered Federal funds for purposes of Federal statutes relating to the proper expenditure of Federal funds.

We also believe that the bill should limit the authority of the LSC Office of Inspector General ("OIG") to impose additional auditing requirements on grantees beyond those required by OMB A-133 and GAS. Although the OIG should have the authority to audit grantees to respond to complaints and to audit to ensure against instances of waste, fraud and abuse, the bill should clarify that regular monitoring for compliance with substantive statutory and regulatory restrictions is the role of OCE, not OIG or grantee auditors ("IPAs"). NLADA is willing to work with the Subcommittee staff as well as with LSC Management and the OIG to address these or any other concerns that they may have about the bill's treatment of grantee audits, ensuring compliance, and any other issues.

Need for Increased Funding

The $750,000,000 authorized by the House Bill is essential to ensure the ability of LSC grantees to close the widening justice gap in America.

Since its inception in 1975, the Legal Services Corporation has been the principle source of financial support for legal aid programs across the country. In its early days, LSC set a "minimum access" goal for federal funding of its grantees that would have provided enough federal dollars to support two LSC-funded lawyers for every 10,000 eligible poor people. Congress responded to LSC's effort, and by 1980 LSC funding had reached $300 million, the "minimum access" goal. By 1981, funding for LSC was $321,300,000, but that success was short lived. In 1982, in response to efforts by the Reagan Administration to eliminate the program in its entirety, Congress cut LSC funding by 25 percent, to $241 million.

Although the program survived, it was not until 1990 that LSC funding again surpassed, in actual dollars, the level it had reached in 1980, with an appropriation of $316,525,000. However, when adjusted for inflation, that amount still represented a cut of one-third from LSC's 1980 funding level. During the early 1990s, funding for LSC rebounded slowly, reaching its all-time high of $400 million in 1995. However, when adjusted for inflation, even that amount still represented a 28 percent cut from its 1980 funding level.

In 1996, Congress again decided to slash LSC funding, this time by 30 percent, to $278 million. When adjusted for inflation, this amount represented more than a 50 percent cut from LSC's 1980 funding level. Since 1996, LSC funding has remained relatively static with small cuts or modest increases in most years. In 2007, Congress provided LSC with $348 million, an increase of $22 million over the 2006 appropriation, its first significant increase in more than a decade. But each year, inflation has continued to eat away at the buying power of LSC grant funds. In 2008 Congress appropriated only $350,490,000, despite bills in both the

House and the Senate that would have provided substantial increases over the amount appropriated for 2007. In 2009, Congress increased LSC funding to $390 million, but after taking account of inflation, the 2009 appropriation still represented a 48.2 percent cut from LSC's 1980 funding level. To keep up with inflation, 2009 LSC funding would have to have reached $752,938,299.

Non-LSC Funding

In part in response to the reductions in LSC funding in the early 1980s and mid 1990s, numerous legal aid programs have aggressively sought resources from non-LSC funding sources. Even though LSC remains the largest single source of legal aid funding, in many states around the country, the legal aid program today is primarily supported by funds from other sources. As a result, over the last twenty years, there has been a radical shift in funding from LSC and other federal programs to a more diversified funding base, including substantial increases from state sources, and the percentage of total legal aid funding provided by the federal government through LSC has shrunk significantly.

Since 1982, legal aid funding from state and local governments has increased from a few million dollars to over $370 million.[3] Most of this increase can be attributed to proceeds from Interest on Lawyer Trust Account ('IOLTA") programs, which have now been implemented in every state. A number of new initiatives resulted in expansions in IOLTA revenue in many states. These initiatives included changes from voluntary to mandatory IOLTA, or from opt-in to opt-out programs, changes in legislation or court rules regarding interest rates that must be paid on IOLTA accounts, and, in some states, aggressive and successful negotiations with financial institutions. In 2007, IOLTA resources rose to $123,924,000. However, because of significant drops in interest rates, increases in bank fees and substantial slowdowns in real estate transactions and general business activity, IOLTA revenues have dropped significantly in the last year from what programs had expected to earn. In addition, because IOLTA programs still vary significantly from state to state, available IOLTA funding for legal aid programs differ greatly, depending on the location. In 2008, IOLTA income was down 23% nationwide, reflecting both dwindling IOLTA fund balances and the miniscule federal funds interest rate. In some states, IOLTA income was down over 60%. While cumulative data is not yet readily available regarding the overall perspective on state and local public appropriations, many states report the potential for significant cuts in these areas as well.

Within the last several years, substantial new state funding for legal aid has come from general state or local governmental appropriations, filing fee surcharges and other state governmental initiatives. Until the recent economic downturn, it appeared that significant state funds would likely continue to be available for legal aid programs because state revenue growth seemed to be strong enough to support spending demands. However, in the last year, states have begun to experience extremely tight fiscal conditions, and these conditions are having a substantial impact on the amount of funds appropriated for civil legal assistance programs. It is impossible to predict future state spending on civil legal aid, as well as on other areas that will have an impact on the demand for legal assistance, because state fiscal conditions may change and the federal government may continue to shift more costs to state governments. With prospects for continued increases in state funding dimming, expanded federal funding becomes even more important.

Significant Geographic Funding Disparities

While LSC funds are distributed according to the 2000 census data on individuals living below the Federal Poverty Line, non-LSC funding sources are not distributed equally among states, and there are enormous disparities in the legal aid resources that are available in different parts of the country. The lowest-funded states are in the South and Rocky Mountain states, and the highest-funded states are in the Northeast, Mid- Atlantic, Midwest, and West.

LSC funding provides the critical foundation for legal aid programs across the country. Those LSC grantees in areas of the country where it is difficult to raise substantial amounts of non-LSC resources are almost wholly dependent on LSC funds for their continued existence. In other states, LSC funding provides the essential foundation to leverage and raise other resources. Regardless of where on the spectrum of non-LSC funding a program lies, increased federal funding is absolutely critical to expanding their ability to provide access to legal assistance for the low-income community and to close the justice gap.

But federal funding has not kept pace, and today the money programs receive from LSC purchases only half of what it did in 1980, when LSC appropriations provided "minimum access," an amount that could support two lawyers for every 10,000 poor people in a geographic area. In order to secure the foundation of the civil legal aid program, federal funding must be increased and secured into the future.

Conclusion

We believe that, if adopted, the House bill will significantly improve the ability of LSC grantees to effectively serve the low-income community. The bill includes a framework to provide additional resources that are sorely needed to help fill the enormous justice gap that exists today. The bill eliminates numerous restrictions that have impeded the ability of LSC grantees to fully serve many financially eligible members of the low- income community and to utilize the tools that attorneys with paying clients can now use to represent their clients. The bill respects the historical role of States to establish and enforce rules of professional responsibility for the attorneys who practice in their jurisdictions

In conclusion, I would like to thank you for holding this hearing and for your support for LSC and the civil legal services community. Providing civil legal aid is an integral part of constructing the foundation for ensuring that the least advantaged among us receive the help they need to build healthy, happy families and live constructive, fulfilling lives. A 48.2 percent reduction in funding for LSC and turning away 50 percent of those who seek legal aid is NOT living up to the constitutional promise of "establish[ing] justice" that we all embrace. The federal government can and should do more. The House Bill will enhance the goal of "justice for all," not erode it with unreasonable restrictions. Our clients and your constituents deserve no less.

End Notes

[1] See 42 USCA§2996 (Section 101 of the LSC Act).

[2] In March of 2009, Senator Harkin introduced the Senate version of the Civil Access to Justice Act of 2009 (S. 718) ("Senate Bill") which is, in most respects very similar to the House version. However, the House Bill differs from its Senate counterpart in several aspects, and the House version improves upon the Senate Bill in a variety of ways.

[3] The exact amount of state funding for civil legal assistance has not been fully documented, because much of this funding has gone to non-LSC funded programs, which, unlike LSC-funded programs, do not have to report to any central funding source.

In: Legal Aid for the Poor and the Legal Services Corporation ISBN: 978-1-61668-939-1
Editor: Carl T. Donovan

Chapter 11

STATEMENT OF H. THOMAS WELLS, JR., SUBMITTED ON BEHALF OF THE AMERICAN BAR ASSOCIATION TO THE COMMITTEE ON THE JUDICIARY, SUBCOMMITTEE ON COMMERCIAL AND ADMINISTRATIVE LAW

H. Thomas Wells

Mr. Chairman and Members of the Committee:

I am Tommy Wells, Immediate Past-President of the *American Bar Association* ("ABA") and a founding member of the law firm of Maynard, Cooper & Gale, PC in Birmingham, Alabama. I submit this testimony at the request of the President of the American Bar Association, Carolyn B. Lamm of Washington, DC, to voice the Association's views with respect to the essential role of the Legal Services Corporation ("LSC" or "Corporation") in closing the "justice gap." LSC is essential to ensure access to justice for all, not just those who can afford a lawyer. The ABA believes that this objective must largely be achieved by strengthening the Legal Services Corporation through bipartisan reauthorization and increased funding. The ABA urges the 111th Congress to enact bipartisan legislation to reauthorize, strengthen and improve the LSC.

The American Bar Association, the world's largest, voluntary professional organization with nearly 400,000 members, is the national representative of the legal profession, serving the public and the profession by promoting justice, professional excellence and respect for the law. The ABA is a "big tent" if you will: we consist of Republicans and Democrats, plaintiff and defense lawyers, corporate general counsel and outside lawyers, prosecutors and defenders. The ABA does not endorse candidates or make political contributions. For these reasons, the ABA brings a strong, non-partisan voice to the table. We appreciate the opportunity to discuss the LSC and the justice gap, and offer our ongoing support and assistance to continuing to improve the delivery of legal services to low-income individuals.

I. ABA IS A LONG-TIME LEADER IN ACCESS TO JUSTICE ISSUES

The American Bar Association has supported the effort to provide legal services to the poor since the establishment of the Standing Committee on Legal Aid and Indigent Defendants in 1920. Supreme Court Justice Lewis F. Powell, while serving as ABA President in 1964, called for a major expansion of the nation's legal services for the poor, ultimately leading in 1974 to the creation of the LSC.

Long before I became ABA President, I began visiting with my Congressional Delegation, both Republicans and Democrats, to explain how important LSC funding is to Alabama and the most vulnerable citizens in our state. Until recently, the only funding for Alabama legal services was federal funding. Over the years, strong bipartisan support for LSC has energized not just in Alabama but around the country. In addition to their year-round work at home, ABA members and state and local bar presidents, many on their own dime, travel to DC every year to remind Congress how important LSC is to their states and districts. These past two years the Bar Presidents of all 50 States, plus the District of Columbia, the U.S. Virgin Islands and Puerto Rico, jointly urged Congress to increase funding for LSC. This past year, the four major bars of color (the National Bar Association, the Hispanic National Bar Association, the National Asian Pacific American Bar Association and the National Native American Bar Association) *added their voices* to this effort.

In addition to the support of the legal community, the American people strongly support a federal legal services program. This past spring, ABA released a newly completed *Harris public opinion poll* which demonstrated strong national support for providing free legal services to qualified low-income families.

Promoting meaningful access for all persons regardless of their income or social condition continues to be one of the ABA's primary organizational goals. The ABA has assisted Congress and state and local entities in the development of the LSC, has assisted the Corporation in becoming the cornerstone for delivery of legal aid to the poor in this nation, and has also worked to build broad understanding of the work of LSC and bipartisan support for it in the Congress and throughout the country. We work closely with a coalition of state and local bars that support the work performed by LSC grantees in their communities and that have joined us in urging policymakers at all levels to support the program.

The ABA has also helped by articulating clear standards for the operation of civil legal aid programs. The ABA set forth these standards in 1961, and updated them several times, including as recently as 2006.

A key resource supplementing the LSC is pro bono contributions by private lawyers. The ABA promotes, as a key professional value, generous contributions of pro bono service and money by private lawyers. ABA Model Rule of Professional Conduct 6.1 states that: "Every lawyer has a professional responsibility to provide legal services to those unable to pay. A lawyer should aspire to render at least (50) hours of pro bono publico legal services per year. In addition, a lawyer should voluntarily contribute financial support to organizations that provide legal services to persons of limited means." With our support and encouragement, 25 states have adopted a version of this rule to emphasize that the professional responsibility of lawyers includes direct representation of the poor. Other states have rules expressing this same sentiment using language other than that of Model Rule 6.1. The ABA itself seeks to catalyze pro bono contributions through its national support center for pro bono activities – the ABA Center for Pro Bono.

Pro bono service is an indispensable element for closing the justice gap. Yet it can never alone meet the legal needs of the poor. Therefore, to supplement the foundation provided by federal resources through the LSC and the pro bono contributions by the private bar, the ABA has also provided support and leadership for charitable giving by lawyers and the profession. Through the "ABA Resource Center for Access to Justice Initiatives," we assist state legal aid systems in identifying and pursuing additional revenue sources to support civil legal aid. The ABA has long advocated Interest on Lawyers' Trust Account (IOLTA) programs as an effective way to raise additional resources for the legal aid system. We provide a clearinghouse of information and operational expertise for those programs, including promulgation of techniques for enhancing revenues which can then be used to supplement federal resources provided through the Corporation.

Last year, the ABA worked with Congress to encourage the FDIC to include IOLTA in the Temporary Liquidity Guarantee Program to ensure that this vital program continued through the economic crisis. My own Congressman, Spencer Bachus, spearheaded the House bipartisan effort and we again thank everyone, including many members of this Committee, who signed letters to the FDIC to express their support.

II. The Poor in America Have Very Limited Access to the Justice System

The Preamble to the U.S. Constitution states that the first enumerated function of government is to "establish justice." President Washington wrote that "the due administration of justice is the firmest pillar of good government." Our system of government cannot retain the respect and popular support so essential to its functioning if it is apparent that access to justice is dependent upon one's wealth or place of residence. A comprehensive, national system is necessary to assure that all persons have access to the justice system. Yet every indicator shows that the efforts described above have proven to be inadequate; access to justice is largely denied to the poor.

We are heartened that there has been increased discussion during the last several years of the "justice gap." But to me this seems to be a misnomer; it is more like a "chasm" than a "gap." Every effort to assess the number of life-altering legal issues that confront poor people in this country, and the capacity of our legal aid system to respond to those problems, leads to the conclusion that much work lies ahead.

ABA 1993 Comprehensive Legal Needs Study & Results

In 1993, a Temple University report commissioned by the ABA reported that, despite the combined effort of legal services programs and the private bar, only 20 % of the civil legal needs of the poor were being met. The ABA Legal Needs study found that, on average, low-income households experience approximately one serious legal problem each year. This study revealed that 79% of these legal needs go unaddressed. An executive summary of this seminal report is located on the ABA website at:

http://www.abalegalservices.org/downloads/sclaid/legalneedstudy.pdf. Unfortunately, for a variety of reasons including an increase in the number of people living in poverty, these statistics have changed little in the last 16 years.

Recent State-Based Legal Needs Studies Find a Large Proportion of the Legal Needs of the Poor Remain Unmet

Since the year 2000, sixteen states have conducted large-scale legal needs studies. These studies were conducted by a variety of respected research and academic institutions, using standard empirical research techniques. They have revealed in every case that only a small fraction, about 20%, of the legal problems experienced by low-income people is addressed with the assistance of a private or legal aid lawyer.

At least one state study suggested that there are likely to be economic returns from providing prophylactic legal aid. The University of Wisconsin LaFollette School of Public Affairs estimated that every dollar spent toward increasing representation for victims of domestic violence will yield about $9 in net benefits to victims or reduction in costs that would otherwise have to be borne by government.

Some observers might say that the legal needs research is too abstract because it depends upon surveys of the quantity of legal problems presenting significant life challenges that are not resolved through the justice system. But in 2005 and 2009, the LSC examined something far less abstract – the demand for its services and the capacity of its grantee programs to respond to this demand. It learned that, due to limited resources, grantees are able to respond to less than half the applications for legal assistance by eligible individuals. LSC-funded programs must turn away one-half the eligible people who seek assistance in resolving legal problems that affect their health, housing, employment or other critical areas of life – problems that keep them mired in poverty. Furthermore, it is clear that the actual level of need is much larger than the current demand for such services would suggest. Many poor people with life-altering legal problems simply do not seek assistance because they are well aware that they have at best a 50-50 chance of getting such help.

The Number of People in Poverty Continues to Grow

Today, more than 51 million Americans (including 18 million children) qualify for federally funded legal assistance through the Legal Services Corporation. The Census Bureau reported in September of this year that the poverty rate rose in 2008 to 13.2 %. This is the highest rise in the poverty rate since 1997. The total number of people in poverty climbed to the highest level since 1960. This is a marked increase in the number of people eligible for legal aid from just ten years ago, when 45 million Americans were eligible for LSC-funded representation.

III. The Legal Services Corporation Provides the Foundation for a System Providing Equal Justice

LSC Provides a Strong Organizational Infrastructure and Foundation for the Legal Aid System; LSC Should Be Reauthorized, and Given Adequate Resources to Close the Justice Gap

It is important that this Congress examine the current situation regarding access to justice in America and enact bipartisan legislation to reauthorize the Legal Services Corporation – which represents the principal federal mechanism through which government seeks to provide some assurance that justice is available to all, regardless of their financial condition. Our nation should be proud of the structure that it has created, but should allocate the resources needed to fully address the needs. LSC is important to your constituents because:

LSC-funded programs provide basic legal services for low-income persons in every Congressional district in the country. LSC disburses 95% of its annual federal appropriation to 137 local legal aid programs nationwide. Boards consisting of leaders in the local business and legal communities set the priorities for and oversee these programs, which provide basic civil legal services to the poor.

LSC-funded programs help those who suddenly qualify for and need legal assistance, including during times of recession and after natural disasters strike. There are continually new issues that require legal assistance that disproportionately affect low-income families, including consumer fraud and now the mortgage foreclosure crisis; foreclosures are forcing both low-income homeowners and renters from their homes.

LSC-funded legal aid lawyers preserve and protect American families; many low-income military families qualify for legal aid. Local legal aid programs make a real difference in the lives of millions of low-income American families by helping them resolve everyday legal matters; these include family law, housing, and consumer issues, and obtaining wrongly denied benefits such as Social Security and veterans' pensions. Soldiers and their families most often seek help with estate planning, consumer and landlord/tenant problems and family law.

LSC-funded programs prevent a long-term reliance on other government programs, many of which have also suffered funding cuts. People who are unable to resolve basic legal problems are more likely to experience greater hardships and require assistance from public social services programs.

LSC-funded programs are the nation's primary source of legal assistance for women who are victims of domestic violence. Legal aid programs identify domestic violence as one of the top priorities in their caseloads. While domestic violence occurs at all income levels, low-income women are significantly more likely to experience violence than other women, according to the U.S. Bureau of Justice Statistics. Recent studies also show that the only public service that reduces domestic abuse in the long term is a woman's access to legal aid.

The LSC is the central foundation for the legal aid system; other components – state and local funding and pro bono contributions by private lawyers – are catalyzed by LSC seed funding and serve to supplement the LSC resources. The Corporation is a model private-public partnership. The core federal funding provides for client intake and screening, referral of cases, responding to emergency matters, training *pro bono* lawyers, and handling cases when no private lawyer can do so. LSC leverages and facilitates the utilization of private resources – both in-kind, pro bono services and private funding.

However, federal resources to support LSC are grossly inadequate. They do not come close to addressing the level of need and have not even kept pace with inflation. In 1981, LSC for the first and only time achieved sufficient funding to reach the longstanding goal of providing 2 lawyers for every 10,000 poor people. If the $321 million 1981 appropriation for LSC had kept pace with inflation, LSC would now be funded at close to $800 million. LSC's FY2009 appropriation is only $390 million.

The resources that are provided to LSC are not able to be used to maximum effect. Impediments have been created by restrictions that have proven to be overreaching. The ABA supports a reexamination and adjustment of these restrictions, as is contemplated in reauthorization legislation in both chambers of Congress.

The ABA strongly urges the Subcommittee to address in reauthorization legislation three measures that have been included in appropriations riders since 1995 that have impeded LSC in fulfilling its mission of providing basic legal services to qualified persons. Specifically, we request that the Subcommittee eliminate (1) the restriction that prevents recipients of LSC funding from freely utilizing – without being subject to federally imposed restrictions – state, local, private and other non-LSC funds to provide needed legal assistance to poor clients; (2) the restriction that prevents LSC recipient programs from obtaining statutorily permitted attorneys' fees, as the House did in its version of the CJS bill; and (3) the restriction on class actions. These changes are sure to expand access to justice for low-income families without imposing unjustifiable costs on defendants.

The restriction on the use of other non-LSC funds by local legal aid recipients of LSC funding greatly diminishes the ability of LSC-funded programs to raise other funds from state and local governments, charitable foundations and private individuals. The restriction prevents these other funders from giving money to LSC-funded programs because the funds often cannot be used as the donor intends. The restriction has created great inefficiency in the legal aid system across the nation; entirely new and separate local legal aid programs had to be created to accept non-LSC funds in order to facilitate the donor's intent. The result has created a situation where hundreds of thousands of dollars in limited resources are squandered on needless duplication.

The restriction barring recovery of statutorily authorized attorneys' fees further diminishes the scarce resources available to support civil legal aid programs. Perhaps more important, it eliminates a critical source of leverage in many cases, putting legal aid lawyers at a grave disadvantage in attempting to negotiate settlements for their clients.

Both restrictions offend basic principles of federalism. They require independent legal aid programs to act in ways that are contrary to the expressed desires of state and local governments, local individuals and charities and state fee-recovery statutes. While it is understandable that the federal government may wish to dictate what can be done with federal funds, it is unacceptable for the federal government to tell local public service programs what they can do with other funds. Furthermore, states have, in their own sovereign wisdom, chosen to permit fee-shifting in certain situations and have therefore structured an appropriate balance between parties operating within their justice systems. Federal interference denies states the right to determine how their justice systems should operate.

The ABA also recommends lifting the restriction on LSC-funded programs using federal funds to file class actions. The ABA strongly believes that class actions should be available to low income victims of unscrupulous practices. Should eliminating this restriction prove controversial, we urge the Subcommittee to consider compromise language that would enable groups of similarly targeted poor people to effectively and efficiently obtain justice in the courts.

The ABA has longstanding policy favoring a legal aid system that does not interfere with poor persons' full access to the courts or deny advocacy that is available to others in our society. Removal of these restrictions will be a modest step toward adjusting the legal aid system so that it once again can approach the promise of ensuring equal access to justice for all.

States and Other Sources Provide Supplemental Resources for Access to Justice – But Resource Levels Vary Greatly by State and Over Time

Most, but not all, state governments are now partners in the efforts to provide legal aid to the poor. Forty-eight states provide public funding in varying amounts that supplement federal funding provided through LSC. However, the amounts contributed by the states vary widely. States with more limited resources, like my own state of Alabama, can contribute very little. We are able to supplement the LSC grant by only $200,000 in state funding to support legal aid.

During the past year to 18 months, several states have sharply reduced state appropriations to support legal aid. A small handful of others have rallied to provide additional funding. We estimate that the system as a whole continues to receive approximately the same amount as in the past from state governmental funding sources, but that is only because of large increases in a small number of states. Access to justice in many states has been dramatically impaired by the current economic downturn.

All states now operate Interest on Lawyer Trust Account (IOLTA) programs that harness the earning power of money that would otherwise lie fallow by aggregating small quantities of funds that would otherwise not be able to earn interest for anyone. However, IOLTA resources are market-driven and therefore are not a stable form of support; they rise and fall quickly with interest rates and the level of deposits to IOLTA accounts. ABA research shows that in the aggregate, IOLTA programs experienced a 23% decline in income in 2008, the most recent year for which full data is available. Thirty-seven jurisdictions saw an actual decrease between 2007 and 2008 income; decreases ranged from 1.4% to 60%. A recent informal poll of IOLTA programs requesting their projections of income for 2009 indicates that, in the aggregate, IOLTA programs expect to see an additional decrease in income from 2008 to 2009 of about 67%. As a result, the amount of supplemental funding available from state IOLTA programs is expected to continue to shrink in the short term.

States are expanding their efforts to improve the legal aid infrastructure by another mechanism – creation of broad-based access to justice commissions. The commissions involve leaders of the bar, the judiciary and other community leaders who are designing and finding resources for more effective civil legal services systems. Approximately 25 states have created such commissions, or similar entities, including my home state of Alabama. These efforts hold promise for the future, as they seek to improve the infrastructure and resources available for legal aid. This is, however, a nascent effort which has not yet begun to bear fruit or to generate significant new resources for the system. The ABA is providing support for these efforts through an ABA Resource Center for Access to Justice Initiatives, established in 2006. The Resource Center provides assistance in the development of the commissions, offers technical assistance in developing effective strategic plans, and sponsors annual national meetings/educational sessions for commission members.

Pro bono service by the private bar provides an invaluable supplemental source of in-kind contributions to the total resources for legal aid. It is difficult to accurately quantify the total amount of pro bono contributions, as much service occurs outside of any organized program; in many cases, lawyers are contacted directly by individuals in their communities who are in need, and the lawyers respond generously and without seeking credit. The ABA began to conduct periodic random surveys of lawyers in 2005 to assess the amount of pro bono service provided both within and outside of organized programs. Our surveys in 2005 and 2008 showed that approximately 70% of members of the private bar report providing at least one hour of pro bono service to persons of limited means during the year preceding their report. Of the lawyers who performed pro bono work, the average amount contributed was about 40 hours of service during the reporting year. Between 2005 and 2008, our surveys showed a slight increase in the number of lawyers who reported providing pro bono service.

We are pleased that the trend appears to be toward increased pro bono participation. Law firms are now hiring pro bono partners and according both associates and partners credit for billable hours for pro bono work; law schools are developing more pro bono projects and clinics per the ABA accreditation standards requiring pro bono efforts; bar associations are supporting their members' participation in pro bono activities; judges are taking a more active role in promoting pro bono work to lawyers in their communities; and government attorneys are doing more pro bono work. Currently, 26 state bar associations have staff dedicated to coordinate statewide pro bono activities. In addition, there are over 1,400 organized pro bono programs in the country, many of which are specialized to focus on certain needs and types of cases (like domestic violence victims, children involved in custody cases, or people living with HIV/AIDS).

Even with these heartening statistics, the ABA, and the organized bar in general, continues efforts to enlist more lawyers in providing pro bono service. For example, the ABA Standing Committee on Legal Assistance for Military Personnel has launched a program, "Operation Enduring LAMP," which is a consortium of state and local bar associations that have made a commitment to recruit volunteer attorneys, and in many cases offer training and facilities to volunteers, in order to assist military legal assistance providers with civil law matters affecting service members. The Committee also has launched the ABA Military Pro Bono Project to connect active-duty military personnel to free legal assistance for civil legal issues that are beyond the scope of services provided available to such personnel through a military legal assistance office.

During my term as President of the ABA, the ABA established a new and innovative project to coordinate an ABA-based national medical-legal partnership pro bono support initiative. Medical-legal partnerships (MLPs) now serve almost 200 sites in the United States, including hospitals, community clinics and other health care facilities. MLPs represent an exciting and unprecedented opportunity for lawyers to join the national health care community in working with key stakeholder organizations to develop partnerships to help identify and resolve diverse legal issues that affect patients' health and well-being and to educate physicians on the impact of unmet legal needs on the health of patients, provide physicians with information on screening for such unmet legal needs in their patients, and provide physicians, hospitals and health-centers with information on establishing a medical-legal partnership.

We know that many low-income families and individuals who receive legal assistance from legal aid or pro bono attorneys have multiple needs well beyond the discreet legal issues we lawyers handle. These patients confront illness that interferes with their ability to meet their basic needs. But, not every illness has a biological remedy. A family forced to choose between food and heat in the winter months cannot be treated with a prescription or a vaccination. Similarly, a child with asthma will never breathe symptom free – no matter how much medication is administered – if he or she returns from the doctor's office to mold-infested housing, as thousands do.

Medical-legal partnerships integrate lawyers in the healthcare setting to help patients navigate the complex legal system that often holds solutions to many social determinants of health – income supports for food-insecure families, utility shut-off protection during cold winter months, and mold removal from the home of asthmatic children.

Bar associations and private lawyers have redoubled their efforts during the current time of economic uncertainty, to try to raise additional funding for legal aid, or to expand pro bono services. Examples include:

Arizona: The state bar association and bar foundation created the "Lawyers Helping Homeowners" program, calling upon volunteer lawyers to assist homeowners in working with their lenders to find appropriate financial arrangements to avoid foreclosure.

California: Among a wide variety of pro bono contributions, notable is the Holocaust Survivors Initiative, a network of over 2,600 lawyers who provide service to survivors, coordinated by the joint efforts of Bet Tzedek Legal Services and the firm of Manatt, Phelps & Phillips.

Iowa: The director of our ABA Young Lawyers Division Disaster Legal Services Project is Craig Cannon, a North Carolina lawyer and Iowa native and graduate of the University of Iowa. His project provided an incredible amount of pro bono service to victims in the aftermath of the recent Iowa floods. Craig is a recipient of the University of Iowa Distinguished Alumnus Award for his work in pro bono and, particularly, for legal assistance to low income disaster survivors.

North Carolina: The North Carolina Bar Association in 2008 launched an innovative "Justice4ALL" campaign to increase access to legal services for the poor through a five-prong approach: educate, legislate, donate, participate and provide loan repayment assistance.

The education campaign focused on informing North Carolina lawyers about the great unmet need for legal services by the poor in the state. The legislative campaign developed a grassroots advocacy network to seek increased public funding for legal services. Through its private bar fundraising efforts, the campaign raised close to $900,000 for Legal Aid of North Carolina. The "4ALL" campaign has also led to increased pro bono participation through its annual statewide "Service Day."

Ohio: The Ohio State Bar Association worked closely with state government and other key institutions to launch the "Save the Dream" foreclosure assistance program: a new initiative that connects qualified homeowners with legal aid lawyers and nearly 1,100 attorneys statewide who have volunteered to provide legal services free of charge. Ohio State Bar President Robert F. Ware, Jr. stated at the program's launch: "Nearly 1,100 Ohio lawyers have volunteered to assist Ohio homeowners facing the potential loss of their homes. These 1,100 lawyers – and more will join their ranks – are being assigned to local legal services providers to be matched with qualified clients and will work with lower income Ohioans who could not otherwise afford legal counsel. These pro bono attorneys will supplement the resources available in the legal services community which alone are inadequate to address the current need. We are committed to helping Ohioans stay in their homes – to save their dreams – wherever possible."

Virginia: The Fairfax Law Foundation and the Fairfax Bar Association support a vibrant and expanding civil pro bono program. Volunteer lawyers, law students, and paralegals give their time to staff diverse projects including: Housing, Consumer, and Employment Pro Bono Law Panels, a Family Legal Assistance Project, a Nonprofit Legal Support Program, and a Wills on Wheels Pro Bono Project. Lawyers contribute a full day's work at any given time when they serve as "lawyer for the day" helping victims of domestic violence obtain protective orders. The Fairfax Law Foundation also hosts an innovative annual fundraiser "Jazz 4 Justice." This year's event, to be held November 13 at George Mason University, is a terrific example of a great community partnership as proceeds go to both the Law Foundation and GMU Jazz Ensemble.

To draw the bar's and the public's attention to the pro bono contributions of lawyers, and to encourage even more lawyers to participate, the ABA is this week sponsoring a National Celebration of Pro Bono. This consists of over 500 events nationwide recognizing the important contributions lawyers make to communities all over America.

Despite the wonderful work demonstrated by lawyers as described above, we again must caution that even with an ongoing strong commitment from the private bar, at best pro bono provides a supplementary resource. Some have suggested over the years that the private bar or state funding alone can ensure access to justice for the poor. Such suggestions would only result in further rationing of justice. The level of need is too overwhelming.

The ABA agrees that pro bono service is an indispensable partner in closing the justice gap. Some have suggested that the lawyers can and should be required to provide pro bono service or even to bear the entire burden of closing the justice gap alone. Such a suggestion is misguided. First, ensuring access to the legal system for all and not just the wealthy is fundamentally a governmental responsibility; one profession cannot be conscripted to fulfill a government obligation without compensation. Second, lawyers as a profession already do more public service than any other profession. As ABA President, I had the wonderful opportunity to travel the country to see firsthand the outstanding pro bono work that I described above which is being done by state and local bar associations and individual lawyers. Many who would place additional responsibility on individual lawyers for closing the justice gap do not realize that America's lawyers are mostly solo or small firm practitioners; they are your constituents who are small business owners trying to make ends meet themselves, including paying off student loan debt and providing for their own families.

Pro bono remains an important part of the delivery system, and we can and should do more to encourage private lawyers to assist in closing the justice gap. The ABA, and state, local, specialty and territorial bar associations will remain tireless in urging members of the profession to voluntarily contribute pro bono legal services to the poor, to build upon the foundation and central infrastructure that is provided through the Legal Services Corporation. This is why the ABA strongly supports the language in H.R. 3467 that encourages LSC to continue its Private Attorney Involvement program.

CONCLUSION

The ABA strongly supports the Legal Services Corporation as essential in helping secure access to justice for all Americans. The ABA urges the Subcommittee (and Congress) to work together to approve bipartisan reauthorization legislation before the 111th Congress adjourns. Despite some dissenters, LSC is not going away – the program enjoys strong bipartisan support in Congress and among the American people. There are many improvements, however, that can be made – LSC has not been reauthorized since 1977 and many things have changed since then. The ABA was indeed part of the compromise in 1995 that imposed the "restrictions" that saved LSC. But it's time to take a hard look at those restrictions, learn from how these restrictions have been in many cases overreaching, and work together to improve the delivery of legal services to the poor. The ABA, our members, and state and local bars nationwide stand ready to help get this important job done.

It is in the interest of all of us to see that these legal needs are resolved in a peaceful manner and that respect for the rule of law is strengthened. "Liberty and justice for all" is our proud national credo, but it is empty rhetoric without a significant increase in resources devoted to the Legal Services Corporation.

H. Thomas Wells Jr., Immediate Past President, American Bar Association

H. Thomas Wells Jr., a partner and founding member at Maynard, Cooper & Gale, P.C., in Birmingham, Alabama, concluded his term as President of the American Bar Association at its annual meeting in Chicago in August 2009.

Wells has a litigation practice with emphasis on complex environmental, toxic tort law and products liability cases.

He has served on numerous committees and in leadership roles in the Alabama State Bar, the Birmingham Bar Association and the American Bar Association.

Wells has served in the ABA's policy-making House of Delegates since 1991 and was chair of the ABA House of Delegates, the second highest office in the American Bar

Association, from 2002 to 2004. He is a former chair of the ABA Section of Litigation, the largest section in the ABA with more than 75,000 members.

In addition, Wells is co-chair of the ABA's Special Committee on Disaster Response, which was commissioned after the devastation of Hurricane Katrina. He also has been a member of the ABA's Commission on the American Jury and the ABA Commission on the Future of the Legal Profession.

Wells is a frequent speaker and participant in state and national programs dealing with trial and litigation issues. He is also listed in the Best Lawyers in America in the areas of Environmental Law, Mass Tort Litigation, Energy Law, Natural Resources Law, and Product Liability Litigation. Wells is a Fellow of the International Academy of Trial Lawyers and was named as one of the Top Ten Lawyers in Alabama for 2008 and 2009 by *Super Lawyers.*

Wells earned his B.A. degree with honors from the University of Alabama, where he was president of the Student Government Association and was elected to *Phi Beta Kappa.* He earned his J.D. degree, Order of the Coif, from the University of Alabama. He also was a member of the *Alabama Law Review* and Hugo Black Scholar while in law school. He was awarded an honorary Doctor of Laws degree in May 2008 from Suffolk University School of Law.

Wells lives in Birmingham with his wife Jan. The couple's two children, Lynlee Wells Palmer and H. Thomas "Trey" Wells III, are also lawyers in Birmingham.

CHAPTER SOURCES

The following chapters have been previously published:

Chapter 1 – This is an edited, reformatted and augmented version of a United States Government Accountability Office publication, Report GAO-10-194T, dated October 27, 2009.

Chapter 2 – This is an edited, excerpted and augmented version of a United States Congressional Research Service publication, Report Order Code R40679, dated November 10, 2009.

Chapter 3 – This is an edited, excerpted and augmented version of a United States Congressional Research Service publication, Report Order Code RL34016, dated November 10, 2009.

Chapter 4 – This is an edited, excerpted and augmented version of a Legal Services Corporation publication, dated September 2009.

Chapter 5 – This is an edited, excerpted and augmented version of a Legal Services Corporation Fact Book, dated August 2009.

Chapter 6 – This is an edited, excerpted and augmented version of a Legal Services Corporation Fact Sheet, dated November 2009.

Chapter 7 – These remarks were delivered as testimony of Helaine M. Barnett, President, Legal Services Corporation, before the Subcommittee on Commercial and Administrative Law, Committee on the Judiciary, United States House of Representatives, dated October 27, 2009.

Chapter 8 – These remarks were delivered as testimony of Harrison D. Mciver, III, Executive Director/CEO, Memphis Area Legal Services, Inc., before the Subcommittee on Commercial and Administrative Law, Committee on the Judiciary, United States House of Representatives, dated October 27, 2009.

Chapter 9 – These remarks were delivered as testimony of Michael D. McKay, Vice Chairman, Board of Directors, Legal Services Corporation, before the Subcommittee on Commercial and Administrative Law, Committee on the Judiciary, United States House of Representatives, dated October 27, 2009.

Chapter 10 – These remarks were delivered as testimony of Donald Saunders, Director of Civil Legal Services on behalf of The National Legal Aid and Defender Association, before the Subcommittee on Commercial and Administrative Law, Committee on the Judiciary, United States House of Representatives, dated October 27, 2009.

Chapter 11 – These remarks were delivered as testimony of H. Thomas Wells, Jr., on behalf of the American Bar Association, before the Subcommittee on Commercial and Administrative Law, Committee on the Judiciary, United States House of Representatives, dated October 27, 2009.

INDEX

A

B

C

F

G

H

I

J

L

M

N

O

P

Q

R

S

T

U

V

W